African Perspectives on Adult Learning

# Foundations of
# Adult Education in Africa

Other books in the Series

- *The Psychology of Adult Learning in Africa*
  Thomas Fasokun, Anne Katahoire and Akpovire Oduaran
- *Research Methods for Adult Educators in Africa*
  Bagele Chilisa and Julia Preece
- *Developing Programmes for Adult Learners in Africa*
  Matthew Gboku and Nthongo Lekoko
- *The Social Context of Adult Learning in Africa*
  Sabo Indabawa with Stanley Mpofu

The Editorial Board for the Series

- Adama Ouane, UNESCO Institute for Education
  (Chairperson)
- Martin Kamwengo, University of Zambia
- David Langhan, Pearson Education South Africa
- Wolfgang Leumer, Institute for International Cooperation,
  German Adult Education Association
- Christopher McIntosh, UNESCO Institute for Education
- Mantina Mohasi, National University of Lesotho
- Stanley Mpofu, Adult Education Consultant, Zimbabwe
- Gabo Ntseane, University of Botswana (Assistant series
  Managing Editor)
- Anthony Okech, Makerere University, Uganda
- Orrin F. Summerell, UNESCO Institute for Education
- Edward Turay, University of Sierra Leone
- Frank Youngman, University of Botswana (series Managing
  Editor)

African Perspectives on Adult Learning

# Foundations of
# Adult Education in Africa

Fredrick Nafukho • Maurice Amutabi • Ruth Otunga

Pearson Education South Africa
Forest Drive, Pinelands, Cape Town

www.pearsoned.co.za

Co-published by the UNESCO Institute for Education, Feldbrunnenstr. 58, 20148,
Hamburg, Germany, and Pearson Education South Africa, corner of Logan Way and
Forest Drive, Pinelands, Cape Town, South Africa, in collaboration with the Institute for
International Cooperation of the German Adult Education Association, Obere Wilhelmstr.
32, 53225 Bonn, Germany, and the Adult Education Department of the University of
Botswana.

First published 2005

ISBN 9282011216

**Acknowledgements**
The authors and publishers are grateful to the following for permission to reproduce
copyright material:
INPRA for the photo on page 51; Benny Gool, Trace Images for the photo on page 109;
FishEye photos for the photos on page 119 and page 122; DKimages for the photo on page
122.

Published by David Langhan
Editorial manager: Lisa Compton
Project manager: Anita van Zyl
Symbol research and selection: Sandie Vahl
Photo research: Carin Lilienfeld
Editor: Mafalda Marchesi
Book design by Graham Arbuckle
Cover design and artwork by Toby Newsome
Typesetting by Robin Taylor
Printed by Clyson Printers, Maitland, Cape Town

# Contents

# ADINKRA SYMBOLS

For the icons in this Series, we have chosen Adinkra symbols that are associated with learning and community in some way. These striking and expressive symbols are used by the people of Ghana and the Ivory Coast in textile and jewellery design, architecture, wood carvings, etc., and represent only one of a number of writing systems found in Africa.

| | Symbol | Meaning | Interpretation |
|---|---|---|---|
| | bese saka | sack of cola nuts | abundance, plenty, affluence, power, unity, togetherness |
| | dame-dame | name of a board game | intelligence, ingenuity, strategy, craftiness |
| | dwennimmen | ram's horns | humility, strength, wisdom, learning |
| | mate masie | what I hear I keep | wisdom, knowledge, learning, prudence, understanding |
| | nkonsonkonson | chain link | unity, human relations, brotherhood, cooperation |
| | nsaa | hand-woven fabric | excellence, authenticity, genuineness |
| | sesa woruban | morning star inside a wheel | life transformation |

# The authors

## Fredrick Nafukho

Fredrick Nafukho obtained a BEd (Hons) degree in Business Education and Economics in 1988 and an MEd (Economics) in 1993 from Kenyatta University, Kenya, and a PhD degree in Training and Development/ Human Resource Development in 1998 from Louisiana State University, USA. He is a Fulbright Scholar and Associate Professor at the Department of Rehabilitation, Human Resources and Communication Disorders of the University of Arkansas, USA. Prior to that he served as a Senior Lecturer and Head, Department of Educational Administration, Planning and Curriculum Development, Moi University, Kenya. He is co-author of *Training of Trainers: Strategies for the 21st Century* and has written more than 60 articles, book chapters and book reviews on the economics of education, adult education, training and development, entrepreneurship education and performance improvement. He wrote Chapters 1, 7, 8 and 10.

## Maurice Amutabi

Maurice Amutabi is a Lecturer in the Department of Development Studies at Moi University, Kenya. He received his undergraduate and graduate education at the University of Nairobi, Kenya. He is currently a Fulbright Fellow in the Department of History, University of Illinois at Urbana-Champaign, USA. He has published chapters in several books, and his articles have appeared in several refereed journals such as *African Studies Review, Canadian Journal of African Studies, International Journal of Educational Development* and *Jenda: A Journal of Culture and African Women Studies.* He is co-author (with E.M. Were) of *Nationalism and Democracy for People-Centred Development in Africa* (Moi University Press, 2000). His book *Islam and the Underdevelopment of Africa* is forthcoming from Moi University Press, Eldoret, Kenya. He wrote Chapters 2, 4 and 9.

## Ruth Otunga

Ruth Otunga has BEd, MEd, PhD degrees and is a Senior Lecturer in curriculum Studies at Moi University, Kenya. She is currently the Department Head of the Department of Educational Administration, Planning and Curriculum Development. She has been lecturing to undergraduate and graduate students for the last 16 years and has supervised and examined over 30 graduate research theses. She has been involved in various research activities in education, gender and entrepreneurship and has attended and presented many papers at national and international workshops and conferences. She has a total of 15 publications to her credit and is a member of several professional associations. She wrote Chapters 3, 5 and 6.

# Foreword

The remedial strategy of borrowing textbooks conceived in contexts of and for students from developed countries with well-established traditions of adult education is no longer viable. The present textbook series, African Perspectives on Adult Learning, represents the outcome of a venture initiated three decades ago by the Institute for International Cooperation of the German Adult Education Association (known by its German acronym as IIZ/DVV). Bringing together non-governmental and civil society organisations, the DVV turned this venture into a creative partnership with academia, aimed at building the training and research capacities of African universities that serve the adult education community. It has become a means of fruitful cooperation with several leading African universities, all partners being concerned with providing textbooks for university departments and institutes of adult education relevant for the African context.

The abiding interest, as well as growing financial support and substantive input of the IIZ/DVV, has provided a key ingredient for the success of this project, along with establishing its potential for expansion. The University of Botswana has been another major contributor right from the beginning. Its Department of Adult Education has given the academic and institutional support needed for such an ambitious undertaking, graciously shouldering the editorial secretariat of the series. The third pillar of this endeavour – and a decisive one – was furnished by the UNESCO Institute for Education (UIE), an international centre of excellence in adult learning enjoying the full backing of UNESCO and boasting extensive publishing experience in the field. UIE brought in vital international and inter-regional expertise coupled with the vision of the Fifth International Conference on Adult Education (CONFINTEA V). The Institute has also mobilised sizeable financial resources of its own, led the Series Editorial Board and assumed responsibility for managing often difficult matters entailed by such a complex venture.

The present Series recommends itself through many distinctive features that reflect the unique manner in which it has come about. One of these has to do with the professional guidance and technical advice provided by the competent, sensitive and broadly representative Series Editorial Board, whose members have displayed the capability and wisdom required to steer a project of this kind. Their intellectual resources, experience and know-how made it possible for the Series to take on its actual form. We wish to express our deep gratitude to all the members of the Editorial Board for their profound involvement, the optimism they brought to the Series and their dedication to its successful completion.

The co-publisher with UIE is Pearson Education South Africa, which has proven to be a partner highly committed to the goals of the project, one prepared to engage in a collaboration of a different order and take risks in exploring new paths in publishing. As a full member of the Series Editorial Board, the co-publisher has offered invaluable assistance, especially in the writers' workshops and in coaching the authors throughout the composition of the chapters. The creative way in which Pearson Education South Africa has integrated the project into its work and its firm dedication to fostering editorial and authorial capacities in Africa deserve special mention. Without this sense of mission, the Series would not have seen the light of day.

The authors of the works in this Series have themselves been selected on the basis of proposals they submitted. We took pleasure in working with all of these devoted partners, and the project greatly benefited from their combination of individual conviction together with teamwork, collective analysis and decision-making. We wish to thank all the authors for their hard work as well as their adherence to a demanding schedule. Their professionalism and competence lie at the heart of this Series and were instrumental in its realisation.

Finally, and most importantly, special recognition is due to Professor Frank Youngman, the Series Managing Editor, and his Assistant, Dr Gabo Ntseane of the University of Botswana, who constitute the Editorial Board Secretariat. Frank Youngman initiated the idea for this Series in 2001, and the Secretariat has been in the front line at all times, carefully guiding the process, monitoring progress and ensuring the quality of the work at all stages without compromise.

This Series addresses the critical lack of textbooks for adult education and the alienating nature of those currently in use in Africa. We have sought to develop a new set of foundational works conceived and developed from an African perspective and written mainly by African scholars. An African perspective, however, is not mere Afrocentrism, although some degree of the latter is required to move beyond the reigning Eurocentrism and general Western domination of all scientific domains and adult education in particular. Injecting a dose of Afrocentrism without prejudice to universal values, elementary scientific knowledge and other cultures and without complacency in the face of retrograde and discriminatory values and traditions, has proven to be a significant challenge. In essence, the African perspective has revealed itself to be both a renaissance of the continent and its manifold traditions, as well as the birth of its own new vision and prospects in the context of a fast-growing, ever-changing and increasingly globalised world.

For the initial volumes in this evolving Series, the following five titles were selected: *The Psychology of Adult Learning in Africa; Foundations of Adult Education in Africa; Research Methods for Adult Educators in Africa; Developing Programmes for Adult Learners in Africa;* and *The Social Context of Adult Learning in Africa.* We will certainly judge the success of these volumes by taking into account the reactions and responses of their users, and we will make any necessary adjustments while striving to widen the scope of the venture to cover other linguistic areas of Africa and to explore new thematic fields for deepening the African perspective. There is no question that IIZ/DVV and UIE are committed to lending their intellectual and financial support to this endeavour. Furthermore, the University of Botswana is committed to providing the academic and administrative base for the Series, while Pearson Education South Africa foresees the ongoing viability of the project. In opening up new approaches to adult education and learning in Africa, the Series meets the needs of governments, non-governmental and civil society organisations, and academia in an area of great importance to UNESCO and the community of nations.

**Adama Ouane**
*Director, UNESCO Institute for Education*

# Preface

During the 1990s it became clear that adult learning must be an important part of all strategies for development. In a series of world conferences between 1990 and 1996, various agencies of the United Nations addressed the issues of education for all, the environment, human rights, population, social development, the status of women, human settlements and food security. Each of these conferences recognised that progress would be dependent on adult members of society transforming their life circumstances and gaining greater control over their lives. To achieve this change, adults require new knowledge, skills and attitudes. This significant insight was highlighted by the Fifth International Conference on Adult Education (CONFINTEA V), that was organised by UNESCO in 1997. CONFINTEA V affirmed that adult learning is potentially a powerful force for promoting people-centred development. It concluded that the education of adults is key to sustainable development in the twenty-first century.

The concept of adult learning articulated by CONFINTEA V is a broad one, embracing formal, non-formal and informal learning processes in all areas of people's lives. This concept is relevant in African contexts, where the learning of adults takes place across their various social roles, in the home, the community, and the workplace, as well as in formal educational and training institutions. Opportunities for learning are availed by a wide variety of providers. The state has a central responsibility to promote and facilitate adult learning. In some countries this responsibility has been diminished by the impact of structural adjustment policies. But in others the state continues to play an important role, with a wide range of government departments organising programmes that involve adult learning. These programmes are multi-sectoral, including activities as varied as agricultural extension, health education, business training, consumer education, community development, and wildlife education. Also, the organisations of civil society are significant sites of adult learning, providing their own educational programmes, as well as a context in which adults acquire new competencies through their active involvement in running such organisations. For example, in many coun-

dame-dame

tries the trade union movement is an important source of adult learning. Increasingly, the private sector is a major provider of learning opportunities for adults. Its role has two dimensions. Firstly, companies are expanding their training and development for employees as they respond to the challenges of technological change and global competition. Secondly, there is a rapid growth of commercial educational institutions such as colleges, academies, and institutes, which are responding to market demands for learning opportunities, especially in work-related fields such as information technology, tourism and business. These institutions are to be found in all the urban centres of Africa. Public and private universities also cater for many adult learners, especially through their part-time, evening, and distance learning programmes. The education and training of adults in Africa therefore takes place in many settings, embraces many content areas and modes of learning, and is provided by many different types of organisations. It is a complex and diverse field of activity.

The successful implementation of adult learning policies and programmes depends in large measure on the availability of knowledgeable, skilful, and socially committed educators of adults. Because they are key agents in the realisation of adult learning, the quality of their initial and continuing training is crucial. The educators of adults in Africa work in a wide variety of organisational and social contexts, from government bureaucracies to community-based projects. They play multiple roles as programme planners, organisers, teachers, researchers and counsellors. While this diversity of situations and roles reflects the reality of adult learning settings, it presents significant conceptual and practical problems in terms of training those who educate adults. One example is that those who work with adults in learning activities identify themselves as adult educators. Rather, they identify themselves as health promoters, business advisers or community workers. Nevertheless, whatever the nomenclature of a particular cadre, it is important that they are proficient in their work of helping adults to learn. The development of their expertise includes a body of knowledge, skills and values that is centred on adult education as a field of study and practice.

The professional training of educators of adults in Africa takes place in institutions of tertiary education across the continent, primarily at diploma and degree level. For example, in every country there are colleges of agriculture that prepare agricultural extension workers, health institutes that train community-based health workers and technical colleges that train vocational teachers. In particular, many African universities have departments or institutes of adult education that train personnel for fields as varied as adult basic education, prison education and human resource development. Although the areas of content specialisation vary from agronomy to literacy, the curricula of the training programmes have many common topics, such as the psychology of adult learning, programme development, communication skills and research methods. This is because all educators of adults require a common body of knowledge (such as an awareness of the historical and philosophical dimensions of adult education practice) and a number of generic skills (for example, in teaching and research). A key learning resource in these training programmes is the prescribed course textbook. However, those who teach these programmes often have difficulty in finding textbooks that are relevant to the work situations and social contexts of their students.

A review of English-language curriculum materials used in the professional training of adult educators in Africa reveals that the majority of textbooks for the courses are published in the United States or the United Kingdom. The content of these books seldom reflects issues of African development or the realities of adult education policy and practice in Africa. The social and organisational contexts, theoretical underpinnings and practical examples are largely derived from the experience of adult education in the advanced industrialised countries of the West. Hence the textbooks currently being used in the training of adult educators in Africa are at best lacking in relevance and, at worst, actively promoting inappropriate models of adult education. Furthermore, because of the cost of these books, student access is often limited.

The post-colonial history of adult education as a field of study in African tertiary education institutions shows that very few indigenous textbooks have been produced over the years. Useful individual books, such as the *Adult Education Handbook* (edited by the Institute of Adult Education, Dar-es-Salaam, 1973) and *A Handbook of Adult Education for West Africa* (edited by Lalage Bown and Sunday Hezekiah Olu Tomori, London, 1979), have been one-off publications that were not followed up and were not widely available. When an institution in one country has consistently produced relevant materials, such as the Department of Adult Education at the University of Ibadan in Nigeria, they have been difficult to obtain in other countries. The problem of a lack of appropriate and accessible textbooks for use in the training of African adult educators remains.

There is, therefore, a need to develop relevant, affordable and available textbooks that reflect African social realities, theoretical and cultural perspectives, policies and modes of practice. This is the need that the series African Perspectives on Adult Learning seeks to meet. The books in the Series place the African context at the centre of discussions on adult education topics. They take into account the impact of colonialism, liberation struggles, neo-colonialism and globalisation. They show the importance to adult learning of African philosophies, indigenous knowledge systems, traditions and cultures. They demonstrate that the realities of class, gender, race and ethnicity in African societies shape the nature of adult learning activities. They provide examples of the policies and practices that characterise adult education across the continent. While referring to international discourses on adult learning, their presentation of issues in adult education is Africa-centred. The Series therefore contributes to the indigenisation of education within the perspective of the African Renaissance.

The books in the African Perspectives on Adult Learning Series cover important subjects for the training of educators of adults in Africa. They are intended to be course textbooks that will be used in face-to-face teaching environments in a way that encourages interactive learning. Each book is designed to provide an overview of the subject, to introduce appropriate theory and to provide discussion and examples rooted in professional practice, policies and research from African contexts. Each chapter features clear learning objectives, practical examples, activities for the reader to do individually or in small groups, a summary, key points, further questions and suggested readings. It is hoped that the use of the books will promote the development of relevant curricula and interactive teaching approaches in adult education training programmes across the continent.

Each book in the Series provides an African perspective on an important area of knowledge and practice for the educator of adults. In *Foundations of Adult Education in Africa*, Fredrick Nafukho, Maurice Amutabi and Ruth Otunga present key concepts, information and principles that should underlie the practice of adult education in African contexts. The book is based on the assumption that there is a body of basic knowledge that all educators should master in order to be effective in their work. Therefore, adult educators should have a historical perspective on what they do. This is particularly true in Africa where the colonial experience had a

negative impact on many indigenous traditions. Adult educators should likewise be aware of the philosophical underpinnings of adult education activities, and should be able to articulate their own philosophy of adult education. The authors also make the assumption that adult learning does not take place in a vacuum, and the educators of adults must be able to analyse the wider environment in which they work. The contemporary impact of information and communication technology and of globalisation in many areas of life in Africa is a case in point of the significance of the ever-changing environment. Therefore, their influence on adult education is discussed in the book. The book is broad in scope but it covers essential topics that all adult educators need to know about.

The aims of the book are:

■ to provide knowledge about the basic concepts and principles of adult education as a developing profession in Africa;
■ to emphasise the need to understand the wider environment in which adult learning takes place.

Chapter 1 considers the meaning of adult education and looks at the forms, purposes and providers of adult education. It introduces the important concept of andragogy and identifies six core principles of adult learning. Chapter 2 explores the historical development of adult education in Africa. It explains the role of indigenous knowledge systems and traditional forms of adult education. It considers the impact of imperialism and colonialism, and the development of adult education in the post-colonial period. Chapter 3 focuses on the discipline of philosophy and its significance for adult education. Influential Western philosophies are considered, and the importance of African philosophies for adult education is emphasised. Chapter 4 analyses how sociocultural, political and economic factors influence the nature of adult education in African contexts. Chapter 5 looks at the learning opportunities that are available for adults, and discusses the factors that limit access to these opportunities. Chapter 6 focuses on the issue of gender, explaining key concepts and the implications of gender patterns for adult education activities. Chapter 7 looks at adult education as a developing profession in Africa. It explains the meaning of a profession and discusses the significance of adult education associations in the professionalisation process. Chapter 8 discusses the role and impact of information and communication technology (ICT) on adult education and identifies various barriers to using ICT in adult education in African contexts. Chapter 9 explores the concept of globalisation and the impact of external influences on adult education programmes and methods in Africa. Finally, Chapter 10 considers the policy environment for the development of lifelong learning in Africa.

A sound understanding of the basic concepts and principles of history and philosophy, and of the wider environment of adult learning, is an essential component of the knowledge base of adult education. *Foundations of Adult Education in Africa* provides an excellent resource for developing the relevant foundational knowledge.

**Frank Youngman**
*Department of Adult Education*
*University of Botswana*

# Acknowledgements

Several individuals, learning institutions and organisations worked together to make the production of this book possible. The many people who influenced, supported and encouraged us in this noble endeavour are too numerous to list in full, however, some deserve special mention. The authors give special thanks to the following:

- The Managing Editor of the African Perspectives Adult Learning Series, Frank Youngman, and members of the Editorial Board, Christopher McIntosh, Wolfgang Leumer and David Langhan, for their timely and scholarly feedback on the drafts. We treasure their useful and encouraging comments. In addition, we thank them for making available all the materials and journal articles that we required in the course of writing this book.
- The organisers of the writers' workshop that was held at the University of Botswana, Frank Youngman, Julie Viljoen and Gabo Ntseane, for the timely and invaluable information provided during the workshop.
- Dean Reed Greenwood, College of Education and Health Professions; Barbara E. Hinton, Department Head and Professor; Professors Bobby Biggs, Buddy Lyle, Kit Brooks and Fred Wills from the University of Arkansas, USA; Nelly Kodero, Dean, Faculty of Education, Moi University, Kenya; Mary C. Lutta-Mukhebi, Dean, Institute of Human Resource Development, Moi University, Kenya; Charles C. Stewart, Dean, College of Liberal Arts and Sciences; and Donald E. Crummey, Department of History; and Jean Allman, Director of the Centre for African Studies, University of Illinois at Urbana-Champaign, USA. We thank these colleagues, mentors and great teachers for their professional support and encouragement.
- Gene Huang Yang and Carroll Graham, our graduate students, who provided tremendous support to us.
- B. Chilisa, J. Preece, M. Gboku, N. Lekoko, T. Fasokun, A. Oduaran, A. Katahoire and S. Indabawa, our fellow writers in the African Perspectives Adult Learning Series, for all the networking and

sharing that strengthened us and enabled us to stay on course even during very trying moments.

- The outside anonymous reviewer for the invaluable insights that helped to shape the final direction of the book.
- The UNESCO Institute for Education, Hamburg; Institute for International Cooperation, German Adult Education Association, Bonn; and the Department of Adult Education, University of Botswana, for producing the African Perspectives Series.
- Our publishers, Pearson Education South Africa and UNESCO, for the timely and excellent production of the book.
- Last but not least, members of our families for their patience, tolerance and encouragement during the period of this work.

All three authors would like to mention that this book is the result of a joint effort encouraged by teamwork and team learning. However, Maurice and Ruth would like to express their appreciation to Fredrick for the significant role he played as coordinating author and mentor in providing impetus and direction. Together they unreservedly applaud him as a great team leader. Fredrick and Maurice also applaud Ruth for her commitment to the book by producing her chapters in spite of a particularly difficult period in her family life when she was beset by tragic bereavement.

**Fredrick Nafukho**
**Maurice Amutabi**
**Ruth Otunga**

African Perspectives on Adult Learning

# Foundations of
# Adult Education in Africa

# Chapter 1

# Introduction

## OVERVIEW

In the African context, who is an adult? How is adult education defined? What forms of adult education exist in Africa? What methods are used for teaching adult students? What are the goals and purposes of adult education? In this chapter, answers to these questions and others will be provided.

This introductory chapter will also provide the reader with valuable information regarding the meaning of adult education, as well as the forms, goals, purposes and providers of adult education programmes. Issues pertaining to adult education within sub-Saharan Africa are addressed. The cultural identity of the African people in sub-Saharan Africa will be taken into account in the course of our exploration.

## LEARNING OBJECTIVES

By the end of this chapter, you should be able to:

1  Explain the meaning of adult education.
2  Identify the forms of adult education.
3  Discuss the goals and purposes of adult education.
4  Differentiate between pedagogy and andragogy as methods of teaching.
5  Identify the six core adult learning principles.
6  Identify the main providers of adult education programmes.

## KEY TERMS

**adult**   An individual whose age and biological state requires an expected form of behaviour and a set of social roles.

**adult education**   Activities designed for the purpose of bringing about learning among those whose age, social roles and self-perception define them as adults.

**andragogy**   The art and science of helping adults learn in which the teacher-facili-

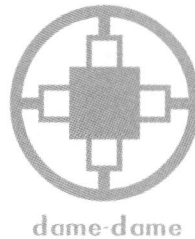

dame-dame

tates the learning process.

**continuing education**   A branch of adult education that aims to link the needs and goals of individuals who have been part of a school system with educational activities that will help to develop their full potential, as well as aid the socio-economic and political development of a nation-state.

**learners' experiences**   Individual differences which learners bring to the classroom related to their work experiences, interests, backgrounds, goals and learning style.

**lifelong learning**   The idea that individuals can engage in learning throughout their life-span in order to cope with life issues.

**motivation to learn**   The interest that a student possesses for learning new material or a particular subject.

**pedagogy**   The art and science of teaching in which the teacher takes a leading role.

**real-life applications**   Knowledge taught and its relevance to the student's world of work.

**self-concept**   An individual's perception of who he/she is.

**self-directed learners**   Self-motivated students with an interest in learning and who seek information through research. The identity of the African individual is shaped by the tendency for African traditional cultures to encourage the interdependence of individuals on each other for the development and fulfilment of those powers that are recognised in African traditional thought.

## ⊞ BEFORE YOU START

Have you ever taught another person how to communicate in your African language, taught a friend how to use that new computer in your workplace or attended orientation training for new employees? In addition, have you ever attended a community development workshop, enrolled in any distance learning or participated in an HIV/AIDS workshop? If you have, then you have participated in some form of adult education. Briefly discuss your experience of adult education.

# THE MEANING OF ADULT EDUCATION

To understand the meaning of adult education it is important to mention Eduard Lindeman, a renowned scholar whose early writings opened the door for debates about what the purposes of adult education should be. He observed that 'this new venture is called adult education not because it is confined to adults but because adulthood and maturity defines its limits' (Lindeman, 1926: 4). Courtney (1989) and Smith (2001) suggested that adult education could be explored from five basic and overlapping perspectives. These include: the work of certain institutions, a special kind of relationship, a profession or a scientific discipline, historical identification with spontaneous social movements, and uniqueness to other kinds of education because of its goals and functions. Detailed explanations of these five perspectives from within the African context are provided below.

1  *The work of certain institutions and organisations.* In Africa, what is referred to as adult education has been shaped by the activities of key organisations such as the trade union for mine workers in South Africa, the *Maendeleo Ya Wanawake* organisation in Kenya and the Commission for Human Rights organisations that exist in nearly all of the African countries. Adult education is what these organisations, which represent different interest groups, do.

2  *A special kind of relationship.* Adult education could be compared to the type of learning that is engaged in for everyday life. It is a relationship between adults in which a conscious effort is taken by the adult to learn something. This could be in a formal setting, such as a school, or an informal setting, such as a community development workshop.

3  *A profession or a scientific discipline.* Smith (2001: 1) noted that 'the focus here is on two attributes of professions: an emphasis on training or preparation, and the notion of a specialised body of knowledge underpinning training and preparation'. Therefore, based on this view, 'the way in which adults are encouraged to learn and aided in that learning is the single most significant ingredient of adult education as a profession' (Brookfield, 1986: 20). For example, when teaching an adult education course, the best way to encourage students to learn is to provide them with projects related to the real world of work. In order to encourage them to learn, flexible schedules should be designed to allow adult students to work while attending school. In 2000, for example, the University of Nairobi in Kenya designed adult education programmes in gender studies, governance and international relations. The programmes were offered in the evening after normal working hours and on weekends. This flexibility in time scheduling enabled diplomats, the then Mayor of Nairobi and Members of Parliament to enrol in these programmes as adult learners. Flexibility in scheduling is a very common element in course offerings at many leading universities in the United States and in Great Britain.

4  *A historical identification with spontaneous social movements.* In Africa, as in many other countries of the world, adult education can be seen as a result of unionism, political parties, political movements, anti-colonial movements and women's social movements (also see Smith, 2001; Lovett, 1988).

5  *Uniqueness in comparison to other kinds of education because of its goals and functions.* This is the most obvious way of differentiating adult education from other forms of education. Darkenwald

and Merriam (1982: 9) have noted that

*adult education is concerned not with preparing people for life, but rather with helping people to live more successfully. Thus, if there is to be an overarching function of the adult education enterprise, it is to assist adults to increase competence, or negotiate transitions in their social roles (worker, parent, retired person), to help them gain greater fulfilment in their personal lives, and to assist them in solving personal and community problems.*

When looking at the five perspectives of adult education, it is clear that adult education is concerned with working with adults to provide them with education essential for their adult lives. However, as a profession, adult education could involve equipping youths who are in the process of growing up with skills and knowledge that will be relevant to their lives. In traditional African societies, as children grew they learnt life and work skills from adults. In contemporary African societies, unemployed youths learn entrepreneurial skills from training institutions to help them become self-employed entrepreneurs (Nafukho, 1998).

Having looked at what adult education involves, the term *adult education* will now be defined. Merriam and Brockett (1997: 4) observed that 'one key to defining adult education lies with the notion of *adult*'. In the African context who is an adult? Traditionally, adulthood as a stage of life is a very old concept in Africa. Every male or female had to be initiated into adulthood before being considered and accepted by the community as an adult. Even today in Nigeria, Ghana, Malawi, Uganda, Zambia and elsewhere, there are initiation rites for young men and women. Initiation rites perform several purposes. Initiation marks the entrance of the initiate into the adult community. It also joins the initiate with all those who have gone before throughout the history of the group. The initiate is able to take part in the rituals of society, that is, to marry and to accept a responsible role within the community. The initiation ceremony also brings the community together for the common purpose of welcoming the young people into its midst (McIntyre, 1996). In South Africa, Ghana and Kenya, for instance, the circumcision of males among several Bantu groups was and still is used as an initiation rite. Every male has to be circumcised as a way of initiation into adulthood (Mbiti, 1991). Adulthood in Africa was also based on fulfilling certain social functions, such as making pottery, hunting, farming and blacksmithing. Adults were expected to marry, raise children and provide for them. This is still the case today.

In traditional African societies, therefore, adulthood was concerned with fulfilling certain sociocultural roles. The concept of adulthood has changed, however, due to Western influence. In contemporary African society, adulthood is based on existing laws. In many independent African countries, one is considered an adult from age 18 years and older. Using the concept of chronological age to define adults in African societies is, however, inadequate. Adulthood is also considered to be a biological issue. Many cultures in Africa consider the puberty stage as the entry to adulthood. When all is said and done, adults are older than children and are expected by their society to behave in a specific manner. Paterson (1979: 13) has noted that

*those people (in most societies, the large majority) to whom we ascribe the status of adults may and do evince the widest possible variety of intellectual gifts, physical powers, character traits, tastes and habits. But we correctly deem them to be adults, because, by virtue of their age, we are justified in requiring them to evince the basic qualities of maturity. Adults are not necessarily mature. But they are supposed to be mature, and it is on this necessary supposition that their adulthood justifiably rests.*

In traditional African societies, if one was already an adult by age but had not been initiated into adulthood through circumcision for instance, then the individual was never considered an adult and could not be allowed to perform certain roles in society. In contemporary society, the definition of an adult is closer to the definition advanced above by Paterson. The meaning of an adult can, therefore, be looked at as a 'biological state, legal state, psychological state, expected form of behaviour and set of social roles' (Smith, 2001: 3). Only adults in traditional African societies would be allowed to participate in such social functions.

## Definition of adult education

Scholars in the field of adult education have defined it in several ways. For the purpose of this book, the definition given by Merriam and Brockett (1997: 13) will be considered to be the most appropriate. They define adult education as 'activities intentionally designed for the purpose of bringing about learning among those whose age, social roles, or self-perception define them as adults'. This definition of adult education captures what it means to be an adult as seen in the previous section of this chapter. UNESCO (1976: 2) provides a more comprehensive definition of adult education:

> *the term* adult education *denotes the entire body of organised educational processes, whatever the content, level, method, whether formal or otherwise, whether they prolong or replace initial education*

*in schools, colleges and universities as well as in apprenticeship, whereby persons regarded as adult by the society to which they belong develop their abilities, enrich their knowledge, improve their technical or professional qualifications or turn in a new direction and bring about changes in their attitudes or behaviour in a twofold perspective of full personal development and participation in balanced and independent social, economic and cultural development.*

Although this definition is broader, it is important to point out that adult education must be considered not as a separate learning experience, but as an integral part of lifelong education and learning. As noted in Chapter 10, for African people to achieve meaningful development and for Africa to survive in the twenty-first century and beyond, adult education and lifelong learning must play a central role. Youngman (2001: 2) observed that 'the necessity for people to learn throughout their life derives from the needs created by the different phases of the life-cycle. Its contemporary urgency is based on the extent and rapidity of the changes taking place in all areas of society'.

## Forms of adult education

In Africa, as in many other parts of the world, several terms and concepts have been used interchangeably with the term *adult education*. These, however, should not replace the important term *adult education* as defined above. While the term *continuing education* has been used to refer to adult education, Tahir (2000: 147) defines continuing education as that 'subset of adult education that seeks to positively link the needs and aspirations of individuals with educational activities for the full development of their potentialities and for the socioeconomic and political development of a nation-state'. He further states that continuing education 'implies that the learners have had some contact with the school system and are striving to build into the knowledge, skills and ideas already acquired' (Tahir, 1985: 4). Youngman (1998) provides a very good summary of the various terms that have been used to refer to adult education in Africa. Some of these terms include:

- agricultural extension;
- in-service training;
- literacy;
- out-of-school education;
- audiovisual education for adults;
- mass media education;
- vocational education;
- in-service personnel training;
- community development; and
- cooperative education.

Adekambi and Modise (2000: 67) note that adult education practices in Africa include 'evening classes, library services, extra-mural education, trade union education, secretarial training and popular theatre'. Other terms that have been used interchangeably with adult education include:

- parallel degree programmes;
- self-sponsored degree programmes;
- mature entry programmes;
- privately sponsored degree programmes;
- prison education;
- non-formal education;
- informal education;
- distance education;
- experiential education;
- human resource development;
- AIDS awareness education;
- herbalists' education; and
- birth attendants' education.

All these forms of adult education reflect the diversity of adult education programmes in Africa.

## Goals and purposes

The goals of adult education in Africa were well articulated in the recommendations to UNESCO during its General Conference at the nineteenth session held in Nairobi, Kenya on 26 November 1976. UNESCO (1976: 2–3) observed that the aims of adult education in Africa and the world over should be to contribute to:

- Promoting work for peace, international understanding and cooperation.
- Developing a critical understanding of major contemporary problems and social changes with a view to achieving social justice.
- Promoting increased awareness of the relationship between people and their physical and cultural environment, and to respecting nature, the common heritage and public property.
- Creating understanding and respect for the diversity of customs and cultures and to developing solidarity at the family, local, national, regional and international levels.
- Acquiring, either individually, in groups or in the context of an educational establishment, new knowledge, qualifications, attitudes or forms of behaviour conducive to the full maturity of the personality.
- Ensuring the individual's conscious and effective incorporation into working life by providing men and women with an advanced technical and vocational education so as to develop the ability to create, individually or in groups, new material goods and new spiritual or aesthetic values.
- Developing an understanding of the problems involved in the upbringing of children.
- Developing an attitude whereby leisure is used creatively for acquiring any

necessary or desired aesthetic values.

■ Developing the ability to critically use mass communication media, in particular radio, television, cinema and the press, so as to be able to interpret the various messages addressed to modern men and women by society.

■ Developing an aptitude for learning how to learn.

The goals and purposes of adult education in Africa have a historical relevance. In traditional African societies, education's purpose was to enable the individual to play societal roles. Both the individual and society were at the centre of learning. With the coming of the colonialists and the missionaries, the goals and purposes of education changed. Colonial administration provided education that would make African adult men and women better labourers. Missionaries, on the other hand, provided education for salvation purposes. All over the world, two general purposes of adult education, namely individual improvement and societal development, as identified by Lindeman (1989), have remained central to the field of adult education. Merriam and Brockett (1997: 17–18), while quoting Lindeman, noted that

> *adult education will become an agency of progress if its short-term goal of self-improvement can be made compatible with a long-term, experiential but resolute policy of changing the social order. Changing individuals in continuing adjustment to social functions – this is the bilateral though unified purpose of adult education.*

Knowles (1980), on the other hand, writes that the mission of adult education is one of satisfying the needs of individuals, institutions and society. Adult educators have the responsibility of helping individuals satisfy their needs and achieve their goals. Although institutions that offer adult education programmes have a need to improve their ability to operate effectively and establish public understanding and involvement, 'the overall development of society requires urgent programmes to equip adults with core competencies that can enable them to perform in an uncertain and changing work environment' (Knowles, 1980).

In summary, the goals and purposes of adult education in contemporary African society, as in many other societies the world over, should include 'the need to meet civic and social responsibilities, political needs, facilitate change, enhance personal and social improvement, promote individual and organisational productivity, career development, remedial and scholastic, and support and maintain the good social order' (Merriam and Brockett, 1997: 19). Many jobs in contemporary African countries require adults to learn new knowledge, skills and attitudes. The University of Botswana's Department of Adult Education website provides the following as examples of where adult education knowledge, skills and attitudes can be applied:

■ the training officer developing human resources in the workplace;

■ the instructor teaching computer skills in a vocational centre;

■ the non-governmental organisation project officer;

■ the extension worker helping farmers to increase their productivity;

■ the community development worker promoting economic projects;

■ the literacy worker teaching adults to read and write; and

■ the instructional designer producing distance learning materials (University of Botswana, 2002).

## ACTIVITY

1 Given the wars and terrorist activities that are taking place the world over, describe what issues adult education programmes should address in order to promote peace, international understanding and cooperation.
2 In traditional African societies education served the purpose of enabling the individual to play societal roles. List the various aspects of traditional African education that still exist today and show their relevance to contemporary African societies.
3 Working alone or in small groups, list five activities that a human resource development manager would create for the purpose of bringing about learning among employees in an organisation.
4 Describe the jobs found in your country that require people to learn throughout their life.

## TEACHING ADULT LEARNERS

In order for adult educators to meet the needs of learners, they must be aware of two important terms associated with teaching and learning: *pedagogy* and *andragogy*. Malcolm Knowles observed that many principles of learning as well as teaching methods have been developed with and for children, and argued that teaching adults requires a different set of instructional strategies (Knowles, 1980). *Pedagogy* refers to the art and science of teaching children. This term has been used in Africa to refer to instructional methods learnt by teacher trainees during their training period. The term *andragogy* (designating the art and science of helping adults learn) was originally used by a German teacher, Alexander Kapp, to describe elements of Plato's education theory (Nottingham Andragogy Group, 1983: v). *Andragogy (ané , genetive andros* – meaning 'man') could be contrasted with *pedagogy (pais*, genetive *paidos* – meaning 'child'), *agógos* meaning 'guide' (Davenport, 1993: 114).

Smith (2002) observes that Kapp's use of the term *andragogy* in German was resisted by other educators until 1921 when Rosenstock argued that adult education required special teachers, instructional strategies and philosophy. This was also true with regard to the teaching of adults in traditional African societies, where only people considered to be experts, with experience and wisdom, were assigned such roles. In the United States, Lindeman picked up Rosenstock's use of the term *andragogy* but only used it on two occasions. In France, Yugoslavia and Holland, the term *andragogy* was used extensively to refer to the discipline which studies the adult education process or the science of adult education (Smith, 2001; Nottingham Andragogy Group, 1983). Knowles learnt the term *andragogy* from Savicevic, a visiting Yugoslav adult educator, and introduced it to North America. Knowles (1970) in his book *The Modern Practice of Adult Education: Andragogy Versus Pedagogy* redefined andragogy as an emerging technology for adult learning. His theory of andragogy is based on five important assumptions about the differences between children and adult learners. These are:

1 *Self-concept*. As people mature, their self-concept moves from one characterised by a dependent personality to one characterised by independence and self-direction.
2 *Experience*. As people mature, a growing reservoir of experience is accumulated that becomes an expanding resource for learning.
3 *Readiness to learn*. As people mature, their readiness to learn becomes focused

on the developmental tasks of their social roles.

4 *Orientation to learning.* As people mature, their time-perspective changes from one where application of knowledge is postponed to one where there is immediate application of knowledge acquired. In the same way, focus towards learning shifts from subject orientation to problem orientation.

5 *Motivation to learn.* As people mature, their motivation to learn becomes an internal drive.

## Six adult learning principles

The five assumptions of the theory of andragogy were later developed into six core adult learning principles which include: 'the need to know, the learner's self-concept, the role of the learner's experiences, readiness to learn, orientation to learning, and motivation' (Knowles, Holton and Swanson, 1998: 64–68). The six principles are based on the psychological definition of what it means to be an adult. As adults, self-direction and responsibility are necessities. In contemporary African society, as in any other society, the following principles of adult learning are especially meaningful.

## Adults need to know why

Knowles, Holton and Swanson (1998: 64–68) noted that 'adults need to know why they need to learn something before they will take the time to learn it.' The need to know could include the benefits to be gained from knowledge acquired or from skills learnt, and any negative effects for not learning new skills or not enrolling in a specific learning programme. As Knowles, Holton and Swanson (1998: 64) stated, 'if adult learners can discover the gap between where they are now and where they want to be, they will become more conscious of their

"need to know" new knowledge and skills'. In many African societies, men learnt skills that were considered necessary to make them useful members of society. During the period 1997–2002 the Mayor of Nairobi enrolled in a philosophy course at the University of Nairobi because he wanted to develop the ability to use logic to solve the many problems facing the city. The need to know and to become an informed member of the Council influenced the Mayor's decision to return to school as an adult learner.

## Responsibility for decisions taken

As an adult, the individual's tendency is to always defend his or her established identity. Adults have a need to be seen by others as being capable of directing themselves. When adults realise others are imposing ideas on them, they may withdraw by not returning to class or they may voice their concerns to the teacher. This is not common with children. Therefore 'when planning for adult learning, efforts must be made to create experiences for adults where they can go from being dependent to independent or self-directed learners' (Knowles, Holton and Swanson, 1998: 65). The concept of *self-directedness* is culturally bound and may vary from one culture to another. In Western culture, the self is often envisaged as something 'inside' a person, or at least as a kind of container of mental characteristics and powers. This distinction, characteristic of much of Western philosophy, is not common in African thinking. In African thought the individual is considered to be bound by society, hence the concept of extended family that is still very strong in many rural African societies. In Africa, the self and the world are united, and the two are part of a web of interdependent relationships (Shutte, 1993: 46–47; Lassiter, 1999). Makgoba (1997: 197–198) argues that throughout the African diaspora, people of African descent

> *are linked by shared values that are fundamental features of African identity and culture. These, for example, include hospitality, friendliness, the consensus and common framework-seeking principle, ubuntu, and the emphasis on community rather than on the individual. These features typically underpin the variations of African culture and identity everywhere. The existence of African identity is not in doubt.*

On the issue of the individual, Mbiti (1969: 109) observes that the individual has little freedom for self-determination outside the context of the traditional African family and community

> *Whatever happens to the individual happens to the whole group, and whatever happens to the whole group happens to the individual. The individual can only say: 'I am, because we are; and since we are, therefore I am.' This is a cardinal point in the understanding of the African view of humankind …*

Although the views expressed above were quite true in traditional African societies, many changes have taken place. It is important to remember that Africa does not exist in isolation and has borrowed heavily (willingly or unwillingly) from other cultures, especially with regard to education. While designing education for adult learners in Africa, an understanding of the African identity and how it has been affected by other world cultures needs to be taken into account. By way of comparison, the African emphasis on the community rather than the individual is in line with the Western concept of teamwork and team learning, while the concept of shared values among various

African communities is in line with Peter Senge's principle of shared visions which learning organisations must nurture and encourage (Senge, 1990). This background is important for designing adult education programmes in Africa.

To illustrate the importance of African traditional societies with regard to adult learning, the renowned Senegalese philosopher, Leopold Senghor, noted that 'the traditional African society was based on the community because it was founded on dialogue and reciprocity. The group had priority over the individual without crushing him/her, but allowing him/her to blossom as a person' (Senghor, 1966: 5). Shutte, a leading South African philosopher, citing a Xhosa proverb, *umuntu ngumuntu ngabantu* (a person is a person through persons), argues that the self in African languages and traditional cultures is concerned both with the interdependence of persons on each other for the exercise, development and fulfilment of the powers that are recognised in African traditional thought, and also with the understanding of what it is to be a person (Shutte, 1993: 46). This saying is similar to that of the Luhyia people in western Kenya, *omundu nomundu wabandu* (an individual is an individual because of other individuals in society). This proverb is relevant in the field of adult education, where learners are encouraged to engage in team learning, group work and group projects.

## Learners' experiences

Lindeman (1989) emphasised the value of the learner's experience with regards to adult education, observing that the approach to teaching adults should be through situations rather than subjects. He noted that 'experience is the adult learner's living textbook' (Lindeman, 1989: 8). Knowles, Holton and Swanson (1998:

26) stated that 'adult learners bring to the classroom a diversified range of individual differences related to their experiences, interests, backgrounds, goals and learning styles. The best way to manage the differences between adult learners is by creating activities that tap into the adults' experience, such as group discussions, problem-solving activities and simulations'. When we apply this principle to the African situation it needs to be critically examined. In traditional African societies, children learnt by performing social roles within the society. For example, when adults went hunting, young boys were required to accompany them; in the same way when women went to collect water from the river, young girls accompanied them. This was a powerful way of learning. When referring to experiences, the learning of social roles in contemporary African society should be taken into consideration. For example, the *Sindikisa* (lifting one another economically) women groups in Kenya have been very successful in helping women learn business skills. In this case, a group of ten to twenty women willingly join together and raise money to support one another. The money is given out on a rotational basis and each recipient is supposed to invest the money in an economic project.

## Coping with real life

This is applicable to many adult learning situations among many African communities. In communities where men are engaged in pastoralism, boys are taught how to survive in the forests many kilometres away from home. This kind of training is relevant to young men as they become adults. The main issue in this principle is not one of age or maturity but what is conducive to effective teaching. Also, the focus on immediate application of skills learnt may not be true with regard to adult literacy classes in many African countries. The majority of learners enrolled in adult literacy classes are often motivated to learn for reasons related to personal growth (internal motivation), rather than for materialistic (external) needs. Adults who missed an opportunity to receive education are often fascinated by their new ability to read and write. For some adults, learning is enjoyable and is motivated by no specific goal in mind.

## Real-life applications

Knowles (1984) suggests that this means that when designing a curriculum for adult learners, courses should be organised around the acquisition of skills necessary for one to earn a living. These skills may include computer skills, farming skills, business skills and teaching skills. In many African countries, following the World Bank and IMF recommendations, many people have been retrenched from the civil service. These retrenched employees need to learn life skills that will provide them with a means to earn a living. In addition, positive aspects of African traditional norms can be applied to the twenty-first century African situation. Lovemore Mbigi, a leading Southern African scholar, has stated that there is a need to apply traditional African concepts to national developmental issues. Mbigi uses expressions such as 'ancient African wisdom,' and persuasively argues that the traditional African concept *ubuntu*, 'I am because we are; I can only be a person through others', is useful for African corporate and organisational executives, managers and others pursuing organisational or national transformation (Mbigi, 1997: 37). Indeed, when designing adult education programmes in Africa, the *ubuntu* concept needs to be considered. For example, learning programmes should encourage groups of evening students to remain intact, share their work experiences, work in learning teams on similar projects and encourage each other to complete the programme without having to drop out.

## Motivation to learn

Knowles, Holton and Swanson (1998: 68) have stated that 'even though adults can be motivated by external factors (such as higher salaries, promotions, better jobs in the future), they are more motivated to learn by internal pressures, such as the desire for increased job satisfaction, self-esteem and quality of life issues'. This principle is in agreement with the tradi-tional African concept of teaching through the social roles expected of the learners. The other important factors that can motivate adult learners as identified by Lieb (1999) may include:

- social relationships, such as making new friends;
- external expectations;
- social welfare, such as improving the ability to serve others;
- personal advancement;
- escape from boredom by providing a break from the routine of work or home; and
- cognitive interests, such as satisfying an inquiring mind and seeking knowledge for its own sake.

Our personal experience as educators of adult students has enabled us to interact with the evening students enrolled in parallel degree programmes offered at various universities in sub-Saharan Africa. We had a unique case of a student who retired after attaining the retirement age for civil servants of 55 years and then enrolled in a privately sponsored degree programme. When asked why he was pursuing a degree after retirement and why he was ready to meet the direct cost of the degree he was

pursuing, he reported that it was purely for the purpose of satisfying an inquiring mind and seeking knowledge for its own sake. Other students have stated that their need to make new friends and escape from boredom motivated them to enrol in degree programmes long after retirement. Besides the internal reasons, adults in Africa are motivated to enrol in adult education programmes in professional areas as well, including education, health, law, and agriculture.

## ⊞ ACTIVITY

From the information presented on the core principles of adult learning, in your opinion, which of the six principles best describe you as a learner? Let a friend in class look over these core principles of adult learning and identify the learning principles that best describe you. Compare your friend's descriptions to your own.

## ADULT EDUCATION PROGRAMMES

In many African countries, the community has played a major role in providing adult education programmes. Providers of adult education in African societies include the family, community and regional organisa-tions, as well as government, trade unions, non-governmental organisations, civic organisations and international organisa-tions. Universities in Africa may be singled out as having played a major role in the pro-vision of adult education. Oduaran (2000: 37) has noted that 'African universities have been at the forefront of strengthening the growth of adult and continuing education through various personnel training and development programmes. While this role has been important, limited data exists to show the exact number of people that the universities have trained'. He notes further that what is available are selected examples of adult education programmes in some of the leading African universities, such as Ibadan University, the University of Benin, Bayero University, Ahmadu Bello University, University of Maiduguri, Obafemi Awolowo University, and the University of Sierra Leone (West Africa); the University of Nairobi, Kenyatta University, Moi University, Egerton University, the University of Dar es Salaam, and Makerere University (East Africa); the University of Swaziland, the National University of Lesotho, the University of Zimbabwe, the University of Botswana, the University of Zambia and the University of Namibia (southern Africa).

It important to point out that these universities train adult educators who are the main implementers of the adult education programmes in many formal and informal learning institutions in Africa. In addition, universities are direct providers of adult education programmes. They fund research in the field of adult education, organise workshops, seminars, conferences and symposia, and host and support adult education professional associations. Besides the universities mentioned above, there are other institutions of higher learning that provide adult education programmes in other African countries, such as Zambia, Egypt, Algeria, Togo, Cameroon, Niger, Mauritius, Sudan and Mozambique. Universities outside Africa, especially from the United States of America, the United Kingdom, Canada, Australia, Germany, Netherlands, Sweden and India, have played a major role in the promotion of adult education in Africa by training leading African scholars (Oduaran, 2000: 40).

Adult education programmes in Africa have also benefited from funding and support from various international bodies.

For example, UNESCO has provided free teaching and learning materials and important data relating to adult education. The writing and production of numerous books in the field of adult education, including the present Series, has benefited from UNESCO funding. The Institute for International Cooperation of the German Adult Education Association (IIZ/DVV) has also played a leading role in the development and promotion of adult education in Africa, including the present Series. Currently, IIZ/DVV provides scholarships to deserving African students who are studying adult education at several African universities. In addition, the IIZ/DVV sponsors *Adult Education and Development*, an important journal that provides a 'forum for dialogue and exchange of professional information between adult educators and writers in Africa, Asia and Latin America. The journal is unique in the sense that it publishes discussions of new experiences and research findings, and thus fulfils an important function in providing both practical and theoretical support for adult education' (Hinzen, 1998: 11–12). The Association also funds several NGOs and university departments of adult and continuing education. To promote scholarship in the field of adult education, IIZ/DVV awards travel grants to African scholars who attend academic meetings around the continent and the world. The World Bank has also played an important role in the development of adult education in Africa. The launching of the Africa Virtual University project in over thirteen African universities has been a single instance of using technology to advance distance learning in Africa.

The Commonwealth Heads of Government created the Commonwealth of Learning (COL) with the main purpose of developing and sharing open learning and distance education knowledge, resources and technologies between the member countries. COL has helped in widening and improving access to quality education and training, especially among African member countries. Other important organisations include: ACTION AID for its REFLECT programme; UNICEF for its active involvement in basic education, especially since Jomtien, 1990; and the Association for the Development of Education in Africa (ADEA), particularly its Non-Formal Education (NFE) Working Group, which has national working groups in many African countries. Leading donor organisations based in the United States have also played an active role in the promotion of adult and distance learning in Africa. Such organisations include the Ford, Rockefeller, MacArthur, Spencer and Kellogg Foundations. The participation of international organisations and universities from outside Africa in adult education programmes shows the need for cooperation in the development of the profession and in the practice of adult education across the world. Africa cannot afford to isolate herself with regard to international trends in the development and practice of adult education.

A discussion on the providers of adult education in Africa cannot be complete without mentioning two important organisations: the African Association for Literacy and Adult Education (AALAE) and the International Council of Adult Education (ICAE). In Chapter 7 the important role played by AALAE in Africa between 1984 and 1994 will be discussed further.

In this book, our definition of adult education is broad and goes beyond the adult literacy programmes that target illiterate people in Africa. Instead, adult education is defined as a field of study which aims at equipping adults with new competencies which can, for example, enable them to fit into the changing world of work. Such programmes also aim at raising people's self-awareness. This is discussed in Chapter 3, which examines the philosophy of adult education in Africa.

## ⌗ ACTIVITY

1  From the definitions of adult education provided in this chapter, list the main providers of adult education in your community.
2  Based on your own knowledge and experience, how would you define adult education?
3  List various reasons why you think adult education programmes should be provided in your country.
4  Using the descriptors ACTION AID, ADEA, AALAE and ICAE search the Internet for additional information relating to these organisations and share the information in class.

## SUMMARY

The meaning of *adult* within the African context was provided in this chapter. This was followed by a working definition of *adult education*. The aims of adult education the world over as defined by UNESCO were presented, and the goals and purposes of adult education were also discussed in detail. *Pedagogy* and *andragogy*, two important terms for adult learning, were explained. The six core principles of adult learning were also presented. The various providers of adult education programmes in Africa were discussed and the important role played in the development of adult education in Africa by universities, as well as by international organisations, was demonstrated. The remainder of the book will expand upon the concepts introduced in this chapter.

## KEY POINTS

- Adulthood and maturity (the individual's ability to fulfil certain roles in
  society) are essential for adult education.
- The wide-ranging forms of adult education reflect the diversity of adult
  education programmes in Africa.
- The central mission of adult education
  is to satisfy the needs and goals of individuals by providing them with important
  competencies that will help them perform more effectively in an insecure and
  changing work environment.
- Teaching adults requires a different set
  of teaching strategies because an adult is
  characterised by self-directed behaviour
  that is not typical of children.
- In traditional African societies the
  individual's identity is bound by the
  interdependent relationship between the
  community and the individual.
- Both local communities and universities
  in Africa have played a major role in providing adult education.

## ACTIVITY

Discuss the role of adult education in contemporary African society by taking into
account the meaning and definitions of
adult education provided in this chapter.

## FURTHER QUESTIONS

1   Give some examples of adult education
    programmes in your country. Why do
    you consider them to be part of adult
    education?
2   Describe at least five ways in which the
    principles of adult learning discussed in
    this chapter can promote adult learning
    programmes.
3   Based on information presented in this
    chapter, list and describe the characteris-
    tics of adult learners that may influence
    training in the workplace.
4   Compare and contrast pedagogical and
    andragogical methods of teaching.

## SUGGESTED READINGS

Knowles, M. S., Holton, E. L. and Swanson,
    R. A. 1998. *The adult learner*. Woburn,
    MA: Butterworth-Heinemann.
Merriam, S. B. and Brockett, R. G. 1997. *The
    profession and practice of adult education*.
    San Francisco: Jossey-Bass.

# Chapter 2

# The history of adult education in Africa

## OVERVIEW

In this chapter the history of adult education in Africa will be discussed by focussing on some selected areas. Several issues relative to the scope of the history of adult education will be explored by examining the potential benefits that can be derived from an understanding of the field's development in Africa. The earliest adult education centres of learning in Africa, that is, before the coming of Europeans, will be examined. This chapter will confirm that Africa had distinguished cultures of learning influenced by rich heritages on which modern adult education programmes were founded and have been built. The role of African indigenous knowledge systems, traditions and religion in adult education will be explained. The impact of imperialism, colonialism, European missionaries and neo-colonialism on adult education in Africa will also be assessed. Finally, the role of the African Union (AU) in the development of adult education will be discussed.

## LEARNING OBJECTIVES

By the end of this chapter, you should be able to:

1 Discuss the historical development of adult education in Africa.
2 Explain the role of African indigenous education systems and traditions in adult education.
3 Describe the impact of imperialism, colonialism, European missionaries and neocolonialism on adult education.
4 Discuss the role of the African Union (AU) in the development of adult education.

dwennimmen

## KEY TERMS

**African Union (AU)**  The successor of the Organisation of African Unity (OAU), which was founded in Addis Ababa, Ethiopia in 1963 and which brought together all the independent states of Africa.

**colonial Africa**  The period between 1884/5 (the partitioning of Africa) and 1994, when South Africa acquired majority rule, Nelson Mandela became president and apartheid was abolished.

**colonialism**  The use of force or diplomacy to bring a foreign people under the rule of a dominant power.

**imperialism**  The desire by a militarily and economically stronger country (or its agents) to conquer and exploit another country whether directly or indirectly.

**indigenous education**  Education that is passed on from parents to children outside formal schooling. It is a part of indigenous knowledge systems that are much wider, in that they encompass the entire survival and coping mechanisms of a community.

**neo-colonialism**  A form of indirect control and domination exercised over former colonial states by their former colonial masters and other powers. It is often subtle and covert in its operations.

**pre-colonial Africa**  Africa before contact with the external world, especially before contact with imperial European powers and before influence by outsiders in Africa, that is, before partitioning.

## ⌗ BEFORE YOU START

Prepare a family tree in which you begin with your own name, then that of your father, then your grandfather's, great grandfather and so forth, and see how far you can go. Find out where and from what your ancestors died, and whether they were poor or rich. Such family history is important because it reveals your identity, your ancestors, inherited traits, family strengths, where you have come from and where you are going. You will notice that weaknesses are often excluded from family histories because only strengths tend to be preserved.

# HISTORICAL DEVELOPMENT

## The meaning and value of history

Why is history important? History is important because much can be learnt from it. History tells us about our past strengths and weaknesses, thereby giving us the opportunity to improve. History functions like a collective mirror to society, pointing out areas of weaknesses and areas which require attention. People with no knowledge of their past are not likely to know their weaknesses and strengths and instead of improving will most likely stagnate because they have no gauge against which to measure their past performance. Knowledge of history enables people to make correct decisions and avoid past mistakes. Studying the history of adult education and learning in Africa is necessary if performance is to improve. It can aid significantly in planning any future course of action. This is because, like other forms of scholarship, history is not neutral. Every historian has a purpose in writing a particular history. Whenever history is read, these questions need to be asked: Whose story is being told and whose is being sidelined? Why is it being told at this time and not before? Why was it told in the past and not now? Why this voice and not another? Whose interests is this narrative serving? Whose voice is getting silenced? and most importantly, Why is there an interest in the past and from whose perspective?

When stories are told including local emotions, needs and wants in a language that people understand and with a deep sense of identity and pride, this approach can inspire and encourage listeners. Personal narratives such as these from insiders tend to focus more on strengths, whereas when told by outsiders, they might focus more on weaknesses. The history of adult education in Africa needs to be told afresh by Africans and from their own perspective.

A historical perspective on the development of adult education in Africa provides information that will facilitate the understanding of who the African people are and where they fit into the maze that is contemporary adult education. This sentiment is also expressed by Welton when he says that 'those of us who think and write about the history of adult education are swept up like everybody else in a maelstrom of contestation, questioning, doubt and revisionism. We are literally being forced to be self-reflective and self-critical. What are historians of adult education actually doing? What are we choosing to write about? What kinds of stories are we telling? To what use are we putting our stories?' (Welton, 1993: 135). In addition to this, how does the history of adult education help us confront the contemporary problems that face a particular sector? How does this help the African continent in general? These are very useful questions, but they are too wide and beyond the scope of this chapter. While it would be tempting to review the historical development of adult education in sub-Saharan Africa, it would be impossible to do justice to such a broad topic in a single chapter. Those readers who seek a comprehensive history of the field should examine other sources (see, for example, Draper, 1998; and Wangoola and Youngman, 1996).

What value does the understanding of history hold for adult education? Whipple has suggested two major aims for making history a part of the study of adult education. Firstly, historical research has contributed to the knowledge base of adult education, and secondly, history can be used as a tool to improve its practice. He has pointed out that history can provide the adult educator with 'a useful supplementary discipline or tool' that can contribute to more efficient practice (Whipple, 1964: 201). Commenting on the history of education in Africa, Fafunwa has reiterated the significance of history when he says that 'history is to a people what memory is to the individual. People with no knowledge of their past would suffer from collective amnesia, groping blindly into the future without guide-posts of precedence to shape their course. Only a thorough awareness of their heritage allows them to make their public decisions ...' (Fafunwa, 1974: 13). It is our belief that knowledge of our past can indeed serve as a useful guide-post to contemporary society. Awareness of people's heritage increases societal cohesion, identity and pride, which are very important for peace and for Africa's survival.

Continuing with the significance of history for adult education, Long has argued that a knowledge of history has two types of practical significance for adult education. The first is concerned with experience, where 'a sense of history helps in the development of the principles that extend beyond mere impressions of current facts, and it improves practice by suggesting what has worked or not worked in practice before, why it did or did not work, and options or alternatives for consideration' (Long, 1990: 7). Another practical value is that history can be useful in understanding trends in adult education by helping educators 'recognize the past in the present form' (Long, 1990: 8). Allison's comments on the importance of history resonate with, and connect very strongly to our African experience, especially when he says 'the point is that who we are as humans, our very concept of reality, is determined by our histories, by what the past has handed down to us. And those who are most ignorant of their history are the most controlled by it because they are the least likely to understand the sources of their beliefs. They are the most

likely to confuse their inherited prejudices with Truth' (Allison, 1995: xiv).

Therefore, as African people, stories about our history give us perspectives on our present, which can help us to understand that adult education has not developed in an empty space without people. Instead, it needs to be understood that the history of adult education in Africa goes back many thousands of years, where its origins are to be found embedded in the life of various African cultures. It makes us realise that this history is inextricably linked to the history of African societies at large, documenting successes and failures. It tells us about how society has dealt with challenges from the environment and often with adult education itself in addressing iniquities and injustices that have been a very real part of the African experience. The narrative is laden simultaneously with excitement, joy, pain, victory, defeat, glory, struggle and triumph. It reveals to us where we stand compared to the rest of the world.

## Education in pre-colonial Africa

Ki-Zerbo captures this triumphant mood when he points out that organised learning started in Africa. It is possible that many Africans have not been told this, believing that learning started elsewhere. He says that 'Africa was the first continent to know literacy and to institute a school system thousands of years before the Greek letters *alpha* and *beta*, the roots of the word *alphabet* were invented, and before the use of the Latin word *schola*, from which the word *school* derives. The scribes of ancient Egypt (used here to include the Nile Valley that begins in Lake Victoria) wrote, read, administered, philosophised, contemplated the beyond and caressed the infinite, using that first aid to writing, papyrus' (Ki-Zerbo, 1990: 17). If we accept the validity of this statement, we can go further and state that adult education in Africa is very old, and that Africans should be proud of their great past. Michael Omolewa is therefore correct in pointing out that 'adult and continuing education in Africa began with the creation of man (sic) on the continent' (Omolewa, 2000: 11). This is because Africa has had well-developed knowledge and educational systems founded in its past. It has had knowledge systems before contact with external cultures in many disciplinary areas equivalent to modern academic disciplines, such as history, geography and mathematics.

A survey of the historical records of adult education in Africa reveals that in some countries, pre-colonial adult education is not given much prominence, whereas in others, adult education appears to have experienced rapid growth during the colonial period, and even after independence. Yet in others, it experienced decline and suffered from neglect in all periods (Shu, 1982; Indire, 1982; Mohapeloa, 1982 and Sherman, 1982), meaning that scholars are not quite agreed on the origins of adult education in Africa. The emergence of Indigenous Knowledge Systems (IKS) as a genre in African studies in the recent past, and the emotions that this has evoked, has re-ignited a lot of interest and is likely to clear some previous misunderstandings on chronology. It is therefore appropriate at this time to fault chronologies that seek to set adult education in Africa as beginning with the arrival of the European presence in Africa. Chronologies that place the West at the centre of knowledge production do Africa a huge injustice for failing to recognise and acknowledge her contributions. There should be a determined effort to find a much earlier presence of adult learning and education in Africa, as well as a much richer Africa-oriented chronology where Africans were at the centre of the action.

Therefore, we agree with Fafunwa when he says that 'no study of education in Africa is complete or meaningful without adequate knowledge of the traditional or indigenous education prevalent in Africa prior to the introduction of Islam and Christianity' (Fafunwa, 1982: 9).

Fafunwa says 'in Old Africa, the warrior, the hunter, the nobleman, the man who combined good character with a specific skill was adjudged to be a well-educated and well-integrated citizen of his community' (Fafunwa, 1982: 9). Fafunwa further points out that education in Africa is 'a means to an end, not an end in itself. Education was generally for an immediate induction into society and preparation for adulthood … and emphasised social responsibility, job orientation, political participation and spiritual and moral values' (Fafunwa, 1982: 9). Omolewa, who pursues aspects that represent Africa's adult education in the past, also echoes Fafunwa's perception. He discusses these pertinent aspects in African educational structures by pointing out that 'apprenticeship training programmes provided an opportunity for the preparation of herbalists, hunters, food gatherers, security officials, rulers, soldiers, traders and so on' (Omolewa, 1998: 11). However, as Ki-Zerbo (1990) has noted, the role of adult education in Africa obviously went beyond these survival skills and included more sophisticated as well as scientifically and technologically advanced pursuits. It traversed a whole array of disciplines including science, technology, social science and the humanities, such as philosophy, various art forms, astrology, astronomy, music, mathematics, anatomy, physiology, sexuality, demography, geomorphology, climatology, geology, medicine, farming and irrigation, engineering, architecture and environment, among others. Fafunwa has correctly stated that 'the aim of traditional African education is multilateral and the end objective is to produce an individual who is honest, respectable, skilled, cooperative and conforms to the societal order of the day' (Fafunwa, 1974: 20).

The knowledge of these 'sciences' is contained in written forms in Ethiopia and the Nile Valley, and in oral forms and narratives in the rest of the continent. The best-known examples of these geniuses of creative ingenuity are the pyramids of Egypt, mummies and their mummification, the great palatial buildings of Meroe and Aksum from Ethiopia, as well as walled cities such as Great Zimbabwe. Cheikh Anta Diop addresses most of these issues in his book, *The African Origin of Civilization*, where he discusses the 'modern falsification of history' (Diop, 1974: 43). Diop points out that the rest of the world later borrowed their science and technology from black Egyptians. He asserts that 'throughout Antiquity [Egypt] would remain the classic land where the Mediterranean people went on pilgrimages to drink at the fountain of scientific, religious, moral and social knowledge, the most ancient such knowledge that mankind had acquired' (Diop, 1974: 10). An American scholar, Martin Bernal (1987), in his four-volume work, *Black Athena*, has confirmed what Diop has reiterated and even what ancient Greeks conceded, that Greek religion, philosophy and science were borrowed from the African world through ancient Egypt and Ethiopia. On this subject, Nabudere has also said 'many of the Greek philosophers and first scientists, such as Solon, Thales, Hecataeus, Democraitus, Herodotus, Plato, and Eudoxus, studied in Ethiopia and Egypt' (Nabudere, 1996: 168). Therefore, we can conclude that adult education in Africa has a rich, independent and diverse historical past.

Africa had other centres of learning, apart from Egypt and Ethiopia. These included Gao and Timbuktu, noted for their learning (Fafunwa, 1967: 2). Many practices in African societies were linked to adult learning as an integral part of life. They developed into a rich knowledge of discourses, such as those experienced at the world's first university at Timbuktu, which in its golden age (2600 BC to 672 AD) boasted not only the impressive libraries of the University of Sankore and places of worship, but also a wealth of private libraries, which must have provided opportunities for education to many (Abun-Nasr, 1975). This was at a time when Europe was still primitive and backward, immersed in superstition and idolatry. For centuries, local families, local officials and scholars in Timbuktu gathered and preserved texts (Djait, 1981). Possibly the most precious legacy of Timbuktu is the surviving manuscripts from its ancient libraries (Levtzion, 1971: 120–157). Therefore, forms of adult learning were already in place in ancient Africa, and any chronological overview of adult education in Africa would be incomplete without reference to these ancient sites of knowledge production. In fact, much of what we refer to in Africa today as Western education has only come full circle, having been incubated in Ethiopia, Egypt and Timbuktu centuries ago (see Ki-Zerbo, 1990; Nabudere, 1996).

Beginning in the seventeenth century, however, for reasons connected to internal upheavals caused by invasions and attacks from abroad (the most serious of all being the slave trade), the school-based education system in Africa was almost totally destroyed. In the pre-colonial period, the educational institutions in Africa were 'schools unenclosed by walls'. The school, in effect, was intimately and intricately intertwined with the family and the village. It was the village itself that was sacked in times of upheavals, and with the arrival of invaders, the inhabitants were scattered and driven away, which destroyed longstanding kingdoms and chiefdoms. New structures and institutions were created in the education sector, mainly to serve imperial projects in Africa.

## Imperialism

Imperialism is represented by the covert or overt intentions of one country for control or manipulation of another. These designs are usually either direct or through proxies. Imperialism in Africa began with ninth century Arab and Persian arrivals, which were confined to small coastal enclaves and did not penetrate to the interior of Africa. Apart from the modest Arabic influence at the coast and the introduction of Islam, many of the Arab spheres of influence were not as enduring, as proselytising or as exploitative as modern imperialism. Modern imperialism, which is what we are interested in and which created large states in Africa, began in the fifteenth century with the onset of the slave trade and later continued through legitimate trade by European powers, especially Portugal, Britain, France, Belgium, Spain and the Netherlands. It was these powers that opened Africa's education to new ideas. These European powers were interested in empire building, and they created spheres of influence all over Africa. They were also interested in overseas products and markets. They spread their European rivalry to Africa, Asia, Latin America and the rest of the New World. Education was one of the means used to control and pacify African people. This was done through missionaries from the respective colonising powers. The result of imperial education was the subjugation and control of the African people. The activities of various European imperialists have often been associated with new educational ideas in Africa, as well as with the beginning of colonial control. The activities of imperialists, such as H. M. Stanley in the Congo

and Carl Peters and William Mackinnon in East Africa, opened up the interior of Africa to European penetration and control, including the spreading of European ideas, especially in the field of education. By the end of the nineteenth century, colonial conquest was virtually complete, and with it came new structures and institutions (Ki-Zerbo, 1990: 18).

It can be argued that the break-up of the African educational system was completed by colonial domination. The missionaries began an onslaught on the African adult education systems by replacing them with modern forms of adult education suitable for meeting their need to evangelise and for reaching their imperial objectives. The colonialists added to this by designing education to serve the overall objective of subjugating the African continent to European needs. What appeared to be transformation by the colonial administrations, as compared to the missionary purposes, was only a shift in emphasis – a shift from a purely religious education to a diluted secular education which emphasised the role of the school in furthering colonial objectives in Africa (Fafunwa, 1982: 21). For African societies, education lost its functional role. Schools were no longer natural organs connected in significant ways to African society. Instead, they were turned into artificial substitutes, real impositions. Since Africa consists of about fifty countries, it is not possible in a space as small as this to do a country-to-country analysis of adult education from the colonial period to the present.

## The colonial period

Perhaps what is most important to note is that many African countries had diverse traditional forms of adult education which merged with the modern forms of adult education introduced to Africa by missionaries (Islam and Christianity) and colonialists, especially after the eighteenth century. Essentially, many African countries have different profiles of the history of adult education because of local differences. Therefore, the reasons given for the choice of a date of origin for adult education vary among scholars. Often, this is dependent on who is doing the analysing and the analyst's understanding of what adult education in Africa means. For instance, Miranda Greenstreet and Kofi Siabi-Mensah place Ghana's profile for adult education as beginning in 1787, whereas Michael Omolewa places that of Nigeria in 1900 (Greenstreet and Siabi-Mensah, 1998; Omolewa, 1998). Greenstreet and Siabi-Mensah see the Toridsoman indigenous society founded at the Cape Coast in 1787 as constituting the first site of adult education in Ghana. On the other hand, Omolewa noted that 'colonialism brought adult education programmes, especially those which prepared the under reached (sic), out-of-school population for a living through in-service, evening classes, and correspondence courses' (Omolewa, 1998: 12). Nineteen hundred is the year in which a European model library was established in the High Court at Lagos 'to provide continuing education facilities for lawyers, judges and others, for the acquisition of skills, knowledge and techniques required for effective job performance' (Omolewa, 1998: 54).

Certainly, the history of adult education in Nigeria is much longer and more extensive. Nigeria was home to one of the highest concentrations of pre-colonial states in Africa and had elaborate structures that included adult education where the art of crafting, storytelling and the preservation of information relating to the family lineage, for example, was passed on from one generation to another. The Hausa and the Fulani in Northern Nigeria received Islamic and Arabic influence in education much earlier on, and established Islamic centres

that became off-shoots of civilisation in the regions under pre-colonial states, such as Kanem-Borno and Kanuri. These culminated in major urban centres such as Kano and Katsina. Early foundations of education such as these were responsible for the special treatment that the region enjoyed under the indirect rule of the British colonial period. The Ibo and Yoruba speaking peoples had also impressive forms of learning before the advent of colonialism. Benin is particularly known for the explosion of artistic creativity following its formation in about 1000 AD and throughout its entire history up to 1897, when it was subdued by European colonialism (Ajayi, 1989).

Turay has chosen 1827 as the starting point for adult education in Sierra Leone, seeing it as coinciding with the European missionary presence. This is when the Church Missionary Society of London first established Fourah Bay College as an institution for training African men as clergy, catechists and schoolmasters. For Botswana, Youngman has chosen to begin the chronology in 1931, when 'the colonial government stationed an agricultural demonstrator with the Bakgatla ethnic group to introduce new methods of crop farming' (Youngman, 1998: 26). Mushi and Bwatwa have pointed to 1860 as the starting point for adult education in Tanzania, when 'Christian missions established literacy classes to enable their converts to read religious literature' (Mushi and Bwatwa, 1998: 87). In the same way in which Turay and Youngman see the missionary and European presence as the starting point for adult education, Mushi and Bwatwa see adult education as beginning with colonial penetration. They do not acknowledge that Tanzania had a sophisticated adult education system before the advent of European missionaries. This was particularly true in Zanzibar, Pemba and the coastal towns, where due to Islamic influence and culture, adult education did take place even though it was for religious instruction only. The writings of Shabaan Robert and Mwana Heri produced in Arabic are examples of the early literacy and adult education culture in Tanzania.

Nondo and Muti have indicated that adult education in Zimbabwe began in 1898 with the activities of the Hope Fountain Mission in Matabeleland when it 'opened the first training school for adults, with the aim of producing elementary school and industrial teachers' (Nondo and Muti, 1998: 98). Even if the activities of the missionary Robert Moffat in the 1850s were taken as a starting point, Nondo and Muti's chronology of adult education in Zimbabwe would still raise eyebrows. Did adults among the Ndebele and Shona not receive an education before Europeans arrived? Surely some form of adult education did exist before then. David Kirui is perhaps accurate to begin his chronology of adult education in Kenya from what he vaguely calls the pre-1895 period when 'traditional education occurred through parents and elders, craftspeople under apprenticeship systems and elders in initiation rites' (Kirui, 1998: 43).

## Post-independent Africa

It has often been argued that even after independence Africa has not escaped the neo-colonial objectives of Western nations, which are today carried out indirectly through economic manipulation and control, among other devices. It is a fact that Africa is still a recipient of Western-controlled education infrastructure that stretches from the Internet to publishing houses. Today, adult education in Africa is often led by Western concerns, such as the contemporary demand for computer literacy in Africa. Adult education programmes in Africa pursue paradigms that are by and large prescribed and funded

by Western nations, such as adult literacy, which is crucial for effective participation in development. Nevertheless, what emerges as crucial in the many analyses of country profiles of adult education in Africa is that after independence, many African countries have placed adult education variously in the Ministry of Education; Cooperative Development; Culture and Social Services; Social Welfare; or Community Development. What is significant to note is that adult education, non-formal education, continuing education, lifelong learning or whatever other names are given to this discipline is a recognised sector in all of the African countries.

Many universities in Africa have set up training programmes in adult education. In fact, university extra-mural departments have grown in strength and have rapidly extended the range and variety of their programmes. Fourah Bay College in Sierra Leone, which started offering degrees in 1876, led the way in Western-type adult education. In the 1940s, some staff members from the college conducted matriculation and commercial classes for adult learners in the major town, Freetown, although it was not until 1951 that a full department of adult education (extra-mural studies) was founded at Fourah Bay College (Turay, 1998: 68). South Africa's University of Cape Town started an extra-mural programme in 1952 (Gush and Walters, 1998: 79). Writing on Botswana, Youngman has noted that 'the University of Botswana, Lesotho and Swaziland opened a country office for its Extension Department (subsequently renamed the School of Adult Learning, and in 1971, the Division of Extra-Mural Services) to provide outreach activities in the community' (Youngman, 1998: 27).

Ghana and Nigeria, like Sierra Leone, received Western-type adult higher education quite early on, after coming under similar Western missionary influence. In

Ghana in 1949, the newly established University College of Gold Coast absorbed the Oxford Delegacy's Office that became the College's Department of Extra-Mural Studies (Greenstreet and Siabi-Mensah, 1998). In 1949 in Nigeria, the same Oxford Delegacy for Extra-Mural Studies helped found the University College, Ibadan, which in turn inherited its extra-mural programmes in Nigeria (Omolewa, 1998). In 1961, the University College of Rhodesia and Nyasaland (then still affiliated with the University of London) established the Institute of Adult Education (Nondo and Muti, 1998). In Kenya, it was in 1967 that the University College, Nairobi (then still under the University of East Africa, together with Makerere and Dar-es-Salaam, previously affiliated with the University of London) established a unit to cater for correspondence courses.

In 1960, the Extension Department of Pius XII University College (now the Institute of Extra-Mural Studies) of the National University of Lesotho was established as the non-formal education arm of the university (Sebatane and Moore, 1998). The University of Zambia at Lusaka established the Department of Extra-Mural Studies and Department of Correspondence Studies in 1966, just two years after independence in 1964 (Mumba, 1998). The University of Namibia has perhaps one of the youngest adult education departments at a university in Africa, dating to only 1997. This delay was caused by the colonial occupation endured by Namibia until its liberation by the South West African People's Organization (SWAPO) in 1990.

Adult education and lifelong learning are closely related and are the fastest growing areas of higher education in Africa. This trend is likely to continue with the arrival of media and web-based education programmes in Africa. There is no doubt that these centres of adult education have made important contributions to Africa's developmental process, especially in the supply of well-trained human resources. Many of these centres have played a leading role in minimising dependence on expatriate labour in Africa.

## ✵ ACTIVITY

**Make your own summary of the most important historical influences on the development of adult education in Africa.**

## INDIGENOUS EDUCATION SYSTEMS

What would constitute an Indigenous Education System (IES) in Africa? Traditional learning and knowledge production form indigenous education. Fafunwa has ably demonstrated the importance of indigenous education in pre-colonial Africa (what Fafunwa refers to as 'Old Africa') before it encountered Western education. He says that 'African education emphasised social responsibility, job orientation, political participation and spiritual and moral values' (Fafunwa, 1982: 9). Moumouni in his book *Education in Africa* provided one of the earliest attempts at conceptualising what amounts to an African indigenous or traditional system of education. He summarised it as involving the following four strands. Firstly, great importance is attached to education in society, especially to its collective social nature, meaning that it is holistic or all-encompassing. Secondly, it is intimately tied to the social life of the people, both in a material and spiritual sense. Thirdly, it is multivalent in character, both in terms of its goals and the means it employs. Finally, it is gradual and progressive in its achievements and in conformity with the successive stages of the physical, emotional and mental development of the learner (Moumouni, 1968: 15). Admittedly, Africa has many cultural areas but there are some similarities in cultural pursuits and objectives.

Indigenous Education Systems are part of Indigenous Knowledge Systems (IKS), which are much wider and utilised by the entire community, and include both specialists and non-specialists. Indigenous education, on the other hand, is passed on from adults to children, and is of a general nature, which is supposed to be disseminated to everyone in society at certain stages of life. Indigenous education systems are very useful areas for understanding contemporary educational issues, especially in adult education. Fafunwa (1974) correctly points out that the aim of traditional African education was multilateral, playing many roles, and that its end objective was to produce an individual who is all-rounded, honest or trustworthy, respectable, skilled, cooperative and who conforms to the societal order of the day. He argues that every society has its own system of training and educating its youth. Fafunwa further points out that 'education in Old Africa (pre-colonial Africa) was not rigidly compartmentalised as is the case in the contemporary system' (Fafunwa, 1974: 16).

In pre-colonial Africa 'Old Africa', education played a practical role. *Functionalism*, as Fafunwa has noted, 'was its guiding principle' (Fafunwa, 1974: 15). Education aimed at providing an immediate induction into society and a preparation for adulthood. It was here that 'children learnt by doing, that is to say, children and adolescents were engaged in participatory education through ceremonies, rituals, imitation, recitation and demonstration' (Fafunwa, 1982: 9). Using Uganda for his analysis, Nabudere has also indicated that learning by doing was at the core of traditional African education (Nabudere, 1996). Therefore, it can be said that indigenous education systems are

a complex set of useful ideas, practices and technologies that enhance the qualitative value of life among the people for whom they have been developed. IES include a holistic set of institutions that covers a wide range of themes in education and other learning processes, both for adults and children. Therefore, IES are communal. They are those ideas that have been long tested and whose efficacy and therapeutic usefulness to people within a given mutually inclusive cultural area have been widely accepted. IES have a role within a holistic community lifestyle that includes both the spiritual/mental and material aspects of a society.

Indigenous Education Systems refer to education developed by and for these populations and used exclusively among them, and which are disseminated at different stages of growth in the life of an individual. Fafunwa has identified seven cardinal goals of traditional African education. They include developing a child's latent physical skills; fostering character; inculcation of respect for elders and those in positions of authority; developing intellectual skills; acquisition of specific vocational training and instilling a positive attitude towards honest labour; promoting a sense of belonging and active participation in family and community affairs; and helping to understand, appreciate and promote the cultural heritage of the community at large (Fafunwa, 1974). Elders, who hold much of societal knowledge in trust, are the only ones that can permit its use outside the cultural area. Therefore, in much of Africa, IES are organised around specific conditions of people congruent to a particular geographic space and location. IES also include ideas developed by individuals but mutually incorporated into communal knowledge banks. The custodians of these knowledge banks are the local societies, who vest their power among the elders and sometimes among local experts. Because of their communal nature, IES are shared widely. The world has been alerted to the presence of IES through the work of anthropologists, sociologists, historians and other scholars who have realised that Africa has a lot to contribute to world education.

However, the creative and innovative traditions in Africa have been masked by historical misrepresentations by outsiders, as well as obscured domestically and internationally for reasons of pedagogy and policy. From an early age students in Africa learn about the major inventions of the Europeans, but they seldom learn about grassroots or higher level inventions and innovations developed by individuals, institutions or communities within Africa. When local contributions are taught in Africa, they are recalled with terminology that generates disdain rather than respect for indigenous genius and innovation. But this is only one reason why the possibility of building upon the grassroots traditions of invention and innovation in Africa has not been pursued. There are several other possible reasons for this:

- there is a lack of awareness about such traditions among policy planners, educationists and members of civil society at large in Africa;
- the influence of foreign Christian missions, foreign languages and foreign aid agencies whose work often results in increased dependency rather than self-reliance;
- Africa has adopted education systems which do not promote curiosity and an experimental ethic, but instead reinforce cultures of compliance and conformity;
- science and technology establishments have emerged that do not encourage local traditions even if they are functional and viable;
- Africa is experiencing the increasing

influence of the media, popularising Western images of progress and so-called 'development' rather than indigenous notions of the same;
- the lifestyles of the elite do not tend to inspire any respect for local knowledge systems;
- there is also declining respect for local therapeutic values, represented by healers and herbalists, as African communities who are exposed to modern medicine are promoting immediate relief regardless of side-effects;
- Africa has also to contend with declining communication between the 'grandparents generation' and the 'grandchildren generation' due to the disappearance of extended families and the appearance of nuclear families;
- there appears to be a lack of incentives for creative people, such as medicine persons, in terms of remuneration and societal recognition and honour; and
- most importantly, there are inadequate intellectual property rights for informal innovators in African communities whose work remains unrecognised. For example, the Kenyan *ciondo* (sisal basket) that has been patented in South Korea, while Nigerian, Senegalese and other African clothes and batik designs have been patented in Taiwan.

Most African technological inventions are not recognised as such, but are regarded as mere cultural phenomena and are assigned to lesser categories of invention, where they are often denied patents in Western nations. African traditional songs are a good example of this tendency, as they are never regarded as material that can be copyrighted despite the creativity that goes into them. Africans find some of their scientific and technological achievements confined to fine art museums. The scientific and technical processes underlying the creation of various inventions are trivialised, and not incorporated in the world of science and discoveries. Creativity in Africa, therefore, has not received adequate attention and recognition. This means that a lack of historical recognition may have influenced the contemporary biased consciousness about creativity and innovation in Africa.

It is noticeable in Africa that the tendency of indigenous knowledge systems to combine traditional skills, culture and artefacts with modern skills, perspectives and tools is not something that has happened only in the recent past. From time immemorial, new crops were introduced from one part of the continent to another, and cultural and ecological knowledge systems evolved while adapting these crops as well as animals, trees and tools to their new contexts. This is an ongoing process, and is similar to what occurs in other parts of the world. What may set the traditional ways of dealing with local resources, external knowledge and inputs apart may be a slower trial and error approach that may not necessarily be unscientific. But, it may not be fully compatible with so-called modern methods of experimentation, validation and drawing inferences. In some cases, the correspondence is close but in many cases it may not be.

For instance, the symmetrical wall decorations in Lesotho and South Africa, and the use of stones and termite clay for house building in Zimbabwe, Mozambique, Liberia and Kenya are styles that evolved simultaneously and were even adopted by early Europeans before cement arrived on the scene. A further example is the weaving of pyramidal baskets using napier grass in the Congo, Uganda, Tanzania, Kenya and Mozambique, among other African countries. Exploration of the hexagonal basket-weaving technique found from the Cameroon to Kenya and from the Congo to Mozambique is fascinating, as it indicates cultural diffusion within Africa. Other examples are the plaited strip patterns from Guinea, Mozambique, Senegal, Uganda and Zimbabwe. Also of significance are the fine geometrical designs from the lower Congo region and northern Zambia. The ancient Egyptian arithmetical and medicinal documents became known as the Rhind, Ebers and Edwin Smith papyri, which were then appropriated by Europe. European predecessors were created where they did not really exist. The fact that the Greek alphabet is largely of African/Syrian/Lebanese origin and that there is a proliferation of loan words from these languages, has not received sufficient attention. The African and Asian origin of many linguistic terms and concepts associated with the Greco-Roman cultural zone is not common knowledge to the unsuspecting layperson (Bernal, 1987; Blaut, 1992; Diop, 1967; Fafunwa, 1974; Ki-Zerbo, 1990 and Nabudere, 1996).

However, it is possible that through mutual respect and trust, traditional knowledge experts can work with those from other knowledge systems to generate more effective solutions for contemporary problems in Africa and the world. After all, the 'tape and weight view' of measuring and weighing science, implying excessive reliance on specific methods of solving problems, has never helped in taking scientific research very far. Traditional contexts reflect and embed certain rules about how interaction with nature, with each other and with our inner selves can help to generate sustainable and compassionate approaches to solving problems. Incentives for creating a sufficiently strong desire for experimentation will become embedded when modern institutions recognise, respect and reward the experiments done in the past, such as with the use of herbal medicine, where the *isangoma* or *mghanga* (healer/doctor) are respected just like those from other knowledge systems.

In many countries in Africa, this knowledge, which is shared among adults orally, is today preserved for eternity and for the benefit of the larger society. The thrust is in indigenous medicine and pharmacology, encompassing human health and even surgery; veterinary medicine and animal health; maternal and child health; and sexual health and disease. Through collaboration, several elements have been • incorporated into mainstream medicine and the previous stereotypes that peripheralised and demonised African medicine have been discarded. Nowadays there are courses at medical schools in Africa that cover African medicine. Moi University has pioneered this in Kenya. Here they teach indigenous taxonomy and systematics; courses on chemical, pharmaceutical and biochemical elements of African medicine; and, most importantly, the psychological, political, economic and sociocultural context of African medicinal plants/herbs and animal products. At the heart of this collaboration is mutuality of trust and respect for each other's knowledge, capability and capacity.

This capability and mutuality is evident in the work of Bible translations into African languages by Africans, which have aided in enhancing literacy in the indigenous languages. The development of African scripts such as the Kiswahili script (Kenya and Tanzania), the Luganda script (Uganda), the Bamun script (Cameroon), the Vai script (Liberia) and the Ki Ka Ku (Sierra Leone) are significant contributions by Africans to literacy efforts in Africa. Many linguistic experts in African languages have recognised the significant contribution that these scripts have made to the study and development of literacy and knowledge in indigenous languages.

Let us bring the discussion in this section to an end by reflecting on the eight pertinent principles that emerge in adult education. The African education system (probably a hybrid between indigenous and European) differs from the Western one and cannot really be separated from life itself, as we have seen that education and training are intricately intertwined. Education is collective, often tailored by culture and embedded in societal norms, is social in nature and is closely associated with life in society. For indigenous knowledge to thrive in the way it has demonstrates how crucial a role society has played, particularly in relation to its preservation arising through continual usage. It is clear then that adult education in Africa operates on the following eight principles:

1   Learning through seeing, observing and doing.
2   Joint and communal custody of knowledge and information.
3   Passing on of information from one generation to another and across cultural borders.
4   Equity, mutuality and respect among members of society in the use of knowledge.
5   Development and improvement of intellectual skills based on need and want.
6   Sparing and joint use of all types of resources.
7   Importance of oral means of transmission, especially through metaphors and riddles.
8   Understanding, appreciating and promoting the cultural heritage of communities.

## ⌗ ACTIVITY

1   **Provide relevant examples of how young people in traditional societies learnt from older members of society. Describe some of the activities that took place in your society when learning took**

place through apprenticeship and when learners acquired knowledge through observation, learning and doing (e.g., circumcision, traditional medicine, blacksmithing, hut building, fishing, hunting).

2  Provide examples of IES in your own community and area.

## COLONIALISM AND MISSIONARIES

Colonialism is a process of subjugation, control and domination by a powerful country over a less powerful one, often resulting in the imposition of structures of control and domination. Colonialism is exploitative and manipulative, and influences economic, social, political and cultural sectors. Colonialism in Africa was a system of administration that was mainly externally operated and served external interests. Whether they were British, French, German, Portuguese, Belgian or Italian, their colonial objectives were similar in many regards and only differed in minor details (Ki-Zerbo, 1990). Colonialism not only fostered a process of exploitation in Africa, but also division and domination. Societies were manipulated and changes were introduced to serve European interests. Colonialism created production systems that were geared towards the creation of capitalist relations and the economic and sociocultural aggrandisement of the coloniser. In more recent cases there are exploitative structures that have been created by neo-colonialism, especially those responsible for creating economic dependence through such supra-national organisations as the World Bank, the International Monetary Fund (IMF) and the World Trade Organisation (WTO). Colonialism and neo-colonialism as forms of exploitation may be perpetrated by covert or overt, direct and indirect, psychological, legal and military mechanisms. For many years African countries have been affected by various problems emanating from the structures and institutions that were inherited from colonialism and European missionaries.

Whereas some scholars have justified colonialism and even pointed out the benefits of this system, others have demonstrated that colonialism was exploitative and inhibited the development of indigenous science and technology in Africa. They have argued that colonial domination brought with it dependence on the production structures of the West. It made Africans net producers of raw materials for the West and net importers of finished products from the West. This led to shifts to cash crop economies and destabilised some of the existing processes of technical and scientific growth in Africa. Therefore, having been handicapped in various ways during the period of colonial rule, many African countries find themselves still affected by colonialism (Zeleza, 1988). A clearly visible legacy is in adult education, where missionaries educated adults for liturgical interests. Colonial governments were interested in adult education in so far as they produced literate people who were used as collaborators and workers for their colonial enterprises.

During colonialism African practices that were not readily understood by colonial officials were branded as magic or superstition, and practitioners were branded as heathens, backward, primitive and even demonic. Adult education was often deployed to disseminate propaganda. It was also utilised for female domestication, for producing women subservient to the needs of the empire, for taking care of the men who worked for colonial enterprises and for producing a future labour force. Adult education was pursued through programmes of hygiene, among others, as if Africans never had such programmes. Colonial manipulations and impositions were so rampant that Africans were often marginalised in decision-making processes. Since then, silence has reigned with respect to non-European predecessors of significant inventions in Africa. The constant interaction between the Ancient Greeks and their African counterparts is ignored, although the Greeks themselves gratefully acknowledged this interaction (Nabudere, 1996).

Colonialism ensured ideological dependence through ideologies such as Christianity and capitalism, among others. Adult education in Africa was changed to reflect the European social process. Christianity was used to prepare Africans for colonisation, best represented in the famous expression: 'the coloniser's flag (or crown) followed the cross (or Bible)'. Missionaries such as David Livingstone did much of the earliest penetration of Africa, and their earliest African converts became their collaborators during colonial domination. Western adult education often comes under attack for promoting elites and has often raised debates in decolonisation movements concerning the educated and uneducated nationalists.

Africa is assailed for not inventing the wheel, as if to imply that it was a European invention. The fact remains, though, that Greek and Roman wheeled vehicles and chariots are the direct heirs of Mesopotamian and Egyptian ingenuity. Moreover, African Saharan rock paintings reveal chariots and wheeled vehicles of great antiquity, yet they are often ignored or attributed to some foreign race that might have moved into Africa and then disappeared (Djait, 1981 and Ki-Zerbo, 1981). Ki-Zerbo therefore insists that 'the tendency to explain all features of African culture by the theory of outside influence must be rejected' (Ki-Zerbo, 1981: 675).

Economic dependence was created causing the African continent to remain a backwater industrial pariah and permanent supplier of raw materials to Europe. Colonialism reinforced the myth that Africa contributed nothing to the development of science and technology, either in terms of hardware or software. Adult education was transformed into an elitist, selective process that earned participants privileges, compared to the previous African approach where adult learning was holistic and served everyone. The colonial powers also implemented outdated teaching methods in Africa, many which had become obsolete in Europe and thereby suffocated Africa with competing theories of learning. African markets were flooded with cheap mass-produced textile, glass and iron products in the context of policies, such as 'the scrap iron policy' of Britain, and was used as a dumping ground for dangerous wastes, especially during experimentation with nuclear and atomic materials. Traditional trades were considered redundant. Indigenous manufacturing was deliberately undermined by these moves, and many strategies were intentionally implemented to facilitate European imports to Africa (Mkandawire, 1988 and Zeleza, 1990). Captive markets were created in Africa through coercive policies and laws aimed at suppressing African indigenous technological development, inventions, innovations and discoveries through indoctrination and education. Adult education was one of the chief means used to further these Eurocentric endeavours (Burke, 1996).

Colonialism ensured the manipulation and appropriation of African ideas. The historical tendency for the majority of the world to passively accept so-called Western science and technology, was perpetuated. Africans have found some of their scientific and technological achievements appropriated or stolen, stored in archives and labelled *possibly Greek* or *unknown*. The scientific and technical processes underlying the creation of various inventions that are associated with Africa have been trivialised. For example, hand woodcarvings, the stirrup, the sternpost rudder, the lateen sail, the abacus, the pendulum, the game of chess, the axle, the bow drill, the chisel and the wedge are all of non-European origin. The latter did for building technology what the Mesopotamian and African sailboat, barge, freight and wheeled vehicle did for navigation and communication (Diop, 1967; Bernal, 1991).

Colonialism made it possible for linguistic domination to take root, to the extent that very few countries encourage education in African languages, and Africa is often divided into the foreign linguistic blocks of Francophone (French-speaking), Anglophone (English-speaking), and Lusophone (Portuguese-speaking). Very few countries in Africa, except Somalia, Tanzania and Kenya, have yet to demonstrate the principle and practice that literacy, even at primary school level, does not necessarily mean knowing how to read and write in a Western language (Blaut, 1993; Fafunwa, 1989; Nyamnjoh, 2001). Knowledge of and fluency in a European language earned one higher status and privilege in the colonial hierarchy, and adult education was the medium through which this was done.

Ethnic, regional and other sectional and sectoral rivalries were developed through colonial rule, especially indirect rule, such as in Uganda and Nigeria. This legacy is still very visible in Africa. As a result of European colonialism, cultural areas were often broken up by setting up artificial boundaries, such as those between the Hausa and Fulani, and between the French and the English in many countries in West Africa. The Masai were divided between Tanzania and Kenya, the Luo between Kenya and Uganda, the Oromo between Ethiopia and Kenya, and the Somali disbursed into four nations (Somalia, Kenya, Ethiopia, and Djibouti). It became virtually impossible to share knowledge across borders, and this led to the intellectual isolation of some areas. A high rate of the obsolescence of education and contemporary technology was created as a result of the dependency created by colonialism, especially Christian mission education which permanently attached Africa to the West.

The creation of the existing structure of capitalism, which creates secrecy in invention through patents and cut-throat competition, is a colonial invention that was minimal in pre-colonial Africa. Furthermore, the creative work of wood and ivory carvers, potters, painters, weavers, mat and basket makers, and of so many other laborious and creative African men and women, were stolen and patented in Europe. Today many are found in Western archives. The birth of modern science is often associated with the seventeenth century, admittedly a period of intensified intellectual activity on the part of European scholars. It may be, however, that modern science predates these Eurocentric boundaries. The high cost of patents, trademarks and licences, and the honour bestowed on European and American property rights perpetuates this inequality. African discoveries, inventions and innovations were totally ignored by colonialism. The imposition of IMF-derived structural adjustment policies, which directly and indirectly affect economic and technological growth in Africa because of neo-colonial structures, also perpetuates this inequality (Mkandawire and Soludo, 1999).

During the colonial period, adult education was used for the creation of classes and elites in Africa through European methods of social mobility, such as education and fluency in European languages, mastery of catechisms and European behaviour. European trades were revered, while African ones were marginalised. Among the first groups to feel the impact of the invaders' new laws and activities were the metallurgists, blacksmiths, weavers, potters, hunters and fishers. These included the blacksmiths who forged iron and whitesmiths who worked with lighter metals, such as tin. Blacksmiths were depended on for implements as much by farmers as by the aristocracy and the political elite. This system of internal self-reliance changed with the arrival of European ways and structures. Even practitioners of indigenous medicine in Africa (*Isangoma* or *Mganga*) were trivialised and demonised. Their medicine was termed *African magic* or *witchcraft*. They were confronted with unjust laws leading to the complete eradication of these forms of treatment in the public sphere. Many withdrew to backstreets and remote areas beyond the law, from where they have only recently started to emerge.

Mental colonisation and mental slavery were created by colonialism, where elites were made to adore and accept everything that emanated from the West as superior. African values were seen as backward and only fit for the uneducated. Hastings Kamuzu Banda of Malawi and Félix Houphouët-Boigny of Côte d'Ivoire best represented this section of African society and have often been known as *comprador bourgeoisie* (i.e. the African elite who collaborated with Europeans to exploit fellow Africans). Traditional African adult education methodologies have disappeared and only recent recuperative efforts are recollecting them under Indigenous Knowledge Systems projects, which is what NEPAD is trying to accomplish under the African Renaissance programme.

## ⊞ ACTIVITY

Imagine that you are a European missionary who has been asked by your Mission head office in Europe to travel to Africa in 1850 to evangelise an ethnic group in the interior. What cultural and physical challenges are you likely to encounter and how would you solve them?

## THE ORGANIZATION OF AFRICAN UNITY

The Organization of African Unity (OAU) was founded in 1963 in Addis Ababa, Ethiopia. The OAU provided a forum in which newly independent states of Africa could discuss common problems. It should be noted that most African states gained independence from European colonisers in the 1960s after varying years of domination and exploitation. A few, such as Sudan and Ghana, had become independent earlier, in 1956 and 1957, respectively. Ethiopia is the only African country that was never colonised, and it is in Ethiopia that Africa's earliest contribution to the world of African civilisation has been found, that is, at Axum and Meroe. Under Emperor Haile Selassie in 1960, Ethiopia was unanimously seen as a natural leader for the rest of Africa. This is where the head office of the Organization of African Unity is located. The change of name to African Union from the OAU, took place at the OAU meeting in Durban, South Africa in 2000, when African leaders felt that there was a need to revamp and revisit the objectives and functions of this body. The change of name is perhaps an attempt to craft a union similar to the European one sometime in the future.

Many African states were just being reborn during UNESCO's World Conference on Adult Education in 1960 in Montreal, Canada. When Ghana became independent in 1957, it launched a massive literacy drive which was to play a crucial reference role in the first OAU meeting in Addis Ababa. It was the Addis Ababa Plan of Action on Education in 1963 that set out the OAU blueprint on education. By the mid-1960s, African states had realised the need for the promotion of adult education, arising from the attention the sector received from the government policy papers at the time. The 1963 OAU Plan of Action on Education was not very strong, but individual states such as Ethiopia, Tanzania and Ghana provided great plans favouring the role of adult education in development. The omission by the OAU was ameliorated by later plans of action. Obviously, these states required more time as they had just inherited colonial education infrastructures that were biased towards formal education systems. In the 1960s, the emphasis of the world supranational organisations was to support Africa's adult education programmes, especially literacy.

By the time the next UNESCO World Conference on Adult Education was held in Tokyo, Japan in 1972, adult education programmes were fairly well established in many independent African states. The emphasis at this time on adult education was placed on access and equity, along with such issues as population explosion and programmes that focused on the protection of the environment. The African continent was registering one of the highest population growth rates as people were released from colonial labour camps that had often isolated men from women for many months within restrictive areas. Family life education activities that focused on family planning were common, and non-governmental organisations (NGOs) actively supported these programmes. After the 1963 OAU Plan of Action, several plans of action followed under the auspices of Conferences of Ministers of Education and those responsible for economic affairs. These included the Lagos Plan of Action on education, which emphasised among other things the use of adult education for decolonisation

and liberation purposes. This became very significant for ideological war and propaganda in Southern Africa, spearheaded by the Frontline States led by Tanzania and Zambia, and which received backing from the liberation committee of the OAU. In Tanzania, many political asylum seekers from southern Africa were given mass adult education. This OAU programme helped with the liberation of Angola and Mozambique in 1975 and Zimbabwe in 1980. Even the African National Congress (ANC) camp within Tanzania benefited from these programmes.

Julius Nyerere, founding president of Tanzania and founder member of the OAU, and Kwame Nkrumah and Kenneth Kaunda, were the leading OAU visionaries for Africa's liberation strategies. Nyerere loved adult education. Popular education became his centre of mobilisation throughout his presidency in Tanzania. He saw education as the development of one's consciousness for thinking, deciding and acting. Nyerere viewed education as a tool to be utilised for improving not only people's physical capacity and potential, but also their mental freedom, in order to increase their discipline over their lives and the environment in which they lived. Nyerere (1976:10) stated that

*the ideas imparted by education, or released in the mind through education, should therefore be liberating ideas; the skill acquired by education should be liberating skills. Nothing else can properly be called education. Teaching which induces a slave mentality or a sense of impotence is not education at all.*

Nyerere established a strong liberation arm under the auspices of the OAU, complete with a fund, that is, the Liberation Fund to which African leaders and friends of Africa contributed generously. Throughout the years, 'Mwalimu' Nyerere incorporated many adult education principles and methods, firstly into the Tanzanian Liberation Movement and secondly into the developmental strategies used after countries in the region, which had been under the grip of colonialism, achieved independence. Many of Africa's liberation heroes such as Samora Machel, Oliver Tambo, Edwardo Mondlane, Agostino Neto, Joshua Nkomo, Robert Mugabe, Yoweri Museveni, Laurent Kabila, Joseph Kabila and Paul Kagamé went to school in Tanzania to study liberation politics under Nyerere and his disciples who included Walter Rodney, Issa Shivji, Ernest Wamba dia Wamba and Dani Nabudere. Walter Rodney taught at the University of Dar-es-Salaam and was one of the leading contributors to the dependency debate of the 1970s. His book *How Europe Underdeveloped Africa,* written during his stay in Tanzania, became a classic and is today compulsory reading in many universities across the world. Yoweri Museveni led the first successful guerilla movement against an African regime in 1986. Museveni's 'partyless' system of governance and his use of political propaganda and public debate resembled Nyerere's rule in Tanzania in many ways. Like Nyerere, Museveni has bred his own imitators such as Paul Kagamé of Rwanda and Laurent Kabila of the Democratic Republic of the Congo (DRC), whose guerilla movements successfully seized power. Issa Shivji continues to ply his trade as an academic ideologue at Dar-es-Salaam, where he still theorises on the state and the peasantry. Wamba dia Wamba is a politician in the Democratic Republic of the Congo.

Other liberation movements in Eastern and Southern Africa also utilised Nyerere's models, since Tanzania, as the leader of the Frontline States, was in a good position to advise Mozambique and Zimbabwe, among other states. Even the African National

Congress (ANC) exiles were to use these models that would later play an important role in a new South Africa after 1994. The framework and strategies of education for independence proposed imaginative and constructive connections between learning and development, between children and parents and between the community and teachers, in ways that were not different from the earlier African education models. Nyerere knew the importance of education as a teacher and student, and was a long-term friend of educators, particularly adult educators. The Adult Education Association of East and Central Africa was founded at a meeting held at Kivukoni College, Dar-es-Salaam, Tanzania in 1964 (Mwenegoha, 1974: 6–7). Nyerere was closely associated with the International Council for Adult Education (ICAE) from its inception and graciously hosted the ICAE's first World Assembly in Dar-es-Salaam in 1976 (Kassam, 1983).

In the 1980s Africa was quickly being overtaken by what would later become known as the Asian 'miracle economies', which in the 1960s and 1970s were on the same level of development as Africa, at least based on GNP (Gross National Product) and GDP (Gross Domestic Product) comparisons. The 1980s were very trying years for Africa, as it was the third decade in its developmental endeavours since independence in 1960. The continent faced many problems, particularly poor governance, declining economies and widespread famine. After the Paris World Conference on Adult Education in 1985, it was clear that the developmental programmes that were being pursued in Africa were not delivering, and needed to be changed. The programmes that required urgent attention included literacy; the promotion of the education of women; linking formal and non-formal education to the perspective of lifelong learning; the impact of the modern media on learning;

and the need for creativity and innovation in adult learning. This was at a time when Africa began to decline in net development indices. It looked as if the development plans were not yielding the desired results and something was amiss.

The OAU played a role in one of the most important regional conferences, that is, MINEDAF V, which was conducted in Harare, Zimbabwe in 1982. The recommendations emanating from this conference authorised the Director-General of UNESCO to launch a regional programme that would see to the eradication of illiteracy in Africa before the end of the twentieth century. This was to be achieved through the generalisation and renovation of basic education and adult literacy programmes. Following this recommendation, 1984 saw the launching of a regional programme by UNESCO with a membership of 42 countries south of the Sahara, and the number of countries involved has continued to increase.

After the Paris conference of 1985, it was clear that Africa needed to attend more to issues of universal literacy, to establishing peace and international cooperation, and to creating a genuine spirit of democracy considering the many military coups that were occurring on the continent together with declarations of one-party regimes. The rate at which leaders were declaring themselves presidents for life was worrying. These were, among others, Hastings Kamuzu Banda in Malawi; 'Emperor' Jean-Bédel Bokassa in Central African Republic; Mobutu Sese Seko in Zaire; Daniel Arap Moi in Kenya; Muamar Gaddafi in Libya; Omar Bongo in Gabon; Gnassingbe Eyadema in Togo; and Félix Houphouët-Boigny in the Côte d'Ivoire. Because of the high levels of out of school children there was a need to increase learning opportunities for all age groups and to promote gender equality. Gender parity has been achieved in primary education in many African countries, but not in adult education, where men still dominate.

The OAU (AU) meeting in Durban, South Africa in 2000 was where the New Partnership for Africa's Development (NEPAD) was born and where the notion of the African Renaissance came into existence after being tabled by South Africa's Thabo Mbeki. NEPAD and the notion of an African Renaissance have continued to attract a lot of interest and enthusiasm among scholars. It is expected that this African Renaissance will be a precursor to Africa's industrial revolution and developmental take-off. Adult education is poised to play a crucial role in these dreams and aspirations for the continent. Already, there is a sub-committee under NEPAD that deals with the role of Africa's IKS in the rebirth of the continent. The role of regional organisations in the promotion of adult education, such as the Economic Community of West African States (ECOWAS), Southern Africa Development Community (SADC) and the East African Community (EAC) among others, must also be recognised.

## ACTIVITY

**You have been requested by the Secretary General of the African Union (AU) to prepare a position paper on the importance of adult education for a heads-of-state meeting. What arguments will you advance in your paper to persuade these leaders to focus more on adult education, compared to the present trend where basic education for children is considered a priority?**

## SUMMARY

This chapter has discussed the origin of adult education in Africa beginning from the earliest times in Egypt, Aksum, Meroe,

Ethiopia and Timbuktu. It has shown that the role of adult education in Africa goes beyond survival skills and includes more sophisticated and scientifically and technologically advanced pursuits. It has been shown that the aim of adult education in Africa is multi-purposed and its end objective is to produce an individual who is honest, respectable, skilled, cooperative and who conforms to the social order of the day. This chapter has discussed the impact of colonialism on adult education in Africa, how it has peripheralised and rejected Africa's educational systems. It has also looked at indigenous education systems (IES) in Africa and their increasing role in society. The role of independent African states since the 1960s and that of the OAU (now AU) in the development of adult education was also discussed. The critical role adult education in Africa will play in realising the aspirations of NEPAD and the African Renaissance was noted.

- The Organization of African Unity (OAU), now the African Union (AU), through its policies, programmes and major ideologues such as Julius Nyerere and Kwame Nkrumah, has played a crucial role in the development of adult education in Africa.
- Compared to the West, adult education in Africa has not been accorded much support and encouragement by governments and is still one of the most underfinanced sectors.
- Adult education cannot be ignored in the world today, especially given the role of lifelong learning in the modern world.

## ACTIVITY

Describe the birth and development of an adult education institution or programme near you. How did it start? Who started it and why?

## KEY POINTS

- History is important because it tells us about our past strengths and weaknesses, thereby giving us the opportunity to improve. Whenever history is read it should be done by asking whose story is being told and whose is being sidelined.
- The history of adult education in Africa can be traced through Africa's ancient civilisations in Egypt, Ethiopia and West Africa, among others.
- Every African society has some form of indigenous education system and traditions that can be used to complement the role of adult education for societal development.
- Imperialism, colonialism, European missionaries and neo-colonialism have impacted on adult education in Africa both negatively and positively.

## FURTHER QUESTIONS

1  Name three of the earliest centres of knowledge in ancient Africa and explain their importance to world civilization.
2  What were some of the accomplishments of adult education in Africa before colonialism?
3  Differentiate between indigenous education systems and adult education in Africa.
4  How did colonialism affect Africa's development and achievements in science and technology?

## SUGGESTED READINGS

Bown, L. and Olu-Tomori, S. H. (eds.) 1979. *A handbook of adult education for West Africa*. London: Hutchinson Lib.

Draper, J. A. (ed.) 1998. *Africa adult education: Chronologies in Commonwealth countries*. Cape Town: University of Western Cape.

Omolewa, M. 1981. *Adult education practice in Nigeria*. Lagos: Evans Brothers Publishers.

National University of Lesotho [n.d.]. *A history of adult education*. Maseru: Institute of Extra-Mural Studies.

Wangoola, P. and Youngman, F. (eds.) 1996. *Towards a transformative political economy of adult education: Theoretical and practical challenges*. DeKalb, IL: LEPS Press.

# Chapter 3

# Philosophy and adult education

## OVERVIEW

As an adult learner, what does philosophy mean to you? What is the discipline of philosophy concerned with? What are the various branches of philosophy? And who are some of the great philosophers in Africa? This chapter seeks to provide answers to these important questions. The origin and the meaning of philosophy (as generally understood) and the various branches of philosophy are explored. The Western schools of philosophical thought and how they influence adult education programmes are also discussed. African philosophy and related trends are explained, including their impact on adult education programmes in Africa. This chapter also examines the issue of ethics and adult education in Africa.

## LEARNING OBJECTIVES

By the end of this chapter you should be able to:

1 Explain the meaning of philosophy.
2 Explain the importance of philosophy to the field of adult education.
3 Evaluate the role of Western philosophy in the development of adult education.
4 Discuss the influence of African philosophies on adult education.
5 Explain the link between ethics and adult education.

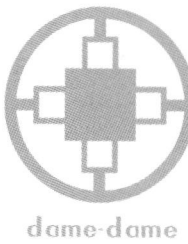

dame-dame

## KEY TERMS

**anarchism**   A political theory that advocates the abolition of the state.

**African philosophy**   African values, beliefs and customs that guide the way of life, perceptions, decisions and choices of African people.

**eclecticism**   A combination of preferred elements from various philosophies that generate a functional approach to designing and implementing adult education programmes.

**ethnophilosophy**   The values, perceptions, decisions and choices of various African communities.

**Eurocentric philosophies**   European-centred or Western philosophies that have influenced adult education programmes in Africa.

**Marxism**   An economic and political theory originated by Karl Marx that holds that actions and human institutions are economically determined, that the class struggle is the basic agency of historical change and that capitalism will ultimately be superseded by communism.

**neo-Freudianism**   A modern way of believing based on the work of Sigmund Freud, an Austrian psychiatrist and originator of psychoanalysis.

**philosophic sagacity**   The individual reflective activity of Africans who, without the benefit of writing or contact with the West, provide philosophic output.

## ▦ BEFORE YOU START

Imagine you are in an agricultural extension classroom in which the focus is on agricultural problems in your local community. You notice a group of students in the class engaged in an argument over civic education and elections while the rest of the class are participating in discussing agricultural problems. Which group of students is engaged in a desirable learning activity and why? Which ones are engaged in an undesirable activity and why? The above scenario in which students consider some things to be desirable (right), as opposed to other things which are considered to be undesirable (wrong), directly relates to the field of philosophy.

# THE DISCIPLINE OF PHILOSOPHY

The term philosophy originated from the Greek word *philosophia* which is made up of two other words, *phileó* (love) and *sophia* (wisdom), which means 'love of wisdom' (Aggarwal, 1985: 42; Chukwu, 2002: 24). A love of wisdom is the essence of any philosophic discussion and investigation. In fact philosophy has come to refer to systems of thought, the academic study of such thought and also particular techniques of study and analysis. It also suggests a 'concern for questions and problems that are "behind" the empirical or experienced world' (Lawson, 1991: 284). At a lower level, it can be said that most people have a philosophy in the sense that they have a set of beliefs and values that govern the way they think, behave and make judgements. A person's philosophy is 'a description, explanation and evaluation of the world as seen from one's own perspective ... shaped by past and contemporary events and experiences ... and social groups ... based on values ... and their knowledge and interpretation of courses, events and their consequences' (Ornestein et al., 1988: 27). These become principles for guiding their actions. Pythagoras, a Greek intellectual who lived between 580–500 BC, is acknowledged as the first person to have used the term 'philosophy' and to have described himself as a philosopher (Chukwu, 2002: 24). Philosophy as a discipline has a number of branches, which are explained below. The five branches are metaphysics, epistemology, ethics, logic and aesthetics (White, 1970).

## Metaphysics

Metaphysics means 'beyond physics' or 'after physics'. It is the branch of philosophy that comes after natural science. It is not concerned with physical being, but with the study of being or existence as such (Chukwu, 2002). It is the philosophical study of the nature of reality, such as the existence of God, the existence of the external world and of things that can be touched, felt, tasted and heard, as well as thought. It is therefore concerned with answers to such questions as: What is real? How does one distinguish between appearances and what actually is? What is the nature of the universe? (White, 1970; Apps, 1973; and Aggarwal, 1985).

## Epistemology

Epistemology is derived from the Greek word *epistémé* which means knowledge in the true and certain sense. This is a branch of philosophy that is concerned with the study of knowledge, what cognition is, its basis and problems, and the process of knowing (Chukwu, 2002). The concern of epistemology is with the nature and possibility of knowledge and focuses on answering such questions as: How do people know? What is knowledge? What are the sources of knowledge? (Apps, 1973).

## Ethics

Ethics is a branch of philosophy that deals 'with what we ought to do and what we ought not to do' (Chukwu, 2002: 69). Some scholars sometimes refer to this branch of philosophy as moral philosophy. Ethics is concerned with basic questions such as: What is of value? How does one decide what is right and what is wrong? What is good or bad? (Apps, 1973: 7). Ethical statements are expressions of value judgements, where such terms as good, bad, right, wrong, obligation, righteousness or wickedness are used.

## Logic

Logic as 'the science of reasoning … has much to do with mathematics' (Chukwu, 2002: 68). It is a science that studies forms of thinking, such as concepts, judgements and proof, with regard to their structure. Aristotle is regarded as the founder of formal logic. Logic is relevant and useful in any discipline, as well as any facet of life because human action is based on reason.

## Aesthetics

The study of the general principles of people's attitude to beauty and values, especially in art, is called aesthetics. Some of the questions raised by aesthetic philosophy include: What is beauty?  Is there an aesthetic way of looking at things? What is aesthetic expression or symbolism?  (Chukwu, 2002: 71).

## The contribution of philosophy

The field of philosophy has made a tremendous contribution to the adult education process. For example, philosophy helps one to think clearly and present arguments with clarity; it helps one to be able to distinguish between sound arguments and faulty arguments; it helps one to understand that there are different ways of perceiving truth and reality and that these can have implications for adult education. Philosophy, specifically, assists in distinguishing that which is real from that which is not real. It also helps to identify knowledge that is appropriate and relevant to adult learners, as well as their methods of knowing. It assists in differentiating between what is right and wrong or good and bad, and in this way helps to clarify moral issues in adult education programmes. Logic is useful, too, because when adult educators interact with their adult learners they should employ systematic reasoning which learners are expected to internalise and develop. Aesthetics as a branch of philosophy is also important to an adult educator in terms of demonstrating through explanations what constitutes beauty or ugliness and how individuality is important in determining what is beautiful and what is ugly. It is also important because the human response to environmental beauty can be harnessed in the educational process, for example, students are likely to learn better in a beautiful learning environment than they are in an ugly one.

Philosophy influences decision-making about issues such as establishing teaching-learning objectives, selecting instructional content, selecting and/or developing instructional materials, choosing teaching-learning methods and evaluating educational outcomes (Zinn, 1990). This applies to all phases and types of education including adult education. In the field of adult education, where the teacher is supposed to be a facilitator of learning, the Socratic method of teaching has been found to be very important. Using the inquiry method of instruction, the teacher as a facilitator of learning guides the learning process by using a set of questions that encourage students to think for themselves. This is in line with the method employed by the great Greek philosopher Socrates.

## ACTIVITY

**Imagine you are involved in the development of an adult education programme in your institution. You are expected to outline the learning objectives, select instructional content, select and develop instructional materials, select appropriate teaching methods and design an evaluation instrument. Outline the various philosophical issues that you will have to address in carrying out all these activities.**

# EUROCENTRIC PHILOSOPHIES

Eurocentric philosophies refer to European-centred or Western philosophies, many of which have influenced the field of adult education. However, for purposes of discussion in this section, only the more influential philosophies are outlined. These include: liberal education philosophy, progressivism, humanism, behaviourism, critical philosophy and eclecticism. In this section we discuss each of these philosophies and their influence on adult education. It should be noted that some of these philosophies relate to each other. For example, progressivism and critical philosophy agree on the issue of learner involvement and active participation in the process of planning, implementing and evaluating the educative experiences. On the other hand, liberalism and humanism agree on the issues of individuality and ethical human values for the process of education.

## Liberalism

Liberal education (also referred to as classical humanism) is the oldest educational philosophy in Western societies (Merriam and Brockett, 1997). According to this philosophy, the aim of education is to produce an intelligent, informed, cultured and moral citizen. In fact, Merriam and Brockett (1997:34) agree that 'Today, there is still evidence of liberal education in college liberal arts curricula and in continuing education programmes sponsored by libraries, museums and institutions of higher education'. Liberal philosophy is relevant to adult education, since the basic argument is that education aims at producing individuals who will make a positive contribution to society. The philosophers in this school of thinking hold the view that the basic beliefs and knowledge of the ancient cultures have

as much application today as they did many years ago.

It is expected that adult learners are exposed to those subjects that have been part of the curriculum over the years and that those subjects should be taught in their customary separate forms with emphasis on the diversification of the curriculum. It is believed that the teacher in an adult education classroom has had an enriched exposure to the content in the discipline and plays the lead role in class interactions. Teachers working within this philosophy of education use classical instructional methods, which include lecturing, memorisation, reading, writing, drill and recitation. These have the capacity to engage and discipline the mind, and to these teachers, it is this that constitutes true education.

## Progressivism

Progressivism favours experience as a basis for knowledge (Apps, 1973). According to this educational philosophy, nothing can be considered to be permanent, as values are relative, subjective and changeable. Adult learners are, therefore, unique individuals who require widely differentiated curricula. Progressivists consider some subjects to be essential for intellectual development and that especially the content selected from the liberal arts, sciences and practical arts can help to develop effectively functioning human beings. This is because subject matter (content) is important as a medium for teaching skills, intellectual processes and applications. The tools of learning include problem-solving methods and scientific inquiry, while the learning experiences include cooperative behaviours and discipline (Ornstein et al., 1988). As teachers they are moderators and guides who relate what they teach to their surroundings by locating, analysing, interpreting and evaluating data to formulate their own conclusions. Adult learners are, therefore, taught how to think rather than what to think and their concern is with improving the quality of life of humankind (Ornstein et al.. 1988). In practice, adult learners are expected to be self-motivated, independent knowledge seekers with the capacity to better themselves and others.

## Humanism

Many philosophers have been excited by something that lies inactive in human beings and which is awoken by education. Plato (427–347 BC) called it 'the Vision of Truth and Goodness', Rousseau (1712–1778 AD) referred to it as 'Natural Goodness and Inner Light of Conscience', while Kant (1724–1804 AD) perceived it as the 'Rational Nature of Man' (Imbo, 1998). From this perspective, to be educated is to be initiated into a new way of life. Humanism is concerned with answering questions such as 'why' and 'how' with a view to understanding human needs and behaviour in the process of education. In dealing with these questions, humanistic philosophy is based on the assumption that humanity is naturally good and free, filled with unique individuality and potential, creating positive differences among people. It emphasises the importance of the self, self-concept and self-actualisation.

Humanistic adult education, therefore, supports liberation, freedom, independence, trust, participatory practice and self-guided or individualised learning. It also concerns itself with the emotional and affective domains of learning and highlights ethical values. Consequently, the expected learning obtained from adult education programmes should be purposeful to the individual, community and nation (Bwatwa, 1990).

In dealing with adult learners, the adult educator needs to be aware that these learners enter the learning situation with well-established ideas and patterns of behaviour, most of which are systematically interconnected with the individual's self-esteem and values (Bwatwa, 1990). These ideas and behaviours served them effectively before the learning experience. Teachers working within this philosophy of education will seek to help the learners develop their own potential and capacity by listening to the learners' demands and by developing a dialogue between the learners' feelings and emotions, so as to allow them to participate freely in the learning process (Bwatwa, 1990). What does this mean? In the first place, it means that teachers working within this philosophy of education strive to meet learners at their own level in terms of knowledge and methodology, in order to create an effective base for a learner-friendly teaching-learning relationship.

## Behaviourism

Behaviourism borrows from a number of philosophical systems, especially logical positivism (Merriam and Brockett, 1997). The main characteristic of this philosophy is the notion that reality exists external to the knower; that it can be known through the senses; is measurable and influences human action (Merriam and Brockett, 1997). According to this philosophy, human actions are the result of past conditioning and the environment. It is associated with the works of psychologists such as Pavlov, Watson, Thorndike and Skinner.

Behaviourism considers that human emotions, feelings, and intellect are the means by which human beings rationalise their responses to environmental stimuli. Thus, in Skinner's works, a carefully designed educational system that controls the environment in which learning takes place is the key to human survival. The methodology to be used in learning includes drilling, repetition and memorisation. According to this philosophy adult learners come to the learning scene with knowledge of what they want and an idea of how they are going to achieve it. This can be very useful to adult educators.

## Critical philosophy

Critical philosophy can be traced to the works of Paulo Freire and Ivan Illich in the late 1960s and 1970s. Sociopolitical movements such as Marxism (superiority of communism), anarchism (no need for the state) and left-wing neo-Freudianism (alternate beliefs to Freud's ideas) laid the foundation for critical philosophy (Elias and Merriam, 1995). According to these sociopolitical movements, adult education is viewed as a means for changing society. The need to change society is based on existing socioeconomic inequalities and oppressive social and political structures within that society (Freire, 1970). According to this philosophy, public schooling ultimately destroys individual freedom and autonomy. Critical educational thought has impacted on adult education in countries like Brazil, where it has been practised.

This philosophy requires that adult learners are the focus when designing programmes with regards to selection of content and materials and identification of functional methods, as well as designing the evaluation tools. The teacher in this situation works hand in hand with adult learners. The adult learners do not have to use ready-made curriculum packages, but should develop appropriate ones for their purposes. This approach is good as far as individual needs and interests and achiever groups are concerned. However, it demands great resources and highly specialised adult teacher skills.

## Eclecticism

It is clear from the above that every educational philosophy has clear prescriptions as to the character of adult education. These prescriptions are likely to impact on adult education in different ways. However, a freestanding philosophy of adult education may not be possible, and a combination from a variety of philosophical standpoints is for some what can reasonably be practical (Lawson, 1991). In this approach the adult educator is encouraged to carefully select practical positive elements from liberalism, progressivism, humanism, behaviourism and critical philosophy that will be functional in a given adult education situation for the benefit of the learners. The adult educator, for example, is expected to ensure that the curriculum is composed of subject matter that helps the adult learners develop their cognitive, psychomotor and affective domains, as well as being applicable to their practical life situations and fostering their interests. On the other hand, the methods to be used in adult classes should, as much as possible, involve the learners while providing the adult educator with the opportunity to provide the necessary guidance as a facilitator of the learning process. It should be noted at this point that the Western philosophies of adult education have adopted more of an existential position, which focuses on the individual as a conscious being aspiring in all undertakings to acquire greater fullness and completeness of being (Paterson, 1979). This may be contrasted with the influence of African philosophies discussed in the next section.

## ❖ ACTIVITY

**Suppose you were required to design an adult education programme for African**

learners. Outline the positive considerations you have gained from the various Eurocentric philosophies that would help you come up with a functional programme. What elements of the Eurocentric philosophies would not have application in designing a programme for African adult learners?

# AFRICAN PHILOSOPHIES

There has been debate among scholars as to whether African philosophies do or do not exist (Letseka, 2000; Chukwu, 2002). However, African philosophies must exist since 'all people have a philosophy that guides the way they live, their perceptions of others, and the decisions and choices they make about every aspect of their lives' (Letseka, 2000: 179). African philosophies exist in both unrecorded and recorded forms. The unrecorded form of African philosophy resides in the memories of the senior members of society (the old) who bring it to the fore only when opportunities for doing so present themselves, such as at funerals and initiation ceremonies. This is reflected in the African communal way of life expressed in *ubuntu* (the humanness inherent in people) as noted in Chapter 1 of this book. The recorded form of African philosophies can be traced in the works of African philosophers such as Paulin Hountondji, Odera Oruka and Julius Nyerere, among others. Africa is surrounded by 'philosophical material … embedded in proverbs, myths and folktales, folksongs, rituals, beliefs, customs, and traditions of the people' (Gyekye in Letseka, 2000: 189).

According to Oruka (1990), there are 'four trends in contemporary African philosophy, that is, ethnophilosophy, nationalistic-ideological philosophy, professional philosophy and philosophic sagacity'.

There is much that these trends in African philosophy have in common in the sense that they are all based on the African way of life with an emphasis on communal harmony. A good example can be seen in the contrast between ethnophilosophy and philosophic sagacity. While ethnophilosophy focuses on the basic principles or forces behind African behaviour, beliefs and customs as they apply to the peoples of specific African communities, philosophic sagacity relates to individual philosophic capacity as it applies to the way of life of a particular African community and can only be tapped as long as the people of that community live. The central issue emphasised in these two trends is the way of life of the African community. As regards the application of African philosophies in adult education, there should be common elements in the planning, implementing and appraisal of adult education programmes. The following section examines each of the above-mentioned trends of African philosophies and their influence on adult education.

## Ethnophilosophy

Ethnophilosophy refers to the views expressed in written texts and oral literature that consider the folktales, communal worldviews and traditions of African communities as well as the philosophies of a group of people, such as the Bantu philosophy. Some of the proponents of this school of African philosophy include Tempels, Mbiti, Kagamé and Ochieng-Odhiambo, among others (Oruka, 1990).

According to this school of thought 'African philosophy is made up of the basic principles that underlie African behaviour, beliefs and customs … and that govern Africans in their day-to-day lives' (Ochieng-Odhiambo, 1997: 46). It centres on people in their social context. The individual is meaningful only as part of the whole society, since 'to be is to participate' (Van der Walt in Ochieng-Odhiambo, 1997: 43). This is true about many African peoples, including the Abaluhya people in Kenya, the Batswana in Botswana and the Mende in Sierra Leone. From the perspective of this philosophy, the overall purpose of adult education in an African context would be to facilitate social harmony at all levels, including the family, clan, village, community, country, region and consequently, the continent. The content or subject matter of adult education is expected to enable the preservation and transmission of values, beliefs and customs of the African people from one generation to the next, facilitating the teaching and learning of valued functional skills and attitudes, as well as taking into account contemporary changes in emerging new knowledge. This calls for a multi-stage procedure in the selection of the knowledge, skills and attitudes that will be offered in adult education programmes in Africa. For example, the content selected should facilitate intelligent and productive functioning within the African environment from the local level to the continental level and up to the international level.

Teachers working within this philosophy of education use a mixture of teaching methods (an eclectic approach) with the emphasis on participatory approaches that encourage and enhance socialisation. Besides lectures, emphasis is placed on practical case studies, individualised instruction and participatory methods. These include: role-play, practical demonstrations, exhibitions, field trips or study tours, discussions, brain-storming, competitions, forums and panel discussions.

In addition, African indigenous instructional methods may utilise where possible and if appropriate, for example, drama, performing arts, theatre, proverbs or sayings. Depending on the level and programme, other instructional methods such as cor-

respondence, newsletters and independent studies can also be used (Bwatwa, 1990). These variations in adult education instructional methods call for both expertise in these methods and flexibility on the part of the adult instructors. In a typical class situation, the teacher would be expected to be versed in the various adult education instructional approaches and be ready to use any of the methods as appropriate.

## Nationalist-ideological philosophy

The nationalist-ideological philosophy emerged as sociopolitical ideologies that were formulated to reflect the vital norms in the culture of traditional Africans that were employed during their campaign for political independence from colonial regimes (Chukwu, 2002). Some of the political visionaries affirmed communalism as the key ethical principle in African culture, upon which African social and political organisations served for political liberation. Some of the well-known African philosophers in this trend include: Kwame Nkrumah (Consciencism), William Abraham (The Mind of Africa), Julius Nyerere (Ujamaa) and Kenneth Kaunda (Zambian Humanism). Included also in this category are the works of Leopold Senghor, Oginga Odinga, Abdel Nasser and Amilcar Cabral. Nationalist-ideological philosophy is similar to ethnophilosophy as both accentuate and centre on African culture prior to colonialism in the form of their communal manner of social existence and worldviews. From this perspective, the purpose, content and methodology of adult education would be similar to those advocated by ethnophilosophers. However, the nationalist-ideological philosopher would go a step further by demanding that the adult learner experiences (learns), understands, and to some extent responds to, existing political structures in their own countries as well as other African states. A good example would be for adult education programmes to be planned in such a way that the learner can fruitfully participate in civic discussions and influence leadership in political settings by participating directly or indirectly in political movements within and beyond the home country.

In addition to the content advocated by ethnophilosophers, nationalist-ideological philosophers would also advocate civic and developmental education for adult education programmes. According to Nyerere, adult education should 'be directed to helping people help themselves and for it to be approached as part of life: "integrated with life and inseparable from it"' (Smith, 2002: 6). Further, this education needs to contribute towards helping people to become 'more conscious and understanding'

*'Mwalimu' Julius Kambarage Nyerere.*

(Smith, 2002: 8). This means that a typical adult education programme aims to help learners solve problems that confront them in their daily lives, as well as to help others improve their lives.

## Professional philosophy

Professional philosophy refers to the works of African professionals trained in Western philosophy who argue that African philosophy should be acknowledged from an academic standpoint. They are of the opinion that philosophy the world over should be perceived from the Western point of view, allowing minor differentiations when discussing philosophy as it relates to the African continent (Chukwu, 2002). Some of the eminent proponents of the professional approach to African philosophy include: Kwasi Wiredu, Paulin Hountondji, Odera Oruka, and Peter Bodunrin, among others. These professionals advocate an integration of all original philosophical works by Africans from all branches of philosophy.

With regard to adult education, this trend in philosophical thought suggests an eclectic approach specifying the purposes of education, the content and methods of instruction. It would also propose an integration of Western and African philosophies in an effort to identify functional overlaps. In a typical African adult education programme there would be evidence of elements of Western and African philosophical trends in terms of outlining the programme objectives; selecting and organising of content; and selecting and using instructional methods and evaluating procedures.

## Philosophic sagacity

Philosophic sagacity has its roots in the works of Odera Oruka who asserts that traditional and modern Africans without the privilege of Western education are people with philosophic acumen (Chukwu, 2002). It is a reflective enterprise that re-evaluates cultural philosophy without the benefit of writing or contact with the West. This philosophy focuses on the philosophical thoughts of individual Africans. Oruka's contention is that African philosophies are the ideas and views of individual African philosophic sages which have been popularised and spontaneously regarded as the communal beliefs of a people. These individual perspectives have been lost over time due to a lack of acknowledgement of the sources and a lack of recording. If this argument is accepted, then the overall purpose of adult education, that is, the selection of content and teaching methodologies, would be that stipulated within the ethnophilosophic paradigm. However, if philosophic sages are viewed as individual African philosophers, then adult education programmes would need to take account of their individual ideas and ideals. The implication according to this philosophy would be that there would be as many variations in purpose, content and methodology in adult education programmes as there are philosophic sages. A typical African adult education programme, for example, that focuses on the administration of initiation ceremonies will be markedly different from one that focuses on all aspects of public service in terms of purpose, content, methods and evaluation procedures.

## Case study

Have you ever attended the traditional African funeral of an elderly man, especially a community leader? In such funerals, you will normally notice the uniqueness of its organisation and of the speeches given. One of the speakers must be an elderly man respected for his philosophical speech-making, referred to as *Omuseni We Kumuse* (a gathering adviser, in the Luhya language of the Bantu of Kenya). The speech made by such a person will touch on critical issues of the community and eventually focus on the issue of being and death. The speech would normally be full of proverbs. The *Omuseni We Kumuse* is a philosophical sage. Philosophic sages are found in many community ceremonies such as funerals, initiation ceremonies, traditional weddings and others. Attend any one of these ceremonies and write a report on the philosophical output from such an individual in your community.

## ACTIVITY

**Assume you are one of the panellists expected to design an adult education programme to be used at a civic education session. How would you bring in elements of African philosophies in identifying the purposes for the programme, selection of subject matter, methods of instruction and evaluation procedures?**

## ETHICS

From the ethical point of view, the concern in adult education is with what is good and right. The ethical issues that are of concern in African adult education relate to: equality, worthwhile activities, consideration of interests, freedom, and respect for persons and community (Peters, 1966). These issues need to be carefully considered in attempting to provide education for adults if meaningful learning is to take place. Each of these issues is discussed below.

## Equality

To what extent are adult education programmes egalitarian? Does adult education increase social divisions by attracting those who already have a measure of education and excluding those who do not have any at all? Equality is the state in which every individual is on a par with all others. With regard to adult education programmes, each learner is equal to another learner in that they all report to the learning situation with their own purposes and expectations, hoping to benefit as a result of attending instruction. This means that adult educators need to be aware of this and must strive to make the adult learner's experiences worth the resource investment. Adult education programmes are placed in specific categories and adult learners will usually report to appropriate programmes depending on their educational needs.

Adult educators are aware that adult students in the same programme are not equal in intelligence, motivation and/or entering behaviour, but the fact that they are interested in a specific type of education implies some kind of homogeneity. It is from this understanding that equality is necessary with regard to exposure to similar learning activities. The question as to whether they enjoy equal experiences in these activities is a different issue. It is thus important that an adult educator in a given class should seek to understand individual learner strengths, weaknesses, opportunities and threats. By so doing, learners will be motivated towards the realisation of their purposes.

In a typical adult education class, the instructor will be required to implement the curriculum, not in an abstract way, but in a manner that takes account of the varying aptitudes inherent in the adult class audience. This will apply to all the other aspects of instructional approaches and evaluation techniques that will be employed.

## Worthwhile activities

The issue of worthwhile activities has to do with the components of an adult education programme. From an African perspective, education constitutes initiation into an activity that the community considers to be worthwhile for life improvement, now and in the future. The curriculum for adult learners should be so planned that learners can acquire the knowledge, skills and attitudes that are important for individual and communal survival. But how are these forms of knowledge, skills and attitudes identified? The significance, relevance and applicability of content for functional living both now and in the future should be the guiding principle. This is so because curriculum activities illuminate other areas of life and contribute much to the quality of living and have a wide-ranging cognitive content. Adult learners, therefore, need to experience worthwhile curriculum activities.

For the purpose of creating a functional African adult education, the content should be significant and relevant to the lives of the adult learners. This will have the effect of engaging learners in their learning activities. The adult educator should identify, select and organise curriculum activities that will be meaningful to the adult learners, as well as provide the tools with which to guide the learning process.

## Consideration of interests

Consideration of interests is an important issue in adult education. The learners' interests determine the effectiveness with which they focus on the curriculum offered. Interests have much to do with the learners' choices. The issue of interests is complicated in the sense that they vary among individuals in the same adult education programme and also for the same individual at different times. These interests could also be directed towards undesirable activities or even towards trivial issues. The concern of the adult educator would be to help adult learners recognise significant interest orientations for achievement. The important issue is that the realisation of the desired goals should be promoted.

In a typical adult education class, some learners could be interested in pursuing further education as opposed to others who may be interested in knowledge relevant to their entrepreneurial activities. The adult educator is expected to recognise interest differentiations and should be in a position to support each learner in achieving their relevant educational objectives.

## Freedom

Freedom means the liberty for an individual to do what he or she wishes. However, there can never be total freedom because individuals or groups may feel like engaging in activities that can arbitrarily destroy human life, and this is not acceptable. In relation to adult education, are teachers free to do anything in a teaching situation? Are students free to do what they want to do within a learning situation? Do women have a right to education, even against the wishes of their husbands, families or communities? Does the teacher have the right, or the duty, to challenge traditional norms where they restrict educational freedom? Should the teacher always avoid making value judgements in the educational context, or are there cases where a value judgement is justified or necessary? Answers to these questions indicate exactly how much freedom is acceptable.

Adult learners have aims that motivate them to attend an education programme, and for these purposes to be realised, it is necessary that they adhere to the requirements of a classroom/learning atmosphere. The freedom to pursue their interests is governed by desirable (good) choices to facilitate the achievement of desirable objectives. The freedom to be exercised by adult learners is guided by the social harmony championed and enforced by African social norms. On the other hand, teachers are not free to teach what they like and leave out what they do not like, and they are not free to put forward their views on certain issues while ignoring learners' views. Teachers are challenged to adopt rational attitudes and exercise acceptable authority, and yet at the same time avoid extremes of authoritarianism and permissiveness.

Using the example of an HIV/AIDS awareness class in any setting, students are not free to engage in a business management discussion while the teacher is explaining behaviour change in an HIV/AIDS management programme. The students are expected to focus on the discussion led by the teacher. On the other hand, the teacher in this class should not assume that the adult learners have no knowledge of the AIDS scourge. The instructor should remember that learners have some knowledge and should utilise such knowledge in an effort to achieve desired objectives.

## Respect for persons and community

Respect for persons and the community relates to attitudes towards others in which people are perceived as worthy beings. This is so whether we are referring to the teacher's attitude towards students or vice versa, or among students themselves. Other people's points of view need to be respected whether they are in agreement with our own or at variance. In an African context this takes place not in isolation, but in relation to community. This means that the individual and the community are interacting entities, each influencing the other in affirming the African truth that 'I am because we are; and since we are, therefore, I am' (Letseka, 2000: 183). Therefore, adult learners have to be viewed as individuals with their own worldviews which of necessity are related to those of the community. As members of the community, they have shared interests, hopes, practices and ideals, and thus the feeling of belonging and loyalty. This is very much in line with African socialism and educating for *botho* or *ubuntu* (humanness) as a major concern of an African philosophy of education (Letsaka, 2000: 179).

A good example is a farmers' extension training class, where individual farmers have farming experiences they bring to the learning situation. Such farmers should be allowed to share their experiences for the benefit of the rest of the class. Such experiences, especially beneficial ones, are shared by even those farmers who may not have attended the extension class through interaction with those who attended the class.

## ACTIVITY

Imagine that you, together with other educators, are invited to run a business start-up and growth workshop in Nairobi alongside other educators. The participants will come from many African countries engaged in different business ventures in their countries. You are therefore required to design a programme that is expected to benefit all. Identify the ethical issues you will need to address in both designing and running the programme.

## SUMMARY

This chapter addresses philosophy and adult education. It explains the origin of the term philosophy and its position as an academic discipline. As a discipline, phi-

losophy has a number of branches which include metaphysics, epistemology, ethics, logic and aesthetics. These branches of philosophy determine the philosophies of education which have a bearing on adult education programmes. This chapter also discusses Eurocentric philosophies of adult education, namely, liberalism, progressivism, humanism, behaviourism, critical philosophy and eclecticism. These philosophies impact on African adult education programmes.

African philosophies and adult education are also dealt with in this chapter. Various African philosophical trends are outlined as well as how they impact on adult education programmes in Africa. African philosophies generally emphasise education for the individual in relation to society. The goal of adult education for the individual should be that learning acquired would create a ripple effect benefiting society in general.

Finally, this chapter underlines ethics as a very important issue in adult education programmes in Africa. The ethical issues that receive attention in this last part of the chapter include equality, worthwhile activities, interests, freedom, and respect for persons and community. It is also posited that adult education in Africa should be for the purpose of *botho* or *ubuntu*, as the individual and the community are closely knit and interacting units.

## KEY POINTS

■ Philosophy as a discipline has various branches that include metaphysics, epistemology, ethics, logic and aesthetics. These have given rise to philosophies of education which are pertinent to adult education programmes in terms of the design, implementation and evaluation of the programmes.
■ Eurocentric philosophies have influenced

the field of adult education and have some relevance with regard to application.

■ African philosophies are relevant in terms of designing, implementing and evaluating adult education programmes within an African environment. However, Africa cannot survive in isolation, and therefore an exchange of philosophical views with the Western world would serve to enrich such programmes.

■ In developing adult education programmes, ethical issues need to be addressed to ensure the functionality of the programmes.

## ⊞ ACTIVITY

Suppose you were involved in designing an adult education programme in your community. Outline the various aspects of Eurocentric philosophies and African philosophies that you would use in the identification of the programme objectives, selection of the content, selection of instructional methods and evaluation procedures. How would you go about determining the feasibility of this programme from an African perspective?

## FURTHER QUESTIONS

1 What is philosophy?
2 In what ways does philosophy apply to the field of adult education?
3 In what respects do Eurocentric philosophies have application to adult education in Africa?
4 Why should adult educators utilise African philosophies in the design, implementation and evaluation of programmes?
5 How is the issue of ethics relevant to adult education in Africa?

## SUGGESTED READINGS

Elias, J. L., and Merriam, S. B. 1995. *Philosophical foundations of adult education*, 2nd edn. Malabaar: Krieger Publishing Company.

Njoroge, R. J. and Bennaars, G. A. 1994. *Philosophy and education in Africa*. Nairobi: Trans-Africa Press.

# Chapter 4

# The impact of the environment on adult education

## OVERVIEW

In the African context what is the role of the social, cultural, political and economic environments in shaping the direction of adult education? What types of African traditional structures, institutions and economic entities are there and how have they impacted adult education? Have you ever participated in the following activities: a town or community forum whose main objective was to discuss employment generation projects in your community; a community meeting to discuss various ways of funding education; a civic meeting to discuss with your community the importance of participation in voting; a community meeting aimed at addressing environmental degradation issues in your community; or a fund-raising meeting to raise funds on a communal basis to pay fees for a member of your community? If you have participated in any of the activities mentioned above, then you have helped in advancing adult education. In this chapter, we use practical examples to demonstrate how adult education is affected by various activities in the social, cultural, political and economic environments.

## LEARNING OBJECTIVES

By the end of this chapter you should be able to:

1 Explain the meaning of social, cultural, political and economic environments, and how they affect adult education.
2 Discuss the impact of social, cultural, economic and political factors on adult education.
3 Using relevant examples, explain how participation in social, cultural, political and economic activities in your community can help promote adult education.

## KEY TERMS

**atomisation** The tendency in current African societies towards the dispersion of family and community members to the cities with the consequent exposure of these individuals to norms, values and rules potentially in opposition to those taught by their culture.

**economic growth** The continuous and steady increase in the production of goods and services in a specific country in a given year.

**egalitarian society** A society where there is equal access and equal opportunity to social services such as education.

**mandated education** Education and training required by employers for all employees in order for them to retain their current jobs.

## ⌗ BEFORE YOU START

Some families in Africa favour boys above girls when providing for education, while other African societies educate boys only. List some of the reasons you think families make such choices. Suggest the various ways that you think such beliefs have affected the development of adult education in your community.

# THE ROLE OF THE ENVIRONMENT

It is important to remember that adult learners are members of various African societies and that these societies play a major role in the way adult education is conducted. For example, a society that values education will invest more resources in the educational sector. Therefore, the sociocultural, political and economic environments prevailing in a given country can help promote adult education. The term environment is used here to refer to the social, cultural, political and economic activities that take place in the African context and how they impact on adult education. The use of the term differs from the manner in which it is used when referring to the natural environment.

Cervero and Wilson (2001: 10–11) have stated that

> *In one direction, the social, cultural, political, economic, racial, and gendered power relations that structure all actions in the world are played out in adult education. These systems of power are almost always asymmetrical, privileging some people and disadvantaging others. This is true of any policy, programme, or practice of adult education, regarding its institutional and social locations or the ideological character of its content.*

In this chapter, we are concerned with understanding how social, cultural, political and economic activities taking place in Africa affect adult education. We cannot talk about social, cultural, political and economic activities without mentioning the role of various African governments. In many African countries, the government collects taxes and determines how the tax revenue will be utilised in the implementation of government policies. Examples of government policies include provision of education for adults. As mentioned in Chapter 10 African governments should prioritise education and play a leading role in promoting partnerships among various organisations engaged in adult education and lifelong learning.

However, Africa's experience in the recent past has shown that the power of the government has been declining. This is due to three major factors. Firstly, there is an increased focus on market economies and their main characteristics of privatisation, liberalisation and globalisation. These forces have weakened African governments in their roles as mediators for conflicting national interests between social and economic classes and between ethnic rivals. The government, which is supposed to deal with legitimising all types of interests and distributing resources equitably, is often unable to establish a recognisable presence for lack of adequate influence and resources (Were and Amutabi, 2000).

Secondly, governments in Africa have been challenged through the emergence of civil society as an alternative area of power and influence in the 1990s through non-governmental organisations (NGOs), especially in rural development. Adult education has contributed to civil society and has been particularly active in advocacy, lobbying, civic education, interest articulation and income-generation (Fowler, 1992; Hall, 1996; Wangoola, 1995). Community based organisations (CBOs) and local NGOs, whose office bearers are mainly literate adults, carry out the work of civil society in many African countries. The number of civil society groups has been rising as more people are educated and informed about their rights and obligations as informed members of nation-states. Women's groups, for example, are challenging some past cultural practices such as female circumcision, the place of women in society and spousal abuse, and are demanding equal treatment and rights with regard to the inheritance of property, among other things. Thirdly, African governments have been further weakened by the introduction of Structural Adjustment Programmes (SAPs), which have in turn led to a reduction in spending on social services, such as health and education (Mkandawire and Soludo, 1999). Left with limited financial resources, many governments have concentrated their energies on basic formal education, catering mainly for children. Adults and adult education have been ignored, and continue to suffer marginalisation in Africa. NGOs and the rest of civil society have stepped in here to help the governments as discussed in Chapters 5 and 10.

In Africa, as elsewhere, the government is supposed to create opportunities for negotiation and sharing of resources amicably among all sectors including education (Poggeler, 1990). Using a political economy approach, Youngman argues that there is reciprocity of meaning and purpose between adult education and the various development spheres of a nation, such as the economic, political and social ones. Youngman (2000: 2) has stated that '… adult education programmes can contribute to the economic, political and social dimensions of development.'

The first president of Tanzania, Julius Nyerere, was opposed to class-enhancing, elitist education. He observed that 'the most central thing about the education we are at present providing is that it is basically an elitist education designed to meet the interests and needs of a very small proportion of those who enter the school system' (Nyerere, 1968: 275). The inequality in formal basic education led Nyerere to favour adult education as a balancing sector. In this respect he said that 'first we must educate adults because our children will not

have an impact on our economic development for five, ten, or even twenty years. The attitudes of the adults, on the other hand, have an impact now' (Nyerere, 1968: 282). According to Nyerere, adult education is an empowering process. It should make formerly neglected men and women more productive and effective in their work, in their social and personal relationship, and as citizens.

As shown in Chapter 2, historically, adult education in Africa has arisen as a response to particular needs in given environments. As a result of this, adult education has a direct and symbiotic relationship with the environment within which it operates. Adult education both responds to societal change and tends to necessitate further change. Regarding the importance of social, cultural, political and economic environments to education in Africa, Fafunwa (1982: 9), noted that 'even when a system is transferred in its purest form from one cultural environment to another, there is bound to be a change due to certain cultural, social and/or economic imperatives.'

## ⊞ ACTIVITY

In your own words, summarise the main points made in the above section.

## THE SOCIAL ENVIRONMENT

The social environment in Africa is defined by certain variables that describe social categories, such as age, gender, class and ethnicity (Nabudere, 1996). For example, older people in African societies are accorded a higher status than young and middle-aged adults. This interferes with the equity and equality that is hoped for in learning situations. The structures and educational models established are not based on the realities of Africa. The learning processes are not dynamically adapted to these African realities through the normal process of socialisation because education is seen as the creator of hierarchies and a privileged class. This elevation of elders contrasts sharply with Western societies where older people are typically accorded lesser status than young and middle age adults. In Africa 'hierarchy of orders is supported by a series of sanctions and taboos in case of breach' (Nabudere, 1996: 163). This comes into play when critical decisions such as those concerning who should receive education in a family are being made.

The social environment in Africa is made rich by various African norms such as the extended family system which is still very strong in rural areas. The social environment is often created out of societal norms and practices, or from groupings that are generated by social processes, such as relatives and friends, workmates, and peer and professional prescriptions. The rich social environment in Africa is also a result of the *ubuntu* concept of life that we mentioned in Chapter 1. In many African societies, there is a common saying that cuts across all communities, that is, 'an individual is an individual because of society'. On the link between education and the social institutions in Africa, Ki-Zerbo (1990: 62) has stated that

*Education is the key to social reproduction. This means that the educational system is the agency that decides which social groups are to advance into the future, and which are to be consigned to the graveyards of history. It is the same process that separates values and customs worth saving in the interests of society, from mores and practices that were better weeded out of the continuing system.*

Also, in Africa, social and economic classes are not as distinguished as in the West. Government policies should be designed with the main objective of minimising class differences, but this is not easily achieved in reality. Some countries have done this through balancing out social classes, by enacting egalitarian constitutions, by avoiding or reducing conflicts that could lead to the elimination of subordinated classes and by checking the influence of new class structures, such as elitism, cartels, secret societies and African versions of the mafia. Mudariki has shown how adult education was used as a government tool for controlling the masses before and after independence in Zimbabwe. He demonstrates how policies were formulated in the early years of independence and especially how progressive policies were stifled at the very top (Mudariki, 1996: 223).

In some African nations, specific ethnic minorities feel neglected and persecuted by the current governments, for example, the Okiek in Kenya, the Ogoni in Nigeria, the Anyuak and Ogaden, Somali in Ethiopia, Issas in Djibouti, the Toposa in Sudan, the Jie in Uganda and the Ndebele in Zimbabwe, among others. At other times, ethnic minorities have also dominated majority groups such as the Tutsi in Rwanda. In Sierra Leone, it has been claimed that Creoles have always dominated the hinterland ethnic groups such as the Mende, Temne, Limba, Koranko, Soso, Kissi, Loko, Mandingo and Vai. In some other countries, two major ethnic groups contend for dominance, as in the case of the Nyanga and Bemba in Zambia, the Mbochi and Ewe in Togo, the Lari and Kabrai in the Congo (Brazzaville) and the Zulu and Xhosa in South Africa (Amutabi, 1995). In Botswana, Youngman (1996: 211) pointed out that

*at least twenty five percent of the population belong to minority ethnic groups, most of which have a subordinate position in society ... As a result, the political and economic dominance of the Batswana has been accompanied by cultural hegemony, articulated in the postcolonial era in terms of the ideology of nation building, which regards assertions of cultural identity by ethnic minorities as negative.*

Datta and Murray (1989: 70) have shown that in Botswana adults from minority ethnic groups mainly fall among the unemployed groups, the low-income strata and the less educated, especially cattle-keepers or pastoralists. These characteristics are correlated with low rates of participation in organised adult education programmes in many African countries (Amutabi, 1997a: 196). The immediate implication is that people from such societies, both young and old, will never participate fully in society or in the decision-making process of government. These people will neither enjoy the benefits of good health, nor education, making it impossible for them to experience the upward mobility needed as adults. Furthermore, they are not likely to be full contributors and partners in effectively shaping and participating in the larger society. As noted earlier, African governments face a major challenge in providing adult education programmes that are inclusive and that promote diversity for the benefit of the entire society.

Given the above scenario, we wish to point out that adult education programmes could be used successfully in these African countries so as to impart positive aspects of ethnicity. For example, civic education programmes should be designed to educate people on the importance of co-existence. In addition, programmes should put emphasis on the strength of African diversity and how it can be successfully tapped in order to strengthen various African com-

munities that have been victims of ethnic discrimination.

Besides problems related to ethnicity, it is perhaps Africa's population growth that has been the most outstanding and long-lasting social problem in Africa. This is so because demographically Africa is changing very fast, making demographics a social reality shaping adult education in contemporary African society. Despite rapid population growth in the past, which the AIDS pandemic is undermining, Africa has a relatively sparse population compared to its land resources. Africa has a population density of 249 per 1 000 hectares. This is quite low when compared to the world average of 442 or the 1 130 found in Asia (World Bank, 2002). There are wide variations of population density within and between countries. Mauritius has the highest population density in Africa, at 5 562 per 1 000 hectares, while Namibia's nineteen people per 1 000 hectares is the lowest (World Bank, 2002). Fertility rates in Africa have declined from 6.5 during 1975–80 to 5.3 during 1995–2000 (World Bank, 2000). Western and Central Africa have the highest fertility rate of 6.6, while Southern and North Africa have the lowest rates of 4.1 and 4.2, respectively. Epidemic diseases have had a serious impact on the African population. In recent years, HIV/AIDS has become one of the major causes of death. In 1996, about 14 million people in sub-Saharan Africa had HIV/AIDS, about 64 per cent of the worldwide total (AIDS Analysis for Africa, 2000). A decade ago Africa was leading the world in birth rate and population growth rate, but since the late 1990s Africa leads the world in HIV/AIDS-related deaths.

At the beginning of the twentieth century, Africa's total population was about 120 million, about 7.5 per cent of the world population. In the following 50 years Africa's population grew slowly as high fertility rates were offset by high death rates due to poor health conditions, infectious diseases and civil wars and the struggle against colonialism. Africa was also recovering from centuries of the ravages caused by slavery and the slave trade, which was responsible for shipping over 12 million Africans to the Americas and Europe.

In Africa, the mortality rates began to decline sharply from the 1950s onwards due to improved health conditions associated with economic development and the decolonisation process. There was, therefore, a dramatic population increase on the continent from that decade, and by 1997 Africa's population was estimated at 780 million, more than 13 per cent of the world's population (United Nations Population Division, 1998). In 2002, Nigeria had an estimated 120 million people, which a mere century earlier in 1900 was the population of the whole continent. It is projected that by the year 2025 the population of Africa will almost double to 1 453 million, representing about 18 per cent of the projected world population, with the youth remaining in the majority.

At the micro-level, Africa as a continent is getting younger with every passing year as people below twenty years continue to occupy over half of the population in many countries. There were indications in the 1980s that people were living longer in Africa, and in fact life expectancy reached 60 in some African countries. This lasted only until the 1990s when the HIV/AIDS pandemic and its related deaths started to ravage the continent. Whereas an estimated three per cent of the African population was sixty-five or older in 1900, ten per cent were that age in 1980, and this has changed since the 1990s. Such actuarial trends are likely to affect adult education in Africa directly and indirectly. Although the elderly are traditionally less likely to participate in adult education programmes, other variables may counteract the traditional non-involvement of the elderly. As retirees generally become better educated and financially more secure, they are more likely to use the average fifteen years of life remaining from age 55 in active pursuits that include adult education activities. The area of imparting entrepreneurial skills to retirees has been a new development in adult education (Amutabi, 1997a).

Compared to populations in the developed nations where the population of older people is increasing, Africa has more people in the younger bracket. This trend has implications for the future since many of Africa's young population do not successfully complete formal schooling. This means that when they become adults they will require further education. African governments must therefore be prepared to provide adult education opportunities for adults who will have missed the opportunity to receive education when they were children. When we add immigrants and refugees such as those displaced by war, the situation becomes more complex. These usually form part of another reservoir of adult learners in refugee camps. Although changing demographics brought about by these new groups offer a tremendous opportunity for capitalising on the merits of many people from different lands, there are risks (Henry, 1990: 29).

There is yet another population-related problem, one which has to do with educational institutions not responding quickly enough to change, for example, by attracting retirees and the elderly, even though adult educators are aware of the positive impact they can have on social systems in Africa. The effects of this population age group on enrolment in parallel degree programmes, evening programmes and the privately sponsored degree programmes discussed in Chapters 1 and 5 are already being felt. Adult education programmes in many universities in Africa have become very popular. State universities have introduced privately sponsored degree programmes which were initiated by private universities (Okech and Amutabi, 2002).

Although statistics are not easily available, household income (exclusive of non-cash components) in 1990 was much lower than in 1980 in many African countries as a result of the reduced national income growth. This has worsened because many households in Africa consist of about eight people on average with only one breadwinner. Even where the household income is high, the distribution of that income is unfair since it favours a few people while the majority of citizens live below the poverty line (Amutabi, 2000). As a result, many families are unable to spend on education as they are preoccupied with meeting basic needs such as food, clothing, shelter and medicine for their own families, as well as their extended families. Among such families, the little money available is more likely to be spent on educating the children rather than the adults. Ki-Zerbo (1990: 40) correctly pointed out that 'sheer population growth, unsupported by a buoyant economy, is likely to impact the education sector in Africa negatively'.

Rural and urban differences also impact negatively on adult education programmes in many African countries. The population in urban areas in Africa grew at a rate double that of the overall population growth of six per cent and over. Ki-Zerbo (1990: 54) observed that 'in these outskirt-cities, African social life and culture slide into depravity, atomistic individualism and unreasoning absurdity... As a result, in terms of lost lives, the new-style initiation into modern life practiced on the city streets costs a great deal more ... while in the clash between the street and classroom, the streets are winning out in the city, a

lot is lost'. Many of the youths leaving the school system have no skills and can easily be lost to urban gangs since the social activities that govern the rural social environment are absent in the city. Also lost are Africa's riches in the form of social capital, consisting of the social networks of relatives and friends and other support groups that are often within reach in rural areas. Many of these youths require skills with which to survive in these urban areas. It is here that adult education could play a vital role.

## ⊞ ACTIVITY

**Discuss what you think are the main social issues that impact on adult education in your community.**

## THE CULTURAL ENVIRONMENT

The cultural environment affects adult education in different ways. This is because African culture involves taboos, practices, habits, mores and values which guide the cultural environment in which adult education operates. There are cultural practices that have persisted from traditional African societies to contemporary societies. Some of these practices are discussed in Chapter 6 of this book. A typical cultural practice in many African contexts is the tendency for many African societies to be based on a predominantly patriarchal base, where the elders are on top of the hierarchy, with the children at the base. A further cultural practice is related to the stages of societal transition, that is, birth, initiation, marriage and death, which are dominated by ceremonies (Ki-Zerbo, 1990). These stages carry with them different kinds of rituals with different implications for the individuals in society. The elders usually set the rules and power structures within which every member of society is supposed to operate, with penalties for violations.

African societies have statutory and non-statutory sanctions that they impose on those who break or go against societal rules. These rules are still respected and followed by many people in Africa. Crime and behaviour that many African governments regard as deviant, such as using alcohol and drugs or smoking or even homosexuality and lesbianism, are becoming more pronounced in major African cities. This could be attributed to the interaction between people from the West and those from Africa. Ki-Zerbo (1990: 51) has noted that 'atomisation is a major problem that seems to be spreading fast in Africa … This atomisation is even more rampant in relationships between African children and their grandparents or the elders in general'. In many African villages men have moved into urban areas and other employment avenues in search of the family bread. This has led to the phenomenon of single-parenthood and female-headed households, which has placed more responsibilities upon women, since they have to raise children on their own.

The separation of African children from their grandparents is a link that has dealt the African family and therefore the socio-cultural fabric a severe blow. The movement back and forth between urban and rural areas has distanced children from the wisdom of their elders (Ki-Zerbo, 1990). This has important implications for adult educators, who should seek to retain the wisdom from African grandparents by collecting tales, proverbs and wise sayings, and writing them in book form for African posterity. The Council for the Development of Social Science Research in Africa (CODESRIA) based in Dakar, Senegal has launched a programme that is documenting all the noble sayings of African scholars

and sages. This is a positive step and should help in promoting African cultural norms and adult education in general. Cultural revivalism and nationalism in Africa have been identified by some scholars as one of the great trends of this millennium. For example, the notion of the African Renaissance and the New Partnerships for Africa's Development (NEPAD) provide some hope for Africa's development agenda (Mamdani, 1990 and Zeleza, 2003). Some African languages have been used positively to promote national development. For example, in Tanzania, Kiswahili has been used as a rallying point for nationalism and national cohesion. On the importance of maintaining cultural identity in this era of globalisation, Naisbitt and Aburdene (1990: 119) observed that 'as our outer worlds grow more similar, there are unmistakable signs of a powerful countertrend: a backlash against uniformity, desire to assert the uniqueness of one's cultural language … while outbreaks of cultural nationalism are happening in every corner of the globe'.

A look at the impact of cultural dynamics on adult education cannot be complete without examining the position of women in adult education in Africa. Women constitute over half of Africa's population, they produce 80 per cent of food eaten in Africa and provide 75 per cent of domestic labour in many countries. Women are now getting absorbed into formal employment sectors in African countries at an encouraging rate. The changing image of African women, particularly in the workplace, is a vital aspect of the contemporary setting for adult education. Historically, women have been greater partakers of non-job-related adult education in Africa, especially through the colonial programmes of female domesticity and 'Victorian' idealism. However, in the 1990s, women became significant participants in job-related training in Africa. In adult education programmes in Kenya and

Uganda, for instance, women represent large majorities in literacy, promotional, demonstration and outreach programmes. Women constitute a large number of the growing enrolment in adult education undergraduate and graduate programmes in Africa. Africa is experiencing a cultural shift with regard to the high participation of women in adult education programmes.

As shown in Chapter 5, as women's roles and influence have expanded, and as their participation in the educational system has increased, they have formed organisations that assume an adult education role. Many countries in Africa have women organisations playing prominent roles, such as the Lesotho National Council of Women, *Maendeleo ya Wanawake* Organisation in Kenya (MYWO) and the *Emang Basadi* Women's Association of Botswana, among others. They promote women's issues through political action and education of their members, and for the public at large. Culturally, women's roles in Africa have expanded beyond that of housewife, nurse, teacher and secretary. This is as a result of societies becoming more egalitarian; the increasing need for a second income; the passage of affirmative action legislation in many countries in Africa; the feminist movement, and, generally, the growing recognition that gender is rarely a predictor of effectiveness in the vast majority of jobs. Many African governments are enacting egalitarian constitutions and encouraging gender-parity in education and other sectors.

## ACTIVITY

1  Based on your knowledge of your community's cultural norms, list the main advantages and disadvantages of these norms and practices.
2  Explain how adult education could

be used positively to promote African culture.

# THE POLITICAL ENVIRONMENT

Africa's post-colonial political environment has been unstable, with ethnic and politically motivated wars in countries such as Sudan, Somalia, Ethiopia, Kenya, Uganda and Sierra Leone. A number of African countries have experienced major political transformations in the past forty years after decolonisation. Politics and adult education interact at various levels since politicians make and implement policies (Jarvis, 1990). For many people in society, adult education often plays a significant role with regard to the right to vote by raising their political consciousness. Production and dissemination of knowledge, which are the main focus of adult education programmes, are important to many people in Africa. As noted in Chapter 8, information and communication technology have become important in this era of knowledge explosion. Knowledge is indeed power, especially when some have it and others are intentionally deprived of it, as in many countries in Africa.

Adult education is an important avenue for creating a conscious citizenry. Knowledge can be used to promote, to enfranchise, and even to liberate the individual by furthering individual self-interest or by enhancing the individual's voice in matters of local or national policy. Adult education's emphasis in Africa should be a liberating rather than a confining role. It should be used to empower people to make conscious political decisions, especially when it comes to choosing leaders. For example, the work of civic education organisations and NGOs in Africa provide a good avenue whereby adult education can be used to bring about political change in Africa.

Egalitarian concerns such as affirmative action have encouraged women and minorities to seek positions for which higher educational levels and continuing education or training are required. At the same time, the idea of getting ahead based on education and ability is an obvious and significant impetus affecting adult education in Africa. These two ideals, promotion based on merit (meritocracy) and egalitarianism, suggest contrast but in fact they may be complementary. Many people in Africa now realise the importance of adult education for improving their productivity in the workplace and as a means of ensuring occupational and job mobility. Adult education in Africa, as in other countries of the world, is used as a criterion for formal and informal job placements by holding constant all other factors over and against such things as nepotism, favouritism and tribalism. This is the only fair means of identifying individuals with competencies for work. This popular meritorious ideal must, however, be founded on the equally popular egalitarian ideal of equal access and opportunity in many African societies. In the same way in which equality of opportunity without liberty is mere privilege, equality of opportunity without the ability to advance is fake. Adult education programmes such as those of the University of South Africa (UNISA), which deal with many non-traditional students (mainly adult learners), are one good example of how adult education can be used to correct past injustices in Africa.

African nations have long embraced bureaucracies based on an educated elite. This has not, however, diminished the role and use of traditional authority structures and institutions that still play a very important role in day-to-day administration. African traditional authority structures with their power-sharing and self-regulating mechanisms are recognised in many nations. For example, in Kenya, the Government has since 1963 entrusted some residual power to clan and family elders who preside over local disputes and quarrels. Here, some kind of power sharing takes place through the council of elders via nominal chiefdoms established when administrative areas are placed under appointed chiefs and assistants. Serving under the chief and assistant chief are many unsalaried officials known as *wazee wa vijiji* (village elders).

These elders preside over cases on the basis of customary law and run village activities using the cultural, social and political ideals of the dominant ethnic group, usually within a patriarchal system. This political arrangement privileges old men, who are often the main custodians of clan or ethnic interests, but who have limited understanding of the educational needs of their societies. Many of the elders are often illiterate or semi-literate and persist in supporting traditional pursuits, such as early marriage and female circumcision. The situation is made worse by the fact that the educated members of the clans are usually away in major cities in salaried employment. This flight of the educated people from rural villages has had a ripple effect on many sectors. It is affecting Africa's education, as the majority of people in Africa are predominantly rural dwellers. This affects the whole education process, especially adult education. Women and youth are often marginalised in the village power structure because of traditional beliefs.

At national level, many African governments are negatively affecting adult education. In the past, many of these regimes were oppressive and dictatorial, causing many people to be imprisoned. Unfortunately, the prison systems in Africa are the most underdeveloped in the world, and inmates are rarely given the full potential to develop their education levels. Governments must ensure that prisoners have access to adult education opportunities. The problems of human rights in Africa have been the concern of international and national human rights NGOs for a long time, and have attracted civic education campaigns throughout the continent. Such activities have been mainly financed by international human rights NGOs, such as Amnesty International. External pressure on Africa's political environment centres on the failure to observe human rights, ethnicity, regionalism and the slow implementation of institutions characterised by quality governance.

Although significant positive steps have been taken to promote democracy in a number of African countries, such as South Africa, Botswana, Zambia, Ghana, Tanzania and Kenya, more still needs to be done. Improvements made in reducing political instability and civil unrest in these countries should be accompanied with the political will to invest in adult education. Adults still form a neglected group, as governments continue to focus on education for children and the youth. With regard to involvement and commitment, much more needs to be done to prepare adults and to develop and impart skills to them, so as to attain and sustain socioeconomic growth, durable peace and equitable income distribution. There are now strong signs of a return to peace and security, and of progress towards democratic governance in several African countries, such as Nigeria, Uganda, and Ethiopia, to mention a few.

For adult education to achieve its objectives in Africa we recommend strong political institutions that have the will to invest in the learning of their own citizens. As shown in Chapter 10, Africa's survival in the twenty-first century will be determined by continued investment in lifelong learning.

## ✕ ACTIVITY

Assume that you are a vote-dependent politician who has just been appointed the Minister of Education in your country. Your first task is to revive the declining adult education sector of your country. However, in your country, you find that urban, elite, white-collar workers in urban areas (few voters) favour spending more on adult education, whereas the majority of workers in urban areas and peasants in rural areas (majority voters) favour spending more on basic primary school education. Explain how you will resolve this dilemma.

## THE ECONOMIC ENVIRONMENT

Training is a vital component in an increasingly competitive world economy. Africa has witnessed economic decline since the 1970s. Ki-Zerbo (1990: 32–34) has noted that 'by 1960, Africa's economies were stable and the per capita income and GNP and GDP very high. However, the 1973 oil crisis and the SAPs introduced in the 1980s eroded any semblance of normal life for Africa'. In recent years many companies based in Africa have reduced their staff, governments have retrenched workers and national economies are recording zero and negative growths. The role of adult education, particularly work-related training, is an important one in the midst of this uncertain economic environment. Some recent union contracts have focused more on job security and job training than on wage increases. All job categories associated with computers (for example, programmers, systems analysts and operators) as well as engineers, accountants, physicians and teachers have experienced growth, and this will create the increasing demand for training and other forms of continuing education in many African countries. Other fast-growing job categories such as cashiers, waiters and waitresses, security guards, drivers, nursing aids and orderlies, hotel workers, bank tellers and switchboard operators also require initial training and continuing education. Clearly, a significant African challenge is the retraining of labour in declining industries for jobs that have a greater demand. Part of this challenge is being met by the rise of adult education programmes at various university and college campuses in Africa and the popularity of distance education such as through UNISA and online learning such as the African Virtual University project of the World Bank mentioned in Chapter 8. In Africa, there exists an ominous knowledge gap between changing technological labour needs and workers with specialised skills that are in low demand, or worse still, workers with limited literacy and inadequate numerical skills. The acceptance of re-certification and refresher courses are likely to help establish a general recognition for the need for adult education and possibly even a greater recognition of its pleasures. At the same time, the popularity of some books examining adult development has helped cement the notion that learning, whether experiential or formal, is an adult education activity.

In Africa as in many parts of the world, education has often been used as a ladder for upward social mobility. In economic terms, education is often looked upon as an important variable for economic progress. Since the oil crisis of the 1970s, the economic growth of many African countries has been negative. In addition, the huge external debt burden, economic instability and corruption experienced in a number of African countries have led to economic stagnation. The debt burden in particular has been a major constraint for

many African nations, which have had to spend more on servicing their debt than providing basic social services. For example in 1997, Africa's total debt stock stood at US$349 000 million, or 67.5 per cent of the GDP (Mkandawire and Soludo, 1999).

During the 1980s and 1990s, many countries embarked on economic reform through Structural Adjustment Programmes. While economic liberalisation may have helped fuel economic recovery, there are indications that economic growth will worsen rather than improve in Africa, especially due to debt burden and debt-building that has been going on for decades (Mkandawire and Soludo, 1999). Clearly, the African economy is changing and with it the learning needs of adults. In particular, there is the inevitability of certain levels of inter-dependence, the continued provision of raw materials and unprocessed industrial contributions to the North, and a change in the composition of the labour force as women are increasingly becoming income earners. As shown in Chapter 9, Africans have become more conscious of the interrelatedness of their lives with the rest of the world. The globalisation of economies worldwide is creating a competitive atmosphere that has dramatic implications for adult learning in Africa. This is especially clear with the intensification of the work of multinational corporations and conglomerates across the globe are the driving forces in globalisation. As pointed out by Naisbitt and Aburdene (1990:19), people the world over 'are in an unprecedented period of accelerated change, perhaps the most breathtaking of which is the swiftness of our rush to all the world's becoming a single economy'. Since the 1990s, African economies have experienced major shake-ups. They have undergone forced market liberalisation, deregulation, privatisation, streamlining and increased structural adjustment, leading to significant reorganisation in the workplace, retrenchments, downsizing and forced or early retirements. African governments have also been forced to reduce spending on service sectors, such as education and health, due to structural adjustment, and to introduce other austerity measures.

The liberalisation and privatisation of African economies has had a significant impact on workers. Government ministries have reduced the number of employees. Many weak private companies have merged with larger ones or have been bought. Thousands have, therefore, been retired involuntarily, and others that have been retrenched or laid off will require new skills in order to survive. In countries such as Ghana, Uganda and Kenya, income generation and entrepreneurship courses have been very popular with those that have been retrenched or retired, and have attracted the attention of the government and private sector (Nafukho, 1998). The changing technological trends around the globe are also a matter for concern in Africa. Tomlin (1997: 20) has noted that 'it does a worker very little good to train specifically for a job with a company that outsources the position, downsizes or sells to a foreign owner, who recognises or "re-engineers" the company, selling off pieces, leaving the worker trained and unemployed' (Tomlin, 1997: 20).

Global realities and influences have led to changing work practices, which require different kinds of preparation and training. This has resulted in a significant influence on adult education. Davis and Boktin (1994: 34) observed that business is 'almost unintentionally evolving new meanings for learning and new methods of delivering education. And it is doing so in ways that are consistent with its fundamental role as business, competitively filling unmet needs in the marketplace. All business visions are anchored in this fundamental belief'. The emphasis now is on improved product and service quality, greater worker responsibility

and teamwork approaches (Senge, 1990). Adult education and human resources development, in particular, have responded with broad-based workplace literacy programmes and training and development packages designed to address a wide range of economy-driven needs. There is a marked increase worldwide in employment-oriented adult education courses, and Africa is no exception.

Bryant and Johnston (1997: 14) have pointed out that the worldwide demand for and supply of education has changed. This shift is evidenced in a changing relationship between educators and learners. They have also noted that

*… Knowledge is exchanged on the performative value it has for the consumer… Educational institutions themselves become part of the market, selling knowledge as a commodity and increasingly constructing themselves as enterprises dedicated to marketing their commodities and to competing in the knowledge business.*

In Chapter 8, we stated that the increased enrolment witnessed by Makerere University, Uganda; the University of Dar-es-Salaam, Tanzania; and the University of Nairobi, Kenya can be attributed to the universities' treatment of students as customers, and a philosophy where education is seen as a commodity that can be adapted to the market's demands (Nafukho, 2002). This is the trend all over Europe and North America (Clark, 1998). Dislocated workers from both the industrial and agricultural sectors, with few if any transferable skills, find themselves in low-skill, low-paying service jobs. This creates a demand for additional training and education among such workers.

Africa's share in world trade is small and is shrinking due to fierce competition from other regions that enjoy faster and more sustained economic growth. In 1995, the continent's terms of trade had fallen to 89 per cent of the 1987 baseline index (Mkandawire and Soludo, 1999). Trade liberalisation in a world market that is not fair towards Africa has worsened the situation. It has been observed that 'where world trade is completely free and open, as in financial markets, it generally works to the benefit of the strongest. Developing countries enter the market as unequal partners and leave with unequal rewards (UNDP, 2002: 1). Growing fiscal constraints and competition for ever-dwindling public resources in Africa have seen the adult education sector being sacrificed in terms of budgetary allocations for the demands of primary and secondary school formal education. As a result, donor funding and NGOs are sustaining many adult education programmes in Africa (Indabawa, 2000).

The workplace and its related activities are also an important site for adult education. Interests and needs generated by the workplace are increasingly becoming the catalyst for adult education in many places in Africa. The private sector in Africa is spending a lot of money in formal training for its employees. Governments in Africa are also involved in employee training (Nafukho and Kang'ethe, 2002). Mandated education and training are especially common in fields such as computer technology, engineering, teaching and education. Employees in these fields, as pointed out in Chapter 8, have to update their skills and knowledge continuously. The most common measure of participation in mandated education is continuing education.

The economic environment prevailing in Africa and in the global economy is shaping the nature of African society and, by extension, the nature of learning that adults are likely to undertake. The shift to a service and information society in the West and rapid changes in the workplace the world over are making adult education and lifelong learning very important. Africa must therefore invest in adult education and lifelong learning programmes.

## ▓ ACTIVITY

**Imagine that you are the Minister of Finance in your country. Your country has a very limited national income of its own and you are expected to share out the national resources among all sectors. Your President has told you that 50 per cent of the money allocated to education should be spent on primary school education, 35 per cent on secondary education, 10 per cent on university education and the remaining 5 per cent must be shared out among other educational sectors, such as vocational and technical education and adult education. Prepare a response to your President in which you justify to him how important adult education is for the development of the country.**

## SUMMARY

This chapter has assessed the impact of various environments on adult education in Africa, that is, social, cultural, economic and political. It was noted that historically adult education has arisen as a response to particular needs. This chapter has demonstrated that adult education is of necessity changing, dynamic, responsive and proactive, in the same way as the society of which it is a part reflects these characteristics. It was also shown that adult education has responded to the various demands of these environments. Adult education programmes have been designed to meet new needs and this has been especially true in the workplace. Both the socioeconomic and the technological trends that are increasingly engulfing Africa pose considerable burdens on Africa's adult education programmes, requiring both ad hoc and ongoing educational responses critical for the development of the existing systems.

## KEY POINTS

- A society that values education will invest more resources in the education sector.
- The social, cultural, economic and political environments prevailing in a given country can help promote adult education.
- African governments must prioritise education and play a leading role in promoting partnerships among various organisations engaged in adult education and lifelong learning.
- Structural Adjustment Programmes have led to a reduction in spending on social services such as health and education in Africa.
- Adult education in Africa responds to societal change and tends to stimulate further change.
- Adult education has an important role in promoting respect for diversity in the social, cultural, economic and political environments in Africa.
- Culturally, African societies have both statutory and non-statutory sanctions that they impose on those who break or go against societal rules.
- Politics in Africa play a significant role in the provision of adult education programmes.
- The ever-changing and competitive economic environments require adults to learn on a continuous basis.

## ☒ ACTIVITY

**Prepare a list of social, cultural, economic and political obstacles to adult education in your own country.**

## FURTHER QUESTIONS

1 Why do African governments often neglect adult education?
2 Briefly describe how culture has hindered the participation of women in adult education activities in Africa.
3 How has economic decline affected adult education in Africa?
4 Why is adult education weak in a continent that clearly has many developmental needs?
5 Explain how participation in adult education programmes in Africa can be enhanced.

## SUGGESTED READINGS

Amutabi, M. N. 1997. 'The plight of adult education in Kenya'. In *Globalization, adult education and training: Impacts and issues*, ed. S. Walters, pp. 189–96. London: Zed Books.

Cervero, R. M. and Wilson, A.L. and Associates. 2001. *Power in practice: Adult education and the struggle for knowledge and power in society*. San Francisco: Jossey-Bass.

Jarvis, P. 1993. *Adult education and the state: Towards a politics of adult education*. London: Routledge.

# Chapter 5

# Opportunities and access for adult learners

## OVERVIEW

This chapter opens with a discussion on the opportunities available to adult learners in Africa. The chapter also discusses the factors that limit adult learners from accessing these opportunities. The role of African governments in the development of adult education is examined. The ministries of education, community development, health and agriculture are identified as significant providers of adult education. Other ministries that play a role in adult education are commerce, industry, cooperatives, tourism and information. Agencies that are important for adult education programmes include universities, national polytechnics, and vocational and technical training institutions. In addition, international organisations such as the World Health Organization, the International Labour Organisation and UNESCO play a key role.

## LEARNING OBJECTIVES

By the end of this chapter you should be able to:

1 Outline the main opportunities available in adult learning.
2 Discuss the factors that limit access to adult education.
3 Explain the role of governments in promoting the development of adult education.
4 Explain the role of universities and international organisations in adult education.

sesa woruban

## KEY TERMS

**continuing education**   A subset of adult education that seeks to positively link the needs and aspirations of learners who have had some prior contact with the school system, to adult education activities that will equip them with relevant knowledge, life skills and attitudes.

**formal adult education**   Education in formal learning institutions, such as schools and colleges for adult learners. This includes those adults who already have some academic certification, but who wish to acquire further education.

**life skills**   Skills that are taught to adults which have relevance to the learners' work and life in general.

**non-formal adult education**   Learning that takes place outside formal learning institutions and that is specifically meant for adult learners. This involves the education provided to adults by non-governmental and private organisations for those adults interested in acquiring specific knowledge and skills for life improvement.

**informal adult education**   The unplanned learning experiences that adult learners encounter in their daily lives.

## ⊞ BEFORE YOU START

1 **In small groups or alone, outline the various forms of adult education provided in your country. In each case, discuss the factors that limit adult learners from attending these adult education programmes.**

2 **Discuss the ways in which universities, national polytechnics, vocational and training institutions, and international organisations are important in the provision of adult education.**

# OPPORTUNITIES FOR ADULT LEARNERS

Prosser (1967) identified four main avenues through which adult learners are provided with opportunities for learning, that is, formal adult education, fundamental (basic) adult education, liberal adult education, and technical and in-service training adult education. Adekambi and Modise (2000) observe that adult education in Africa can be formal, non-formal and informal. Formal adult education takes place in formal institutions of learning such as schools and colleges. Contrary to this, non-formal adult education comprises out-of-school activities that involve various forms of learning, such as literacy education, remedial education for drop-outs, extension services, health education and community development. However, informal adult learning takes place throughout an individual's life.

For the purposes of this discussion, focus will be placed on the categories of formal and non-formal adult education and the opportunities that exist for adult learners in Africa.

## Formal adult education

There are various channels through which adult learners can formally access adult education in sub-Saharan African countries. There are adults who did not have opportunities as children to go through the formal education system. Such adult learners can join the appropriate levels of the mainstream formal education system and follow the syllabi for the various levels at which they are registered, such as primary, secondary and tertiary. This has happened in Kenya following the government's announcement of free and compulsory primary education in 2002. However, it should be remembered that this type of main-

streaming in Africa is, for the most part, restricted by the availability of facilities and resources, as well as the sociocultural factors that distinguish the young from the adults.

There are also adults who have attained sufficient academic certificates in formal education but still have a positive interest in pursuing learning. These are people who wish to gain more knowledge for the noble self-satisfaction that comes from a greater understanding of the world in which they live and the people with which they share it. Self-fulfilment and the extension of the learner's powers to the utmost act as incentives for further disciplined study. It is this section of society that holds the culture of dynamism, experimentation, adaptation and understanding. Important educational issues to be included in the curriculum for this category of the adult learner may include leadership skills to facilitate the exercise of sound judgement and implementation at all levels. These adult learners attain certificates signifying achievement in the various disciplines that are offered at institutions of higher learning in many African countries.

There are adults who are in employment, that is, formally or through self-employment, and who wish to become more proficient technically or more skilled in the basic methods of their own special craft, trade or industry. In our contemporary dynamic world, new knowledge, skills and techniques in specialised fields are necessary to keep abreast of changes. With these changes, technical education must grow and opportunities should be offered for the acquisition of new techniques. In this regard, opportunities for adult learners are found at many national polytechnics, institutes of technology and technical training institutes in Africa.

In Kenya, there is the College of Education and External Studies (CEES) of the University of Nairobi, the national polytechnics which include the Kenya Polytechnic (Nairobi), the Mombasa Polytechnic, the Kisumu Polytechnic and the Eldoret Polytechnic. In addition, there are a number of technology and technical training institutes throughout various parts of the country. In Lesotho, adult education organisations that provide continuing education through in-service training include the Institute of Extra-Mural Studies of the National University of Lesotho, the National Teacher Training College, the Ministry of Education, the Institute of Development Management (IDM) and the Lesotho Institute of Public Administration (Manthoto et al., 2000). In Namibia, there is the Council of Churches of Namibia, the Rossing Foundation Adult Education Centre, Ehafo Vocational Skills Training Centre and the Penduka Development Organisation, which all play a key role in providing adult education opportunities.

There are also adults who are illiterate and semi-literate whose interest lies in adult basic (fundamental) education. Adult basic education is concerned with teaching basic techniques of reading, writing and arithmetic which are important for enhancing personal and community development through participation in economic activities. The concern is generally with community or social development and focuses on new ideas, skills and techniques, new ways of thinking and new methods of organisation. Adult learners in these programmes usually have no previous educational pattern or experience to follow and the programmes target large sections of the community that have little or no formal education. This type of education embraces various aspects of life, such as health, the home, economics, politics and many others, and often leads to a certificate of attainment.

Responsibility for the provision of this type of programme lies mainly with the ministries of community development which have different names in various African countries. In Kenya, it is called the Ministry of Gender, Sports and Social Services. Such ministries provide opportunities for adult learners in conjunction with other ministries, such as health, agriculture, trade and industry, education and those which have an interest in adult literacy and development.

## Non-formal adult education

Non-formal adult education programmes are those that bring adult learners together depending on their interests in certain knowledge and skills. These are adult learners who may be functionally literate, and may or may not have academic certificates in formal education. They are interested in acquiring knowledge and skills in certain fields for their day-to-day functioning, such as music, entrepreneurship, computer skills, design and tailoring, agricultural skills, carpentry and many others.

These adult education programmes are offered by government institutions such as agricultural extension centres; NGOs such as church organisations; entrepreneurship development NGOs such as the Kenya Management Assistance Programme (K-MAP); the Kenya Rural Enterprise Programme (K-REP); and the Women in Development (WID) NGOs that are found in many African countries. Besides the government institutions and NGOs that provide opportunities for adult learners, there are also private training institutions, such as music schools, schools of hairdressing, and design and tailoring schools.

## ▩ ACTIVITY

1 Outline the various opportunities provided for adult learners in your country.
2 Identify individuals in your community who are enrolled in adult education

programmes. Find out the form of adult education programmes they attend and their experiences as adult learners.

# LIMITING FACTORS

It has been emphasised in the CONFINTEA V Midterm Review Conference of 2003 that 'a key to sustainable development in the twenty-first century and a means to bringing about justice, peace and solidarity around the globe are adult education and learning' (UNESCO, 2003). However, despite the promises made at the Fifth International Conference on Adult Education (CONFINTEA V), held in July 1997 in Hamburg (Germany), in which the Hamburg Declaration and the Agenda for the Future was formulated, adult education and learning have not yet received the attention warranted. In response to this, the participants at the CONFINTEA V Midterm Review in 2003, in their Call for Action and Accountability, reaffirmed their commitment to the Hamburg Declaration and the Agenda for the Future. They also reminded the world that adult education and learning are and must remain a collective responsibility shared by all learners, adult educators, governments, non-governmental and civil-society organisations, as well as the entire family of the United Nations.

There are a number of factors and conditions that limit adult learners' access to adult education programmes. These factors may be categorised as programme-based factors, community-based factors and learner-based factors.

## Programme-based factors

There are a number of factors relating to adult education programmes that may contribute to limiting their accessibility to adult learners. One of these factors relates to the nature of the programme developed for adult learners. Is the programme formal or non-formal? Is the target group of adult learners attending the appropriate programme? If the right groups of adult learners are in the right programme, then there will be interest in the programme, as well as sustained attendance. On the other hand, if the reverse is true, then the adult learners will have limited access. Accessibility will also be limited by the mode of instruction. This has to do with whether the programme is residential-based, in which case there is direct teacher instruction, or distance-based, in which communication technologies have to be used. The residential programme requires that adult learners have the time and the facilities to attend the programme. This condition limits students in the African setting who come from poor family backgrounds and are denied opportunities to enrol in adult education programmes when they cannot afford the direct and indirect costs of the programmes. On the other hand, due to the limited financial resources in most African countries, the communications technologies that would facilitate education for adult learners are also limited, as pointed out in Chapter 8. While distance education programmes that use online instruction are now becoming available in various African countries, only students from wealthier economic backgrounds can enrol in such programmes, as shown in Chapter 4.

The location of the adult education programme and availability of programme materials also determines accessibility for the adult learner. If the adult education programme is located far from the target learner, accessibility will be a problem because sacrifices will have to be made on the part of the learner in order to attend the programme. On the other hand, when there are no relevant programme materials for learners to use, they become discouraged and attendance is also diminished. Availability of programme materials and equipment, such as books, journals, periodicals, computers and Internet facilities, is a major factor in determining the accessibility of adult education programmes for learners in Africa. Other equally important factors include the type of adult education programme, the nature of the learners, their literacy levels and the expected monetary and non-monetary returns from enrolment in the programme.

Other programme-related factors that limit accessibility for adult learners include teacher skills and the language of instruction. Content delivery may be easier for the teacher if the learners are literate, but with illiterate learners the teacher needs to be tactful in the use of instructional procedures. Often learners have to be encouraged and convinced to stay on, and if the teacher is lacking in this aspect, the learners will be easily discouraged. The majority of adult learners in sub-Saharan Africa fall within this category. Depending on the type of adult education programme, the language of instruction may also limit accessibility for adult learners. There are many languages in African countries and the choice of language of instruction determines the attitude towards the programme. In Kenya, for example, the use of English and Kiswahili as languages of instruction in various adult education programmes should not be a problem. However, if some adult learners are not conversant in these languages they will experience resentment and discouragement, as opposed to the experience of learners familiar with the language of instruction.

## Community-based factors

Community-based factors which limit participation in adult education programmes in Africa include community appreciation for adult education, cultural factors, cultural institutions, and wars and conflicts. The adult community's appreciation for education motivates adult learners to seek education. However, if the reverse is true, then the adult's motivation to study falls very low and no matter how many adult education programmes exist in that country, the attendance level will be very low. Community appreciation is relevant especially in nomadic communities, such as the Masai people of Tanzania and Kenya. When the entire community keeps shifting in search of pasture for their animals, the provision of adult education for such adults becomes a problem.

The culture of the community is also significant in determining whether adults commit to education or not. The effect of these cultural factors will also depend on the types of adult education programmes available. As discussed in Chapter 6, in the African setting, men are generally considered superior to women in all spheres of life, except the domestic sphere. If the organisation of learning in an adult education programme is insensitive to this fact (especially in literacy programmes) and allows males and females to participate in one class, or worse still, uses female teachers for instruction, males may become resentful and may even drop out of the programme (Republic of Kenya, 1989). These same cultural issues constrain many adult learners from joining mainstream formal education. Cultural institutions such as radio, television, museums, archives and churches can do a lot to encourage participation in adult education. However, if not properly used they can be a hindrance.

Wars and conflicts in some African states drive the adult community to concentrate on survival. Rwanda, Burundi, Liberia, Nigeria, Sudan, Zimbabwe and Kenya have experienced war and conflict which have created vulnerable citizens. In such situations education becomes secondary to survival.

## Learner-based factors

Learner-based factors tend to limit access to adult education programmes. As shown in Chapter 1, adult learners have unique characteristics which adult educators must recognise in order for them to enrol and complete their programmes successfully. These characteristics, such as the nature of adult learners and their objectives for attending adult education programmes, are important factors in determining motivation. In many sub-Saharan African countries, if adult learners do not see a connection between attending adult education programmes and improvement of life, they are not likely to seek enrolment in adult education programmes.

Other factors that limit access to adult education include marital status, the stage in the lifespan, size of the family and family problems. In Africa, a married female student will often need the permission of the husband to attend adult education. African families also tend to have large families with several children in addition to extended family members. These responsibilities place pressures on adult time, finances and energy, and this limits their accessibility to adult education. This is further compounded if there are marital and family problems, because adults will not have the energy, interest and time to seek education.

Furthermore, the current occupation and financial status of prospective adult learners determine whether or not they will seek education. Adults who are fully occupied in their current employment stations and have no time available will tend not to seek education. Attendance is also limited by the students' financial status because in many adult education programmes funds are required for registration, tuition, trans-port and the purchase of relevant reading materials. If prospective students have a weak financial base they are unlikely to seek education. This is a common feature in most African countries. In addition, there is a lack of government policies in many African countries that encourage individual students to enrol in adult education programmes. In Chapter 10, we argue that policies and legislation must be passed in order to support adult education, continuing education and lifelong learning. Workplace learning has become necessary for all workers and there is a need for employers to provide incentives for employees so as to motivate them to learn on a continuous basis (Nafukho and Kang'ethe, 2002).

## ⧉ ACTIVITY

**Reflect on the adult education programmes existing in your country. Give examples of the various factors that limit adult learners from attending these programmes.**

## THE ROLE OF GOVERNMENTS

The role of governments in improving the conditions and quality of adult education programmes and in providing adult education programmes are well articulated in the Hamburg Declaration and The Agenda for the Future. In the Declaration (UNESCO, 1997: 11–14), governments of member countries committed themselves to

> *creating conditions for the expression of people's demand for learning; ensuring accessibility and quality; opening schools, colleges and universities to adult learners; improving conditions for the professional development of adult educators; improving*

*the relevance of initial education within a lifelong learning perspective; promoting policy-driven and action-oriented research and studies on adult learning; and recognising the new role of the state and social partners in the provision of adult education*

Since this declaration a number of governments in Africa have initiated several positive policies aimed at promoting adult education. These include the governments of Botswana, South Africa, Kenya and Namibia. In fact, immediately after independence, the chief responsibility of the governments of various independent African countries lay in the provision of adult education. In practice, all ministries play some role in adult education. However, the ministries of education, community development, health, and agriculture play significant roles, and can safely be referred to as the main adult education ministries (Indabawa et al, 2000). Let us now turn to each of these ministries and briefly examine their roles in the provision of adult education.

## Ministries of education

The main responsibility of the ministries of education is child education or formal types of education that begin with kindergarten and continue up to tertiary levels. The issues and responsibilities which these ministries must attend to are universal and include fee-free education (where applicable, for example, in Uganda and Kenya); the supply and distribution of teachers; the increase in the number of schools in response to the increase in the number of students; the pattern of child education; the examination system and many others. In addition, these ministries provide a component of adult education for those adults

wishing to join mainstream formal education at appropriate levels.

Using Kenya as an example, the Ministry of Education, Science and Technology facilitates adult education through the Kenya Institute of Education (KIE) and the Teachers' Training Colleges (TTC). The KIE provides adult education in terms of orientation courses, in-service courses and seminars in matters relating to curriculum development, while TTCs provide pre-service and in-service education for teachers. The Ministry of Education, Science and Technology also funds public universities that have become important providers of adult and continuing education as a way of ensuring workforce development.

## Ministries of community development

These ministries bear different names in various African countries. Some of these names include the Ministry of Social Development; the Ministry of Community Development; the Ministry of Culture and Social Services; the Ministry of Gender, Sports and Social Services; and the Ministry of Housing and Social Services. The basic function of these ministries is social fostering and the encouraging of the growth of a common culture enriched by the numerous cultural groupings existent in African countries. These ministries are also responsible for self-help schemes that are sometimes based on the concept of African socialism.

These ministries provide further education and training for youths who have left the formal education system but have no gainful employment. The other most important responsibility is the provision of basic life skills, such as improved housing, hygiene, diet and childcare. Most workers in these ministries have social science training and are normally referred to as community development officers or social workers, and their work is mainly to create and sustain a community through adult education. In Kenya, this ministry is currently called the Ministry of Gender, Sports and Social Services, which includes the Department of Adult Education that deals with all community-based adult education programmes. In Mali and Senegal there are ministries of women's affairs and youth development that have components of adult education (Afrik, 2000).

## Ministries of health

The ministries of health are concerned with basic adult education and their workers are normally skilled in health education. Doctors, nurses, community health officers, clinical officers, nutritionists and even health assistants are all involved in one way or another in adult education. Their focus in adult education is on the benefits of disease prevention; basic hygiene; diet improvement; family life education; environmental education; maternal and child care; and the most current health concern, HIV/AIDS education.

## Ministries of agriculture

In all African countries, ministries of agriculture have a major role to play in adult education efforts. Most African countries are primarily agricultural, and their economic development depends on improved agricultural methods and the introduction of new crops while improving on those already in existence. The veterinary and agricultural extension officers are all adult education teachers in this regard.

## Other ministries

Other government ministries that are involved in adult education include the Ministry of Commerce, Tourism and Information; the Ministry of Science and Technology; and the Ministry of Industry and Cooperative Development. These ministries are concerned with teaching basic business principles; industrial relations; methods of cooperative effort for producer and consumer organisations; and entrepreneurship development.

## ⊞ ACTIVITY

**Select one government ministry you are familiar with in your country. Outline and discuss the adult education programmes that are organised and run by this ministry.**

## UNIVERSITIES AND OTHER AGENCIES

In most African universities, especially in English-speaking Africa, there are programmes for adult education. Examples of countries that have colleges and departments of adult education include Botswana, Lesotho, Uganda, South Africa, Nigeria, Ghana, Sierra Leone, Kenya, Tanzania and Namibia (Omolewa, 2000). Chapter 1 provides examples of several universities offering adult education programmes in Anglophone Africa. Universities, adult education colleges and departments provide liberal and formal adult education. Some of these universities provide degree and diploma courses by correspondence, evening part-time study or school-based/ holiday programmes. Distance education programmes are quite strong in Kenya, Swaziland, Lesotho, Botswana, South Africa,

Tanzania, Nigeria, Ivory Coast, Ethiopia, Mauritius and Namibia. Other countries such as Sierra Leone, Gambia, Senegal, Zimbabwe, Zambia, Uganda and Malawi are also moving in the same direction (Afrik, 2000). Further responsibilities of the universities include research, publication and the servicing of adult and continuing education (Omolewa, 2000). Universities should provide leadership in adult education in Africa. In addition, universities should produce cutting-edge research on the importance of adult education in promoting workplace learning in Africa. As mentioned in Chapter 10, universities in Africa should play a pivotal role in promoting lifelong learning and in creating learning communities.

Besides the universities, Omolewa (2000) identifies other important organisations that play a key role in the provision of adult education opportunities in Africa. These organisations include UNESCO, FAO, the Ford Foundation, Friedrich Ebert Foundation, the International Labour Organization (ILO), Oxfam, UNICEF, USAID, World Health Organization (WHO), the German Agency for Technical Cooperation (GTZ), the British Council, the British Department for International Development (DFID), the Economic Commission for Africa (ECA), the World Bank, the German Adult Education Association (IIZ/DVV), the European Union and the Laubach Literacy International (USA). Chapter 1 also identifies several other international and non-governmental organisations that influence policies related to adult education in Africa.

based in your country and discuss the various ways in which this organisation promotes adult education.

## NON-GOVERNMENTAL ORGANISATIONS

Non-government organisations (NGOs) have become increasingly active in adult education work in Africa. These include churches and missionary organisations such as the Catholic Relief Service and Christian Aid (Omolewa, 2000). Besides providing education in the beliefs of the churches, they also offer adult education in all its various forms. Basic adult education forms their main interest through the formation of discussion and church social clubs. The churches have been known to spend huge sums of money to facilitate adult education in terms of self-employment skills, formal employment skills and community development projects. Other NGOs that have an interest in and have contributed to the development of adult education in Africa include the Employers' Associations, Zanta International, Soroptimist International, the Rotary Club and the Boys Brigades (Omolewa, 2000). Chapter 7 of this book discusses the various civil society organisations, such as the trade unions in South Africa and in Kenya, women's organisations and political pressure groups that play a key role in providing adult learning programmes to their members and to members of the general public.

## ✺ ACTIVITY

1 Discuss the adult education programmes offered at universities in your country. Identify the strengths and weaknesses of these programmes.
2 Choose one international organisation

## ✺ ACTIVITY

List the various NGOs involved in adult education programmes in your country. Discuss their strengths and weaknesses as agents of adult education.

## SUMMARY

Opportunities for adult learning are found both in formal and non-formal education programmes. Various institutions in African countries provide these adult education programmes.

There are numerous factors that limit access to adult education programmes. These relate to the community, the adult students and the programmes themselves. The programme-based factors include the nature of the programme, the mode of instruction, the location of the programme, the availability of programme materials, teacher skills and the language of instruction. The community-based factors which limit access to adult education programmes include the community's appreciation for adult education, cultural factors, cultural institutions, and wars and conflicts in African countries. Finally, student-based factors are concerned with the adult learners' nature and their objectives for attending adult education programmes; their marital status; their stage in the lifespan; the size of the family; family problems; current occupation and the adult student's financial base.

A number of African governments have contributed significantly to the development of adult education in their respective countries. They have done so through various government ministries, such as education, community development, health, agriculture, livestock development, commerce, industry, cooperative development, and tourism and information. Besides government ministries, universities in African countries have played important roles in the development of adult education. Other agencies which have supported and facilitated adult education in many African countries include UNESCO and a range of NGOs.

## KEY POINTS

■ Opportunities for adult learners are found in formal adult education, as well as in non-formal programmes.
■ A large proportion of adult learners have opportunities for learning outside the formal education system.
■ There are many adult learners in African countries that require basic adult education. Important components of this type of education are literacy skills (reading, writing and arithmetic).
■ According to the CONFINTEA V Mid-term Review (UNESCO, 2003), adult education and learning the world over have not yet received the attention they deserve.
■ There are factors which limit adult learners from gaining access to adult education programmes in African countries, and these factors relate to the adult education programme itself, the community and the adult learners themselves.
■ African governments have made deliberate positive efforts for the development of adult education in their respective countries through various ministries.
■ Universities in African countries play important roles in adult education.
■ Since the early 1960s UNESCO and other international organisations have played an important role in the development of adult education programmes in Africa.
■ NGOs have an important role to play in the development of adult education programmes in Africa.

## ⊞ ACTIVITY

1   **Suppose you were a member of the adult education commission in your country. What proposals would you provide to help expand opportunities for adult learners?**

2 Think of the adult education programmes in your local community and
identify the factors and influences that
limit adults from attending these programmes.

## FURTHER QUESTIONS

1 What steps can African countries take to
increase opportunities for adult education?
2 In what ways can the cultural identities and diversities in Africa be used to
strengthen adult education programmes?

## SUGGESTED READINGS

Afrik, T. 2000. 'Significant post-inde-
pendence developments in adult and
continuing education in sub-Saharan
Africa'. In *The state of adult and con-
tinuing education in Africa*, eds. S. A.
Indabawa, A. Oduran, T. Afrik and
S. Walters, pp. 19–30. Windhoek:
Department of Adult and Non-formal
Education, University of Namibia.

Indabawa, S. A., Oduaran, A., Afrik, T. and
Walters, S. (eds.). 2000. *The state of
adult and continuing education in Africa*.
Windhoek: Department of Adult and
Non-formal Education, University of
Namibia.

Omolewa, M. 2000. 'Setting the tone
of adult and continuing education
in Africa'. In *The state of adult and
continuing education in Africa*, eds.
S. A. Indabawa, A. Oduran, T. Afrik
and S. Walters, pp. 11–16. Windhoek:
Department of Adult and Non-formal
Education, University of Namibia.

UNESCO. 1997. *Adult education. The Hamburg declaration. The Agenda for the
future*. Confintea. Fifth International
Conference on Adult Education, 14–18
July 1997. Hamburg: UNESCO Institute
of Education.

# Chapter 6

# Gender and development in adult education

## OVERVIEW

Various individuals and groups of individuals have interpreted the term gender in several ways. The types of education offered at different stages in the development of Africa have influenced gender roles. How is gender defined? How are gender relations built and nurtured in African societies? What role should adult education play in promoting gender relations and the development of African societies? What kind of knowledge has been passed on to the various groups of people in your respective communities? For what purposes was the knowledge passed on? What role did male or female members of your community play in the transmission of knowledge? This chapter provides the reader with pertinent information that should assist in answering these questions. An exposition of adult education and gender is also provided. The concepts of gender, patriarchy and matriarchy, as well as women's and men's movements and their influence on adult education in Africa, will also be explored. This chapter also examines gender and lifelong learning.

## LEARNING OBJECTIVES

By the end of this chapter you should be able to:

1 Understand the concept of gender and related concepts.
2 Explain the role of education in promoting gender relations and gender roles in Africa.
3 Discuss the effect of patriarchy and matriarchy on the development of adult education.
4 Explain the gender disparities in adult education.
5 Discuss gender relations and lifelong learning.

bese saka

## KEY TERMS

**femininity**   A socially constructed quality of womanhood and the social expectations arising from this.

**gender**   The significance of being male or female in a given society and its corresponding attributes, roles and positions.

**gender relations**   The social and hierarchical relationship between the male and female sex.

**masculinity**   A socially constructed quality of manhood and the social expectations arising from this.

**matriarchy**   A form of social organisation in which a female is head of the family or society, and descent and kinship are traced through the female line.

**maternalism**   A husband-wife relationship where the woman is more powerful than the man and he resides at the woman's residence.

**paternalism**   A husband-wife relationship where the man is more powerful than the woman and she resides at the man's residence.

**patriarchy**   A form of social organisation in which a male is head of the family or society, and kinship is mainly traced through the male line.

## ❖ BEFORE YOU START

Reflect on the cultural and social set up in your community. Outline the various roles played by women and men in this community. How do these roles determine the positioning of women and men in community life? How does this positioning influence the choice of which adult education programme to be enrolled in?

# GENDER

Being a male or female member of a given African society has certain accompanying qualitative characteristics assigned to you by your social and cultural community. These characteristics constitute gender. Gender is therefore 'the qualitative and interdependent character of women's and men's positions in society' (Ostergaard, 1992: 6). From the onset, gender relations are built and nurtured on the basis of biological functions and related roles and responsibilities, such as the human capacity for love, affection, sexual pleasure and mutual respect. In African contexts, these relations translate into power and dominance, where men are considered superior and the women inferior in most societies. However, in some African societies women own property and are therefore considered equal to or superior to men.

The male gender is associated with masculinity, leadership, decision-making, superiority and the control of economic resources, such as land, money and houses (production). On the other hand, the female gender carries the expectation of femininity, guidance (mostly by males), subordination and focuses on economically unaccounted for chores, such as giving birth, nurturing children as well as other family members, cooking, cleaning and reproduction. Gender divisions of labour are rooted in the conditions of production and reproduction that are reinforced by the cultural, religious and ideological systems prevailing in a given society. On the subject of male-female relations and their role in African societies, it must be mentioned, however, that in some countries women have been more advantaged because of historical occurrences. For example, in some circumstances African men continue to suffer from former gender-related humiliation. Before independence, men in workplaces which were owned or managed by white males in South Africa, Namibia, and Zimbabwe were disadvantaged when compared to women. In addition, males encountered a lot of suffering in some African countries, especially during the colonial era. During the struggle for independence, for instance, the majority of political prisoners in Africa were mainly men.

## ▧ ACTIVITY

Group into pairs to read this case study and discuss your answers to the questions.

Two young people, male and female, fell in love while completing their undergraduate studies in medicine at the same university. Soon after college, they got married and were both employed as doctors. Each of them earned a modest salary, and they agreed that they would invest some of their monthly income after paying their monthly household expenses. They lived in rented premises close to where they worked. The man learnt how to drive and they bought a car. At the end of the first year they had one child and also purchased a plot that they hoped to develop into their future residence.

The rented premises, the car and the purchased residential plot were all in the man's name. The woman did not know how to drive. She also did all the household chores such as shopping, cleaning and cooking, besides her occupation as a doctor. The couple started off on a mutually supportive note.

1 Why should the man be the owner of the car and the plot?
2 Why should the woman be doing all the household duties?
3 Who determined what each one of them should be doing in their home?
4 From the case study presented here, who

do you think has the superior status, who has an inferior status, and why?

## ADULT EDUCATION AND GENDER

Africa forms a part of what is generally referred to as the Third World. The Third World is sometimes used interchangeably with terms such as developing countries, ex-colonies, less developed nations, under-privileged nations, poor countries, newly freed countries, the South or lower-income countries. All of these terms connote material deprivation and technological underdevelopment. The major problems in these nations can be summarised as 'illiteracy, disease, poverty, famine and militarism' (Alemayehu, 1988: 284). Of all these problems, illiteracy appears to be the most serious as it largely determines how each of the other problems are approached and dealt with. In situations where there is widespread illiteracy there is usually widespread famine, unsanitary living conditions, oppression and exploitation (Alemayehu, 1988). It is therefore true that in trying to address each of these problems, the starting point should be literacy. Illiteracy should be addressed through adult education in an effort to transform the rest of the serious problems facing Africa. Adult education can help to prevent and eliminate gender disparity and gender-related social problems, such as violence against women, female genital mutilation and the sexual abuse of children by male and female adults. Wagner (2000: 133) has stated that

*According to UNESCO, there were an estimated 962 million illiterates in the world in 1990, 885 million in 1995, and an estimated 887 million in 2000, constituting 27% of the adult population in the developing countries. Of these illiterates, the*

*majority are women, in some countries accounting for up to two-thirds of adult illiteracy.*

Adult illiteracy rates are high in much of Africa. Due to the inadequacy of resources, basic adult literacy is very expensive. Most countries find themselves in vicious cycles of poverty, and their priority is to meet their basic needs (food, shelter and clothing), rather than literacy. This is true of East African countries such as Kenya, Uganda and Tanzania, Rwanda, Burundi and Ethiopia; West African countries such as Senegal, Côte d'Ivoire, Nigeria, Ghana and Mali; or southern African countries, such as South Africa, Namibia and Swaziland.

Where high rates of illiteracy exist, both males and females are disadvantaged. The adult males in households are usually culturally designated heads of households and are expected to make decisions on behalf of everybody in the household. Illiteracy disables household heads and decisions taken could disadvantage the entire household. If the adult females in these households are also illiterate they are even further disadvantaged, as they are the primary candidates for experiencing the effects of the decisions made by illiterate male household heads. Consequently, both male and female children will suffer equally in these environments. The situation is the same for those households headed by illiterate females. On the other hand, the situation is a little better if one of the spouses is literate, in which case informed decisions that benefit the entire household can be made.

In most parts of Africa the illiteracy rates for females have remained higher than those of the males (Ngo-Birm et al., 2002). In Kenya, for example, the number of illiterate females has always been higher than that of illiterate males (Women's Bureau, 1989). In other parts of Africa, the reverse situation has applied. In South Africa for example, during the apartheid era, black African men were confined largely to manual labour in mines, in factories and on farms, living far away from their families in single sex hostels. This happened while most women remained in relatively 'normal' domestic environments, albeit without their husbands, brothers or older sons. Some worked as live-in domestic servants in white suburbs and thereby found opportunities to enter formal education, becoming teachers and nurses. As a result of this legacy, there are many single parent African homes in South Africa financially managed by female professionals (mainly teachers and nurses), while many of the men remain unskilled, illiterate and unemployed. Adult educators in South Africa face a major challenge in designing programmes that can enrol men who were most disadvantaged during the apartheid era.

In the next few sections, the different family arrangements in Africa and how they relate to adult education programmes will be explored.

## Patriarchy

Most African marriages and families are patrilineal, meaning that when the spouses marry they live at the man's home or at a place belonging to the male spouse. This arrangement from the onset means that the man is superior while the woman is inferior. Paternalism is a husband-wife relationship in which the man is more powerful than the woman and where the woman lives at the man's place of residence. Patriarchy is related to paternalism in as much as the former is 'a set of social relations between men, which have a material base and … establish or create interdependence and solidarity among men that enable them to dominate women' (Hartmann, 1981: 14). Generally, men are dependent on one another to maintain control over women.

The material base upon which patriarchy rests lies most fundamentally on men's control over women's labour power. They maintain this control by excluding women from access to some essential productive resources such as land, money, various forms of capital and certain types of education.

In most traditional African societies, women only owned productive resources through their husbands, fathers, brothers, sons or other male relatives. The women's wealth was subsumed under the patriarchal system. In many African countries, the legal structures have been reorganised in such a manner that women can now own productive resources. However, most still suffer from the effects of the traditional structures. For example, African customary law in the legal structures often places women at a disadvantage in relation to property ownership, unless a woman directly buys the property.

The traditional ideologies that surrounded the home and family in Africa categorised women as homemakers in relation to domesticity and motherhood. Women were mainly tied to the private world of the home, hidden and invisible. Viewed in this way, they were passive elements against which men measured their power, wealth and productivity.

In patriarchal social relations, men appear on the domestic scene only rarely, and even then they are still the superiors. Children raised in this environment learn and internalise these gender roles. Other social structures outside the home where gender roles are taught and reinforced include churches, schools, sports, clubs, unions, factories, offices, health centres and the media. Modern Western education has for a long time included patriarchal elements reinforcing the domestic ideology of women, for example, reading materials provided in learning institutions often place men on a superior level to women. The learning material might, for example, depict a male sitting and reading a newspaper, while the female is portrayed preparing food, cleaning and serving the man.

In patriarchal households in Africa men were expected to provide for the wife, or wives, and all their children. This meant that women were not expected to participate in paid employment. During the colonial period in African countries, women were relegated mainly to the home while men went out to work for payment. In the process, men were more often absent from home and the women took over the leadership of households. This brought about conflict and a demand for adult education that would provide relevant skills for their households' improvement. This is partly what has given rise to increased enrolment among females in adult literacy programmes in countries like Kenya, Uganda and Tanzania. A good example of this scenario is Kenya, where over a long period of time, more women enrolled in adult literacy programmes than men.

Given that both women and men in Africa are now expected to provide for their families, it is important that adult education programmes are designed to equip learners with core competencies such as critical thinking skills, problem-solving skills, analytical and writing skills, leadership and coordination skills, interpersonal, collaboration and negotiation skills and computer skills, among others. Knowledge, skills and attitudes valued by many organisations can be acquired through adult education programmes.

## Matriarchy

Matriarchy is a form of social organisation in which a female is head of the family or society, and descent and kinship are traced through the female line (*The Collins English Dictionary*, 1979). In such a family structure, the oldest female member of the family is the authority figure. Matriarchal family structures existed in some African societies. Good examples of this can be traced among the Ashanti in Ghana, West Africa; the Kikuyu in Kenya, East Africa; and the Bemba in Malawi and Zambia, Southern Africa. In this family arrangement the women are visible and active in the public arena.

To illustrate how the matriarchal system has worked in some African countries, consider an example from the Kikuyu people of Central Kenya. Before, during and even after colonial influence, every Kikuyu was seen as either a son or a daughter of Mumbi, the mother of the Kikuyu community. Girls and women were generally expected to take the leadership role while children were considered as belonging to the women, and the men were considered only as having fathered them. The Kikuyu women's leadership has been felt in a variety of spheres in Kenya over the years. When compared to other ethnic groups in Kenya, the women from the Kikuyu community have performed better in many spheres of the economy. In addition, when compared to other women from forty ethnic groups in Kenya, the visibility of Kikuyu women as heads of households has led them to enjoy the benefits of a modern type of education at an earlier stage than their counterparts in other patriarchal communities.

As regards adult education, the Kikuyu women have the lowest illiteracy rates compared to the rest of the communities in Kenya. Central province in Kenya is the original home of the Kikuyu people. Although the female illiteracy rate in this province in the early 1980s was higher than that of the males in the same province, it was the lowest female illiteracy rate nationally among the rest of the provinces (Republic of Kenya, 1993a). It is therefore evident that matriarchal family structures make women more visible, which in turn has advantages when it comes to investment in adult education.

## ⊞ ACTIVITY

Examine the family structure in your community and identify whether it is a matriarchal or patriarchal family arrangement. What gender relations are evident in the family structure identified? How do these gender relations influence access to opportunities for adult education? What steps can be taken to ensure parity of participation in adult education between men and women?

## PRE-COLONIAL AFRICA

Chapter 2 provides important information regarding the historical development of education in Africa before the coming of the Europeans and during colonial times. In this chapter, an effort is made to show how the historical development of education in Africa affected gender roles. In pre-colonial Africa education was a lifelong activity and people learnt skills and knowledge related to their roles in society. Education was inclusive in nature and catered for both male and female members of society.

In general, the adult members of the community were in charge of all the youth, while education was characterised by its collective and social nature because every member was learning and teaching at the same time. It was a lifelong process in which an individual progressed through predetermined stages from birth to death (Bogonko, 1992). Both male and female members of the society had different roles in educating other members of the community.

There were some common elements in the content of education for all adults.

However, there was differentiation in the kind of education that was specific to females and males (Shiundu and Omulando, 1992). In general, the adult males learnt survival skills, including approaches to hunting and killing wild animals for their meat and their skins, as well as for the defence of their communities. They learnt these skills through observation and practice (Bogonko, 1992). The education of women was also vocation-specific in that the young women imitated and emulated their mothers and other female adults. They learnt about women's family roles by engaging in such skills as pottery, basket weaving, fetching water and firewood, and gathering and preparing food for the family. They also internalised the fact that men were the heads of households.

An important characteristic of African traditional education was continued learning. To the indigenous African perception learning was a lifelong experience and an ongoing engagement that only stopped with the ending of life. It was generally understood that adults were both learners and teachers simultaneously. The question as to when an adult was a learner or a teacher depended on the specific environment and circumstances in which adults found themselves at a particular time.

While it is appreciated that the education provided to adults at that stage was functional within specific communities, it was disadvantageous in that this education was not functional throughout Africa. Africa is an enormous continent with diverse climate and environments. Survival skills for example, in East Africa would not be functional in West Africa and vice versa. Adult education was functional on the premise that people were limited to their local communities and probably their neighbours.

Think of your own local community during pre-colonial times. What was the content of adult education in this community? What differentiation was there in content for adult males and females? Find out more information on content and methods of adult education from the older members of this community.

## COLONIAL AFRICA

As pointed out in Chapter 2, Western education was a non-indigenous system introduced initially by the Christian missionaries. For most African countries, this was the case at the turn of the twentieth century, except for Ethiopia, which was never colonised. The Christian missionaries were more interested in teaching Christianity than anything else. It was after the establishment of colonial rule that the colonial governments began taking an interest in African education (Bogonko, 1992). The kind of education provided at the time was at an elementary level, focusing mainly on literacy skills to enable Africans to perform clerical work.

The adult African male preferred an academic type of education as opposed to one related or linked to manual work. The adult females mainly followed the African indigenous type of education. The few women who attended formal Western-type education were limited to learning subjects that would make them better wives for their husbands and that would improve their homemaking skills.

To the African people, the Western type of education disrupted and interfered with the balanced indigenous way of life (Bogonko, 1992). While this may have been true, it should be appreciated that Western-type education also alerted Africans to

social and technological advancements in other parts of the world and that these benefited them. African males and females who have a Western education can function in any technology-based society in the world. Western education has also helped women in Africa by pointing out the negative aspects of practices such as female genital mutilation that is still being practised among many communities in Africa today. Consequently, adult education programmes should be designed to promote the positive aspects of African cultures while discouraging the negative practices.

## ⌗ ACTIVITY

Think of your own country during colonial times; outline the elements of the content of adult education during that time. What differences existed between the curriculum for adult males and females in your country? What advantages and disadvantages were evident with the introduction of Western-type adult education programmes in your country?

## POST-COLONIAL AFRICA

In the last section, it was noted that during colonial times, Western-type adult education was introduced to various African countries. At that time, there were certain elements of this education that were perceived to be more suited for the different genders. Alongside this Western type of adult education was the indigenous adult education system that was also essentially gender-specific.

In post-colonial Africa men and women are perceived as being mutually supportive to each other, and opportunities for adult education are open to both genders. As discussed in Chapter 1, there are many forms of adult education to which both men and women are admitted including agricultural extension programmes, in-service training, literacy, out-of-school education, audiovisual education, mass media education, vocational education, in-service personnel training, community development, cooperative education, evening classes, library services, extra-mural education, trade union education, secretarial training and popular theatre (Youngman, 1998; Adekanmbi and Modise, 2000). However, gender relations in a given African community regulate who enrols in which programme. For example, it is possible to find that more women are enrolled in literacy programmes than men. On the other hand, one would find that there are more men registered in agricultural extension programmes than women.

Within this modern framework of adult education there are gender-specific movements that have enhanced its development. These movements are discussed in the next section.

## Women's movements

Post-colonial Africa retained and followed colonial educational systems. These have, for the most part, confined women to courses of training that only reflect their roles in service areas such as mothering, teaching, nursing and secretarial jobs. Beginning in the twentieth century, women the world over began campaigning for specific societal reforms because of circumstances in their own lives which forced them to question the male dominated societies in which they lived. There have been a number of UN women's conferences held (1965, 1975, 1985 and 1995) to reflect on the progress made in this regard. Particularly important was the third UN women's conference held in 1985 in Nairobi (Kenya) whose agenda was 'Forward Looking Strategies for the

Advancement of Women'. These conferences generally focused on the plight of women and reflected on possible emancipation strategies. Adult education has been viewed as an effective strategy for enabling women to deal with their situation.

In many African countries, women's movements have been formed to echo women's empowerment through adult education. Prominent among these movements is the Association of African Women for Research and Development (AAWORD), an all-Africa organisation that focuses on research on women and dissemination of findings at local, regional and worldwide levels. African chapters that coordinate country activities reach out to all learning institutions in various countries in order to strengthen the activities of AAWORD. AAWORD has its headquarters in Dakar, Senegal, and is housed by the Council for the Development of Social Science Research in Africa (CODESRIA). There are other women's movements in various African countries that emphasise adult education for women's empowerment, for example, the Women in Development (WID) movement. The *Maendeleo ya Wanawake* (women in development) movement in Kenya plays an important role in reaching rural women through their local branches. A further example is the market women in Nigeria, who utilise adult education as a tool for empowerment in their trading activities. There is also Soroptimist International, a movement of professional women and executive businesswomen in many African countries. Part of the concerns of this organisation is the empowerment of women in the economic and social spheres.

## ▓ ACTIVITY

Think of a gender-specific movement in your country. Identify and outline the various activities that the movement concentrates on in its day-to-day operations. What adult education programmes does this movement utilise? In what aspects are adult education programmes beneficial to the movement's membership?

# GENDER AND LIFELONG LEARNING

It has been said that 'literacy is the right of every human being' (Alemayahu, 1988: 297) and the informed and effective participation of women and men in every sphere of life is needed if humanity is to survive and meet the challenges of the future (*Hamburg Declaration*, UNESCO, 1997). This is very important because it enables an individual to live meaningfully. Adult education is necessary not only for preserving useful old values and knowledge, but more importantly for facilitating the creation of new social values and knowledge. Adult education is necessary for the fostering of harmonious and peaceful living and the maintenance of a healthy environment, as well as in matters of gender.

Africa has a rich cultural diversity and the complexity of adult life makes it difficult to have a common tool for estimating success. However, the success of adult education programmes can be quantified in terms of positive change in attitudes, and particularly so for adult members of society. This is evident in the approach to human tragedies such as pollution, drug addiction, desertification, environmental degradation, population explosion, violence against women and the HIV/AIDS pandemic. Such human tragedies impact on both genders in ways which necessitate lifelong learning for both men and women.

Lifelong learning includes learning which takes place in schools, but it is a com-

prehensive phenomenon which includes traditional learning and vocational learning that leads to self-development or self-actualisation. Learning is therefore lifelong and lifewide.

Lifelong learning is necessary for both genders due to the rapid changes taking place in contemporary society, such as changes in job skills, interpersonal relations, social standards and norms, science and technology and other domains. Because change is so pervasive and rapid, learning should be linked to everyday life-making use of all available resources. In addition, both genders need to learn in a more purposeful, systematic way throughout their lives. Consequently, lifelong education should be encouraged, fostered and improved as it focuses on the management of emerging life challenges for all people. This is well articulated in Ki-Zerbo's book entitled *Educate or perish* (1990).

## Case study

An African couple were living in a rural setting with their six children in a country in Africa. The man was a secondary school head teacher, while the woman was an ordinary teacher at the same school. The man was an alcoholic and habitually abused his wife physically because of his frustration relating to his inability to adequately support his family financially. Generally, he had no time for his wife and children. The wife was a member of the Women in Development (WID) organisation where gender relations were part of the concerns of the organisation. The man was a member of a social club where guest speakers were invited. At the beginning of last year, he attended a club meeting with a guest speaker on the topic 'Gender and responsible family resource management' delivered by a fellow head teacher from an urban setting. Since that time he has not physically abused his wife and he makes time for his family.

From your assessment of the situation:

1 Why did the man change?
2 What are the likely issues that were brought to his attention by the guest speaker?
3 When the woman was being abused what were the likely thoughts that crossed her mind?
4 What changes are likely to have taken place in her thoughts since the change in her husband's behaviour towards her and the children?

## ACTIVITY

**Think of an adult education programme in your community that has helped both men and women.**

1 **What elements of gender are incorporated in this programme?**
2 **What kinds of ongoing gender awareness programmes are there in this community?**

## SUMMARY

This chapter has focused on the need to recognise gender in all adult education programmes. It commenced with a discussion on the concept of gender noting that this is a culturally and socially constructed phenomenon. The issue of adult education and gender was also discussed. It was noted here that illiteracy rates for females have remained higher than those of males in a number of African countries. The concepts of patriarchy and matriarchy in relation to adult education were also explored. In a patriarchal family arrangement, the male members of the family have advantages over the females and therefore have greater access to adult education. In a matriarchal family structure, the reverse is true.

This chapter also discussed adult education and gender in pre-colonial, colonial and post-colonial Africa. Women's movements in post-colonial Africa were examined, noting that such movements take advantage of adult education programmes. The chapter closed with an exposition on gender and lifelong learning. This kind of learning is essential due to the rapid changes taking place in contemporary society and should be linked to everyday life.

## KEY POINTS

- Gender is a culturally and socially constructed phenomenon in all human societies.
- There was effective indigenous adult education before and even after the introduction of Western education in Africa, with differentiated curricula for men and women.
- The introduction of Western education through colonialism relegated women mainly to the domestic sphere. Adult educational programmes were aimed at enhancing the performance of these activities. However, Western modes of adult education also brought with them advantages for both genders, for example, in relation to social and technological advancements.
- In post-colonial Africa men and women are perceived as being mutually supportive of each other and opportunities for adult education are open to both genders.
- Women's movements in Africa have helped raise the participation rates of

women in adult education programmes.

- Adult education is a lifelong engagement and has advantages for both men and women.
- Adult education is an effective tool in shaping people's attitudes and perceptions with regard to human issues such as pollution, environmental degradation, population explosion, gender violence and the HIV/AIDS pandemic.

## ⊞ ACTIVITY

1 Explain how gender relations are constructed in your community.
2 How do these gender relations impact on the current adult education programmes?
3 Outline the advantages and disadvantages of gender relations in Africa with regard to the development of adult education programmes.

## FURTHER QUESTIONS

1 Name the various adult education programmes in your country.

2 What are the gender participation rates in adult education programmes in your country?
3 What factors determine gender participation rates in various adult education programmes in your community?

## SUGGESTED READINGS

Afsher, H. 1991. 'Women and development: Myths and realities: Some introductory notes'. In *Women, development and survival in the Third World*, ed., H. Afsher, pp. 1–10. New York: Longman.

Dennis, C. 1991. 'Constructing a "career" under conditions of economic crisis and structural adjustment: The survival strategies of Nigerian women'. In *Women, development and survival in the Third World*, ed. H. Afsher, pp. 88–103. New York: Longman.

Ki-Zerbo, J. 1990. *Educate or perish: Africa's impasse and prospects*. Dakar: UNESCO and UNICEF.

Visanathan, N. et al. 1997. *The women, gender and development reader*. London: Zed Press.

# Chapter 7

# Adult education as a developing profession

## OVERVIEW

In the previous chapters of this book the definition, the meaning and the forms of adult education were discussed. The philosophical foundations and historical development of adult education in sub-Saharan Africa were also addressed. It has been explained that adult education does not operate in a vacuum and is affected by social, cultural, political and economic factors. These factors in turn affect opportunities and access to adult education programmes. Leading on from these findings, in this chapter an attempt is made to provide answers to the following questions: What is the meaning of a profession? Can adult education be considered to be a profession in contemporary African societies? What professional adult education associations exist in Africa?

## LEARNING OBJECTIVES

By the end of this chapter, you should be able to:

1 Explain the meaning of the adult education profession in Africa.
2 Discuss the professionalisation of adult education in Africa.
3 Describe how the field of adult education in Africa can benefit from the lessons learnt by the rest of the world.

dame-dame

## KEY TERMS

**credentialing**   The instruction, examination and certification required by members of a profession in order to offer the services associated with the profession.

**ethical practice**   Adherence to the standards for behaviour in a given profession as stipulated in the profession's rules and regulations.

**formal training**   Planned instruction that takes place in an organised setting which follows a well-designed curriculum.

**process approach**   The definition of a profession based on the circumstances by means of which an occupation becomes a profession.

**professionalisation**   The process that any specific profession goes through from its inception to full growth.

**self-enhancement**   The idea that individuals can invest in themselves by receiving further education and training in order to acquire additional knowledge, skills and attitudes that will improve their productivity in the workplace or in society.

**socioeconomic approach**   The definition of a profession based on how that profession is viewed and regarded by the general public.

**static approach**   The definition of a profession based on a set of specific objectives and performance standards.

**vocation**   What an individual does for a living, for example, teaching, practising law or cabinet making.

## ▦ BEFORE YOU START

List some of the professions that you know currently exist in your country. Describe the various activities carried out by these professions.

# TRADITIONAL AFRICAN SOCIETIES

The research literature indicates that Africa had very advanced indigenous knowledge systems before colonisation. Discoveries by archaeologists and anthropologists reveal that Africans were involved in some of the most intricate technological processes centuries before the colonial encounter (Seepe, 2000). Schmidt and Avery in Seepe (2000: 24) announced in 1978 that between 1 500 and 2 000 years ago, Africans living on the western shores of Lake Victoria in Tanzania produced carbon steel by means of sophisticated technological processes. In their examination of thirteen Iron Age furnaces dug up during excavations near Lake Victoria, the two researchers found that temperatures achieved in the blast furnaces were higher than those achieved in European machines in modern times.

According to Seepe (2000: 124–125), Africans were advanced in the field of astronomy and mathematics during the pre-Stone Age period. He notes that in 1978, Lynch and Robbins uncovered an astronomical observatory dated 300 BC on the edge of Lake Turkana in Kenya. Seepe (2000: 124) reports the site 'constituted the ruins of an African Stonehenge'. Regarding the calendar year, Lynch and Robbins discovered that modern Cushites in East Africa had a calendar based on the rising of certain stars and constellations. When the arrangement of the stones making up this calendar was examined, they found that 'this was no random pattern but that a definite relationship existed between the pillars at Namoratunga and the stars' (Seepe, 2000: 125). This enabled the team to conclude that a 'complex calendar system based on astronomical reckoning was developed by the first millennium BC in Eastern Africa' (Van Sertima, 1999: 309 in Seepe, 2004: 125).

As discussed in Chapter 2, Africa has made significant contributions to world civilisation. To show the contribution of African cultural practices to modern science, examples from Egypt will be used. Although the focus of this book is on sub-Saharan Africa, these examples are compelling and relevant to the entire African continent. When studying the cultural practices of the African people, iron, tin, gold and bronze artefacts can be found in the North with the Egyptian pyramids, in the empires and kingdoms of Nubia (Sudan), in Kemet (Pharaonic Egypt), in Aksum (Ethiopia), and in Punt (Somalia), including East and West Africa (Emeagwali, 1989). The past practices of the African people indicate the knowledge and creative ingenuity of these practices.

In Chapter 2 it was illustrated that in the case of agricultural science, Africa has been found to have been the first continent to have devised a science of agriculture. Seepe (2000: 128) has noted that 'the earliest technological leap from hunting and gathering activities to the scientific cultivation of crops occurred in Africa at least 7 000 years before it did on any other continent'. Citing Fred Wendorf, as reported in 1979 in *Science Magazine*, Van Sertima (1999: 320) alludes to 'the discovery of agricultural sites near the Nile river that go back more than 10 000 years before the dynasties of Egypt. Africans were first not only in crop science, but also the first in the domestication of cattle'. This is supported by the work of Charles Nelson, a University of Massachusetts anthropologist, and his team. In 1980, Nelson announced in the *New York Times* that his team had unearthed evidence in the Lukenya Hill district in the Kenya Highlands, about 40 kilometres from Nairobi, that 'Africans had been domesticating cattle 15,000 years ago'. Their findings led them to conclude that 'the pre-Iron Age African in that area had a relatively sophisticated society and could have spread their mores, living modes and philosophy, eventually reaching the fertile crescent of the Euphrates River valley, which many had once thought was the cradle of civilization' (Van Sertima, 1999: 322 in Seepe, 2004).

In the area of medicine, empirical evidence shows that several supposedly Western medicines were known to Africans before Europeans discovered them. African medicinal practices are disappearing very fast because the herbalists never wrote down the formulations for the various types of medicine. They also kept their knowledge secret and passed on this knowledge to only a few of their offspring. To show the importance of herbal medicine, Van Sertima (1999: 325) observed that

> The Africans had their own aspirin. The Bantu-speaking peoples use the bark of salix capensis *to treat musculoskeletal pains and this family of plants yields salicylic acid, the active ingredient in aspirin. In Mali they had one of the most effective cures for diarrhoea, using kaolin, the active ingredient in the American brand Kaopectate. Nigerian doctors developed a herbal preparation to treat skin infections which rivals the best in the modern world …*

The cases cited above demonstrate that there were significant indigenous knowledge and learning systems in traditional African societies. Adults played a major role in this learning process. In traditional African societies, a profession was associated with an individual's vocation – what the individual did for a living. There were professional fishermen, hunters, blacksmiths, singers, house builders, circumcisers, pot makers, midwives, brewers, firewood gatherers, medicine men and women, as well as tradesmen and tradeswomen, among others. In order to attain the status of these profes-

sions, individuals were required to observe, participate, become inducted and work in an apprenticeship setting before being allowed to perform their expected roles as a professional. There was no organised school system or certification process as it is known today.

The notion of a profession with regard to adult education in Africa raises some critical issues. First, there needs to be clarity with regard to what is meant by a profession in contemporary African societies. Merriam and Brockett, in *The Profession and Practice of Adult Education*, observe that professions have become a central force in contemporary society. Merriam and Brockett (1997: 218) have noted that 'professionals wield great power in determining what goes on in our society'. While Merriam and Brockett think professionals are important in North American society, professionals are equally important in modern African societies. This brings us to the next question: What is the meaning of a profession?

## ✖ ACTIVITY

1  Give examples of the traditional professional activities that still exist in Africa today. Why do you think these activities have remained important in contemporary African societies?
2  Describe the various strategies that should be implemented to restore positive African professions that are disappearing due to Western influence and globalisation.

## THE MEANING OF A PROFESSION

The meaning of the word *profession* transcends all societies and countries. Different languages can be used to refer to the same thing with similar activities. To have a clear meaning of a profession requires one to understand what constitutes a profession. This means that we should be able to define the word. However, with regard to the definition of a profession, Cervero (1988: 1) observes that 'the problem of defining professions has a long and controversial history'. This controversy is more pronounced when it comes to defining emerging professions such as adult education in Africa. Flexner (1915), one of the pioneering scholars in defining professions, observed that professions must '(1) involve intellectual operations; (2) derive their material from science; (3) involve definite and practical ends; (4) possess an educationally communicable technique; (5) tend to self-organisation; and (6) be altruistic' (Cervero, 1988: 6). When a profession is looked at in this way, then it is referred to by Cervero as 'a static approach' since the definition is based on specific objective standards (Merriam and Brockett, 1997: 218). The second approach for defining a profession is known as 'the process approach'. In this approach, 'emphasis is placed on the circumstances by which an occupation professionalises' (Merriam and Brockett, 1997: 219). To understand the meaning of a profession, the fourteen characteristics of the professionalisation process advanced by one of the renowned scholars in the field of adult education need to be examined. Houle (1980: 35–70) observed that the professionalisation process has the following core characteristics:

- clarifying the functions of a profession;
- mastery of theoretical knowledge;
- the capacity to solve problems;
- use of practical knowledge;
- self-enhancement;
- formal training;
- credentialing;
- creation of a subculture;

- legal reinforcement;
- public acceptance;
- ethical practice;
- penalties;
- relation to other vocations; and
- relation to the users of the service.

Hamilton (2002) noted that members of a profession must maintain high standards of performance, restrain self-interest and promote the ideals of public service in the area of their responsibilities. In return, society accords them substantial autonomy with which to regulate themselves. For the characteristics of a profession to have meaning in the present discussion they will be further discussed from within the African context.

## The professionalisation process

Using the fourteen concepts identified by Houle (1980) as characterising the professionalisation process, specific African examples will be used to explain the meaning of these concepts. Adult education professionals in Africa are faced with the difficult challenge of explaining the core functions of this new and developing profession. As professionals, they must make a great effort to explain the main functions and tasks of various adult and continuing education professional associations that exist in sub-Saharan Africa. When they do this they are clarifying the functions of their professional associations to existing members, potential members and to the general public.

When examining the background information of the members of adult education professional associations in Africa, they can be found to possess some form of knowledge learnt over a period of time. Acquiring knowledge through learning provides members of a specific profession with a common identity and also gives them a common language that enables them to communicate effectively within the profession. A mastery of knowledge also enables professionals to be competent in their work. For example, theory related to workplace learning, meta-cognition, action learning, adult learning, andragogy and experiential learning needs to be studied.

The problems the world experiences arise from several dimensions that may be economic, social, political or technological in nature. In the case of Africa there are poverty issues, health problems, political problems and social problems, to mention a few. Members of a profession should be able to use their theoretical knowledge to explain and interpret the many problems existing in African societies with the aim of finding solutions. The knowledge and skills possessed by members of a given professional association such as the Pan African Association for Literacy and Adult Education (PAALAE) should be used to address problems facing African societies.

While theoretical knowledge is important to a profession, not all problems are theory based. Most problems are practical in nature and therefore require practical solutions. Members of professional associations in Africa should use their knowledge to address practical problems facing their communities, families, societies, countries and the world at large. For example, the Severe Acute Respiratory Syndrome (SARS) disease that started in China in 2003 and spread the world over required an efficient and practical way of addressing it. Both theoretical and practical knowledge were critical in finding a solution to the fast-spreading disease. The World Health Organization (WHO), a respected health organisation run by professionals, took a leading role in addressing the SARS problem. This is an example of the practical way in which professionals can use knowledge to address current problems facing society.

Self-enhancement is in agreement with self-directed learning – a very important concept in the field of adult education. The professionalisation process requires members of a profession to continuously learn new information, skills and attitudes that may not be related to their profession. Our society is becoming increasingly complex. Professions require members to learn on a continuous basis, to be curious and to seek to understand the workings of other professions and how professions affect each other. Individual growth is a necessity in this knowledge explosion era. Teachers need to have an interest in medicine, while doctors need to have an interest in law and vice versa. This characteristic is well explained by Master in Business Administration (MBA) programmes offered at many universities. In the United States of America, for instance, there are universities offering an MBA degree in divinity, the rationale being that Church ministers need fund-raising and financial management skills. Then there are also special MBA programmes for doctors and scientists. This is also true in a number of African universities, where a multi-disciplinary approach is being emphasised in the training of professionals. For example, lawyers need knowledge of accounting, while doctors require communication skills to be able to communicate effectively with their patients. Many of these skills can be acquired in adult education degree programmes that currently exist in several African countries, as discussed in Chapter 1. Other areas where degrees are being offered to adult learners in Africa include education, law, agriculture and extension education, education technology, computer studies, marketing and entrepreneurship.

Training, on the other hand, is very important to members of any profession. Training equips trainees with knowledge, skills and attitudes that enable them to be competent at their jobs. In traditional African societies, vocations were learned at appropriate times and places. In contemporary societies, adult education training programmes in Africa take place in formal organised settings. Well-established procedures to transmit an essential body of knowledge and skills are necessary during the professionalisation process.

The other important concept associated with the professionalisation process – credentialing – refers to the notion that before one qualifies to be an adult educator, for example, one has to be examined and certified in order to offer the services associated with the profession and practice of adult education. The University of Botswana and the University of Namibia offer undergraduate degree programmes in adult education. This is an innovation that is totally different from North America, where most adult education programmes only offer graduate degrees. To qualify as a graduate with a degree in adult education in Botswana, the student has to be examined and certified in order to undertake the role of an adult educator.

Every professional association must create and nurture its own culture for its members. This may include the language of research, recognition awards, publications including journals and other peer-reviewed publications, norms, honours, traditions, roles and personal prestige systems, to mention a few. With regard to adult education, Bhola observed that 'in all human societies, developed or developing, adult education is first a culture and then a sector' (Bhola, 1997: 207). Regarding cultural aspects of adult education in Africa, he noted 'adults educate other adults and socialise the youth by beating drums and dancing, telling folktales and other stories, reciting oral histories and praise-singing, by playing games, organising initiation ceremonies and offering divinations, and in more

recent times, by putting up posters, holding public meetings, organizing exhibitions, and by broadcasting over radio and television' (Bhola 1997: 207). Adult education, as a sector, should be a formally organised establishment that includes the national ministry of education with its bureau or directorate of adult education and adult literacy; and departments and centres of adult education in provinces, districts, zones, blocks and communities. Bhola (1997) also adds that the adult education sector includes non-governmental organisations and other institutions of civil society paralleling state institutions at various levels, from national to local community-based organisations. With globalisation, adult education goes beyond national boundaries and includes regional and international organisations. Thus, the field of adult education itself is a culture that covers the entire world. A further discussion on adult education and globalisation is presented in Chapter 9.

In traditional African societies, every vocation had its own laws that guided the members of that vocation. In contemporary societies, laws exist to maintain order. In the same way, professional associations have laws to ensure order and the smooth operation of the associations. Therefore, every profession must have legal support or formal administrative rules that protect the special rights and privileges of practitioners. Houle (1980) noted that professions in North America try to influence public policy in the field of the work in which they are involved. This is referred to as lobbying. In Africa, lobbying as a concept is not yet well developed with regard to the adult education profession.

Professions do not exist in a vacuum. In order to have influence on society, professions need to be recognised by the society in which they are operating. In this regard Becker (1962: 34) has suggested that 'we view a profession as an honorific symbol in use in our society and analyse the characteristics of that symbol … We want to know what people have in mind when they say an occupation is a profession, or that it is becoming more professional, or that it is not a profession'. As discussed in Chapter 9, because of globalisation our society needs to be seen as an international entity. A profession should therefore be accepted and understood by the international community. This is important for promoting international peace and understanding, the core values that UNESCO, for example, seeks to promote worldwide.

Every profession should have ethical standards that must be observed by members of that profession. For the public and international society to have confidence in a profession, it has to build its own reputation based on set ethical standards. Ethics are important for the successful operation of any organisation (Hatcher, 2002). The professionalisation process is faced with several challenges, creating the need for ethical standards to guide the behaviour of the members of a profession. While ethical standards are meant to guide the behaviour of members, at times these standards are broken or not followed at all. When this happens, then some punishment has to be offered. This may include paying a fine, denial of the right to practise or suspension from membership for a specified period of time. Such punishment is meant to instil discipline and to serve as a warning to other members of the profession.

As a vocation professionalises, it grows in membership, theories, knowledge, skills, rules and regulations. The profession, therefore, becomes an entity in itself. To function efficiently, it must be able to establish a working relationship with other professions. The members of a given profession will usually belong to other professions. It is therefore important to remember that there are other professions whose functions and practices will have an impact on the adult education profession in Africa. While the profession may be very strong in southern Africa, its members should be interested in what is happening in West and East Africa, as well as the rest of the world.

For any professional association to meet its core functions, there is a need to establish formal relations between practitioners of a profession and the people who use their services, namely, the clients. This relationship needs to be clearly defined since the service users are the clients. If a profession has to grow, then its clients must be satisfied with the services provided. This creates client confidence in the professionals. In the case of the adult education profession in Africa, the clients are the participants who prove to be very conscious consumers since they are interested in an intangible product-knowledge. To maintain client satisfaction, the adult education profession has to package the product being offered in an attractive manner. This is even more important in our competitive world, where each profession is continuously challenged to recruit and retrain clients. The adult education programmes being offered must reflect changes taking place in society. For instance, as the knowledge revolution brings radical change to organisations, this change requires the workforce to respond by acquiring additional knowledge and skills so as to improve its functioning in the workplace. This calls for continuous programme reviews, for example, courses in managing change, lifelong learning, learning organisation, organisational learning and entrepreneurship. These have become not only important but also necessary for many adult education programmes currently being offered in Africa.

The fourteen characteristics identified by Houle (1980) and discussed above define a profession from 'the process approach'. This perspective differs from 'the static approach' in that it defines a profession by the extent to which criteria are met, and not from specific objectives and standards. Merriam and Brockett (1997:219) provide a third definition of a profession, 'the socioeconomic approach', which views a profession as a 'folk' concept in that an occupation is a profession only to the degree to which it is regarded as such by the general public. This approach relates to the tenth characteristic of a profession, that is, public acceptance. This characteristic has social, political and cultural implications for the developing profession. Cervero (1988: 9–10) explains the professionalisation process by noting the following:

> *In this process, occupations attempt to negotiate the boundaries of a market for their services and establish their control over it. … Unlike industrial labour, most professions produce intangible goods in that their product is inextricably bound to the person who produces it. Therefore the producers themselves have to be 'produced' if the products are to be given a distinctive form. In other words, professionals must be adequately trained and socialised to provide recognisably distinct services. … Therefore, an occupation's level of professionalisation can be assessed by the extent to which public and political authorities accept its credentials as necessary for providing a specific type of service.*

This quotation has a great deal of significance for the professionalisation process of the adult education profession in Africa. To what extent are adult educators collaborating with the political systems in power? And how does society view the field of adult education in Africa? What are adult educators doing to market the field and to show its relevance to the current social, political, cultural, environmental, health and economic problems facing several African countries?

Answers to these questions are still in line with the professionalisation process. While professions that have existed for many years may be easy to market, new and emerging professions in Africa face difficult challenges. The profession of adult education in Africa faces a challenge of identity. Adult education has been associated with adult literacy classes meant for illiterate people who need to learn how to read and write. But, as defined in Chapter 1, adult education includes many learning programmes designed to equip the workforce with core competencies, knowledge, skills and attitudes required to make individuals more productive in the workplace, for it is productivity that makes organisations more competitive. One of the tasks of the adult education profession, therefore, focuses on managing competition and improving competitiveness through workplace learning.

## ⧉ ACTIVITY

Make a list of your friends, role models, family members and their professions. Identify five role models from the list you have made and arrange to interview them. In your interview seek answers to the following questions:

- How did they get into the profession?
- What formal preparation did they participate in to prepare for their current position?
- What do they find most challenging in performing their professional duties?
- What is the 'good news' and the 'bad news' about their job?
- What local, national, regional and international professional organisations do they belong to?
- How do they keep up with the changes taking place in their organisations and professions?

- What do they find most rewarding about their careers?
- What advice would they give to a person who plans to become a professional?
- Prepare a report from each interview and submit it to your facilitator. Your report should include:
  a. A summary of the questions and answers.
  b. What you learned from the interview.
  c. Additional questions the interview raised in your mind.
  d. Any additional action steps generated from the interview.

# THE ADULT EDUCATION PROFESSION

The process approach of defining the adult education profession is quite relevant to what is happening in Africa. As seen above, adult education is a developing profession in Africa faced with several challenges. Bhola (2000: 208) has observed that

> The challenge of adult education today is to create a vibrant sector of adult education without devaluing and weakening the character and content of the indigenous culture of adult education. Indeed, the adult education sector should receive its agenda of research and training from the culture of adult education and in the process should contribute to the enrichment and renewal of the culture of adult education ... but on the other hand it is also argued that the modern sector of adult education may have dismissed the traditional culture of adult education out of hand and without thought and borrowed indiscriminately from the West irrelevant ideologies, missions, and methods of adult education simply to keep up appearances of modernity or only because the donors donated and demanded.

From the above sentiments, the adult education profession in Africa faces a challenge with regard to retaining the positive aspects of adult education that have existed for a long time in African societies. For instance, the teaching of moral values, which was mainly an adult responsibility, has now been taken over by schools. Scholars in this field with an interest in studying Africa need to focus on the positive aspects of adult education that should be incorporated in the curriculum. Chapter 3 of this book mentioned the African sages who are respected because of their philosophical knowledge and wisdom and play important roles during ceremonies in transmitting societal knowledge and values. When teaching adult education courses, teachers should create opportunities to invite renowned scholars in the field of adult education to visit their classes and to share their wealth of knowledge and experience. Professionals from various fields should be invited to speak to students about their fields of learning and what they stand for. As noted earlier, politics plays an important role in the recognition and acceptance of a profession. This means that in the teaching situation opportunities should be created to invite politicians, respected professionals and community leaders to our classrooms and share with them our learning experiences. Besides inviting guest speakers, there is a need to include field trips to business and industry establishments, community projects, historical sites and places of significance. As seen earlier, a profession needs to receive public acceptance and to build strong relations with other vocations. This is part of the professionalisation process.

To develop the adult education profession in Africa also requires the design and implementation of adult education projects by professionals working in Africa or those in the Diaspora with an interest in Africa. Bhola (2000: 214) observes that 'the responsibility for inventing a future for adult education in Africa lies squarely with stakeholders in and out of Africa'. The vanguard for the struggle will have to be the professoriate of adult education at African universities. Their task should begin with self-education. As correctly observed, scholars with an interest in Africa are challenged to make a contribution. The history of adult education, philosophy of adult education, and the social, political and economic aspects of adult education in Africa need to be recorded. The development of this series of textbooks attempts to do this as a contribution to the professionalisation of adult education in Africa.

The other important step in the professionalisation of adult education in Africa is the offering of a variety of adult education programmes in several learning institutions. Currently, adult education training programmes are offered at farmers' training centres and technical training institutions, institutions of research, science and technology, health training institutions and teacher-training institutions at colleges and universities. The programmes offered include certificate programmes, diploma programmes (also known as associate degrees in North America) and degree programmes. Besides these formal programmes, there are many adult education training programmes offered at the community level in the rural areas and in urban areas. There exist several modes through which adult education training programmes are offered. Examples include conferences, workshops, seminars and instruction in formal classroom settings. All these learning processes focus on the acquisition of knowledge, skills and attitudes considered very important to adult educators in Africa.

## ACTIVITY

1 List ten adult education training programmes currently operating in your country. Give reasons why you think these are adult education training programmes.
2 Identify and discuss the main challenges facing the adult education training programmes that you have listed. Identify practical steps that can be taken to address these challenges.

## PROFESSIONAL ASSOCIATIONS

Professional associations are very important the world over in the professionalisation process. All professionals need an organisation with which they can identify. On the importance of professional associations, Houle (1980: 171–172) observes that people belong to professional associations for the following reasons: 'Membership may be essential for the practice of a profession; a need for status; a sense of commitment or calling; a desire to share in policy formation and implementation both within the profession and in the society in which it exists; a feeling of duty; a wish for fellowship and community; and a zest for education'.

Professional associations meet some of these needs through the publication of journals, newsletters, bulletins, digests, forum papers, books, conference proceedings, working papers and occasional papers. These may be in printed or electronic versions. In addition, associations sponsor and organise conferences, workshops, clinics, conventions, symposia and seminars. All these activities ensure continued learning and professional growth of members and the professions.

In Africa, several professional associations in the field of adult education exist.

*Nelson Mandela, former president of South Africa, received a degree through distance education as an adult learner while in prison.*

They are continental, regional or country-based. Selected examples of some of the professional associations and their specific roles are now provided. At the continental level, the African Association for Literacy and Adult Education (PAALAE) played a leading role from 1984 to 1994. In 2000 a successor organisation was established, the Pan-African Association for Literacy and Adult Education with a Secretariat based in Dakar, Senegal. The founding of this association is in support of the views expressed by Bhola, who argues that the only way the adult education profession can be promoted in Africa is through the establishment of continental professional associations. Bhola (2000: 214) has noted that 'the professorate must develop all-Africa, national, regional and local associations for adult education which adult educators can join for discourses that include both academic and policy issues'.

In the Southern Africa region, several organisations have focused on adult edu-cation issues. Indabawa (2000: 138–141) provides examples in Namibia of associations mainly concerned with the adult education profession in Namibia. These include:

1  *Namibian Association for Literacy and Adult Education (NALAE)* – This is a national association that seeks to pro-mote adult and non-formal education in Namibia. As an umbrella organisation, it brings together academicians, practitioners and all stakeholders in the profession. It plays an advocacy role and helps in developing policy framework planning and implementation of adult education programmes.
2  *Council of Churches in Namibia (CCN)* – This is an umbrella body of Christian churches in Namibia that has played a key role in the promotion of literacy education.
3  *Rossing Foundation* – This is a strong non-governmental organisation that has

made contributions to the provision of non-formal adult education, with the aim of improving the quality of life of average citizens through non-formal educational programmes.

4 *Namibia Non-Governmental Organizations' Forum (NANGOF)* – This organisation brings together all NGOs including those involved in non-formal education. It plays an advocacy role and conducts research in the area of adult education.

In Lesotho, Manthoto, Braimoh and Adeola (2000: 119–122) have identified several organisations providing adult education programmes focusing on basic education needs, technical-vocational training needs, socioeconomic educational needs, ideological-political education needs and improving the quality of life. Examples of these organisations include:

1 *The Lesotho Distance Teaching Centre (LDTC)* offers a wide variety of afternoon and night schools, after formal school time.
2 *The Lesotho Association of Non-Formal Education (LANFE)* offers literacy and basic continuing education programmes.
3 *The Lesotho National Council of Women (LNCW)* promotes community development in urban and rural areas and strives to promote literacy among young women and mothers.
4 *Lesotho Congress of Free Trade Unions (LCFTU)* is a workers' organisation.
5 *Lesotho Federation of Trade Unions (LFTU)* is a workers' organisation.
6 *The Lesotho Planned Parenthood Association (LPPA)* provides family education and clinical services and also promotes good family-planning practices.

In Madagascar, the Madagascar Association for Adult Education (AMEA) is the main association concerned with adult education training and literacy. In collaboration with the Institute for International Cooperation of the German Adult Education Association (IIZ/DVV), AMEA has played a major role in the promotion of adult education (Rabakoarivelo, Rakotozafy-Harrison and Randriamahaleo, 2000: 127).

In the West Africa region, several bodies exist that are associated with the development and promotion of adult and continuing education. In Nigeria, the Nigerian National Council for Adult Education and the Community and Adult Education Research Society of Nigeria (CARESON) have been actively involved in the advocacy, research, publication and professional development of adult educators. In Ghana, the Adult Education Association (AEA) has been actively involved with the promotion of adult education. In Senegal, the National Literacy Directorate (NLD) is a national body that was established in 1971 with the main objective of promoting the development of adult education programmes. To show commitment to the development of adult education, the Government of Senegal established the Ministry of Literacy and National Languages in 1993 (Kane, 2000). In the case of Sierra Leone, the Sierra Leone Adult Education Association (SLADEA) partners with IIZ/DVV. SLADEA has 16 branches and its main focus is the promotion of literacy in indigenous languages; environmental education through its ecological promotion programme; promotion of women's participation at all levels of adult education activities; the building of institutional capacities; the promotion of democracy and civic education for the production of grassroots teaching and learning materials; and the training of facilitators for literacy classes. IIZ/DVV provides funding for these programmes (Koroma, 1998: 66–67).

In the East Africa region, the following associations in Kenya are concerned with adult education activities:

- *Board of Adult Education (AEB)* – Its main functions include the expansion of adult literacy programmes, registration of adult education teachers, inspection of adult education activities especially in non-formal adult education programmes, and the registration of providers of Adult and Continuing Education (ACE) programmes with non-governmental organisations and the private sector.
- *Adult Education Association (AEA)* – This is a national association that promotes adult and non-formal education activities in Kenya. It is an umbrella organisation that brings together academicians, practitioners and all stakeholders in the profession. It also plays an advocacy role and helps in developing policy framework, planning and implementation of adult education programmes.
- *The National Council of Churches (NCCK)* – This is an umbrella body of Christian churches in Kenya which has played a key role in the promotion of civic education and community development activities.
- *The Kenya Institute of Management* – It draws membership from industry and educational institutions promoting excellence in management practices.

In Uganda, Oxenham (2000) notes that the Uganda Joint Action for Adult Education (UJAFE), together with the Department of Adult and Communication Studies of the Makerere University, have played a major role in the promotion of adult education. In Ethiopia, the Christian Relief and Development Association (CRDA) provides its members with training through workshops and seminars, and the Agri-Service Ethiopia (ASE), which started rural adult education in 1969, provides training for farmers. The Adult and Non-formal Education Association in Ethiopia (ANFEAE), which was launched in 1997, plays an important role in the advocacy and promotion of adult education (Hilderbrand, 1998).

## ▓ ACTIVITY

1 Identify any statutory regulatory agencies of adult education programmes in your country. Describe the main activities of these agencies.
2 Find out from the adult education association in your country whether there are any codes of ethics guiding adult education practice.
3 Find out the employment opportunities for adult educators that exist in your country, community or town.

## WORLD-WIDE ADULT EDUCATION ASSOCIATIONS

Besides the various associations based in Africa, there are many associations based in Europe, Asia, North America, South America and in Australia. A few examples of these associations are now provided.

- Asian South Pacific Bureau of Adult Education (ASPBAE);
- International Council for Adult Education (ICEA);
- American Association for Adult Education, Academy of Human Resource Development;
- Academy of Management, American Society for Training and Development (ASTD);

- Association of World Education (AWE) based in Denmark;
- National Institute of Adult Continuing Education (NIACE) based in the United Kingdom;
- Adult Community Education in Australia;
- German Adult Education Association; and
- European Adult Education Association.

The existence of adult education associations all over the world shows the importance of continued learning and for adult educators to organise themselves as a profession. The fact that knowledge and skills acquired become obsolete in a very short time makes adult education and lifelong learning very important. Learning needs to be a continuous process. This is now popularly known as lifelong learning. The issue of lifelong learning is discussed fully in Chapter 10, which focuses on the future of adult education in Africa.

## ⌘ ACTIVITY

1  Using the Internet, identify fifteen professional associations that seek to promote adult and continuing education in the world. Use the following descriptors in your search: adult education, continuing education, lifelong education, non-formal education, adult literacy, human resource development, training, organisational development, workplace learning and the learning organisation, UNESCO.
2  Identify twenty learning institutions in Africa that provide adult education training programmes at certificate, diploma and degree levels.

## SUMMARY

In this chapter it has been shown that in traditional African societies, the adult learning process was based on different vocations and there existed professionals in various fields, such as herbal medicine, astronomy, mathematics, architecture, music, hunting, house construction, surgery and pot-making. The difficulty associated with defining a profession was discussed. The three approaches used to describe the professionalisation process, namely, the static approach, the process approach and the socioeconomic approach, were looked at. Having a clear understanding of the professionalisation process of adult education in Africa is important for providing clarity with regard to the functions and tasks of the profession. In this regard, fourteen main characteristics of professions as identified by Houle (1980) were presented, discussed and supported with relevant African examples. The status of the adult education profession in Africa as a developing profession was also discussed along with the challenges that need to be faced. Also addressed in the chapter were examples of adult education professional associations in Africa and in other parts of the world.

## KEY POINTS

- Before colonisation or any European influence, Africa had indigenous knowledge systems that were advanced in the fields of astronomy, mathematics, agricultural science and medicine.
- Members of several professional associations in Africa should use their knowledge to address practical problems facing their communities, families, societies, countries and the world at large.

- Every professional association has key characteristics that guide the core functions of the association.
- A profession is defined by looking at the static, process and socioeconomic approaches to professionalisation.

## ✕ ACTIVITY

The learning organisation paradigm has become important in managing change in organisations. Based on the information discussed in this chapter, explain the importance of professional organisations in Africa in helping their members manage the rapid change occurring at the workplace.

## FURTHER QUESTIONS

1 What is the meaning of a profession and why do you think the adult education field is a profession?

2 Make a distinction between the static, process and socioeconomic approaches of defining a profession.

3 Identify and discuss the main characteristics of the adult education profession. Use relevant examples from Africa.

## SUGGESTED READINGS

Cervero, R. M. 1988. *Effective continuing education for professionals*. San Francisco: Jossey-Bass.

Houle, C. O. 1980. *Continuing learning in the professions*. San Francisco: Jossey-Bass.

Merriam, S. B. and Brockett, R. G. 1997. *The profession and practice of adult education*. San Francisco: Jossey-Bass.

# Chapter 8

# Information and communication technology

## OVERVIEW

In the twentieth century, adult education experienced a worldwide revolution. This revolution can mainly be attributed to technological advancements associated with computer technology. While information and communication technology (ICT) has changed the distribution and accessibility of information and has led to innovations in teaching and learning processes, this is not often the case in Africa. Acquisition and use of computers in many African educational settings is still a major problem. While the rest of the world is witnessing the benefits associated with technological revolutions, many African countries have yet to see these benefits. Key information is provided in this chapter that explains what a computer is and how it functions. This is followed by a discussion of the Internet and how it works. It is argued in this chapter that computers, the Internet and instructional media tools should be used in Africa to empower adult students, raise their consciousness, promote equality and human rights, and to expose the many injustices occurring in society.

## LEARNING OBJECTIVES

By the end of this chapter, you should be able to:

1  Explain the status of computer access and usage in the context of African adult education.
2  Define a computer and how it works.
3  Explain the importance of the Internet and why its cost of operation is very high in Africa.
4  Explain the role of information and communication technology in adult learning.
5  Discuss the practical applications of information and communication technology for adult education within the African context.

dwennimmen

## KEY TERMS

**application software**   A program or combination of programs sold together as a package.

**computer**   A machine used electronically to process and store information.

**data**   The raw information that needs to be processed.

**data processing**   The methods and procedures whereby information is converted into a systematic and retrievable form.

**hardware**   The physical equipment that processes information for usage.

**operating system software**   The software that is required to run the computer.

**program**   A set of instructions that tells the computer what to do.

**software**   A pre-packaged program used to perform specific jobs on computers.

• Additional key terms can be found on pages 131–132.

## ⊞ BEFORE YOU START

Can you remember when you first saw or used a computer? Was it at your workplace, at school, at the Internet café in town or at the post office? Think about the people in your village, town or community who have never seen or used a computer. Write down what you think are the factors that contribute to people not using computers in your village, community, town or college.

# USING COMPUTERS

In Chapter 5, it was explained that adult education in African contexts might be offered in formal, informal or non-formal settings. This is quite in agreement with the way information and communication technology (ICT) is used, especially in the Western world. The best way to promote the use of computers in Africa is to begin with the individual. The disparity in the supply of computers in many African countries has led to several problems associated with computer access and usage. For example, on the lighter side, in some African countries a computer is considered to be mystical equipment that causes delays in the payment of salaries for teachers and civil servants. In other more serious cases, people using a computer for the first time experience some fear. This creates a problem referred to as computer anxiety. For adult learners in Africa to make full use of computers, they first need to manage the problem of anxiety. The computer is a mere working tool and is not more intelligent than human beings. As a working tool, it should therefore not be feared. Its use in learning and work should be fun. Adult learners in Africa need to know this. Both current and potential users of computers in Africa must learn to demystify the computer by trying out the many functions that a computer is capable of performing. One of the rules of thumb in teaching and learning is to move from the known to the unknown. This is important because not all adult learners in Africa have been exposed to computers. If you have never used a computer in your life, as a new learner do not be turned off the first day you come in contact with a computer. Remember, you are more intelligent and smarter than the computer.

As a computer user or student you need to have a positive attitude towards technology. Attitude is everything, and it determines what people finally become or are able to do. Believe in your own ability to learn and that of your teacher to help you learn. Do not let your initial confusion, fear or lack of interest in computers and in technology in general scare you – soon you will be a computer wizard or an Internet-user expert. For you to become a competent and discerning user of the computer, use instructions available in the computer itself, that is under the 'help function', or from the person teaching you to use the computer for the first time.

A positive psychological learning environment is important for learning. As a student or worker using a computer bring some humour into the class or at the workplace. The best kind of humour could come from your own experiences in learning how to use the computer and Internet. When you visit the popular Internet cafés in the towns where you live, what do you observe? At work, how do your bosses or work colleagues who have never used computers behave when computers are installed in their offices? Share these experiences with fellow students. Also, share your own fears and experiences with other learners. Many people have interesting stories to tell regarding the use of computers. Some people could not print their work and were afraid to ask for fear of being laughed at. Others started typing using one finger and were laughed at by computer experts. There is no computer user that does not have a story to tell. Remember, you are not alone. The popular saying 'practice makes perfect' holds true when it comes to using the computer. As a learner or a worker using computers, find several opportunities to practise what you have learned. In addition, participate in group practice sessions. These have worked very well with the students we have instructed. We have also observed many adults in African settings who never want to learn how to send or receive e-mail messages. Instead, they prefer somebody else to do this for them. Avoid this and do it yourself. That is the best approach to learn how to use computers. In addition, we encourage you to use the Socratic method of learning. As a student or an employee using computers, always ask questions. Do not be afraid or merely pretend that you are following the instructions when you are not.

In Chapter 5, the issue of access and opportunities for students in adult education was discussed. We believe that ICT can be used positively to address the problem of access. African governments and organisations should be able to open up more learning opportunities for adult learners. Computer costs should be lowered by removing duty on computers and computer accessories. Computer assembly plants should be established in Africa as a means of lowering the cost of these precious technological tools. At an individual level, people should be encouraged to save and purchase computers for use at home. This is only possible for urban dwellers that have access to electricity supply. It is a truism that there is a digital divide between countries in the North and the South, but within Africa there is also a digital divide between people living in large cities like Lagos, Nairobi, Harare, Kampala, Johannesburg, Abuja, Accra and Gaborone, and those people living in the rural areas. African governments should make a deliberate effort to equip schools and all learning institutions with computers. In Chapter 10 we talk about *learning societies*. There is a need to set up community computer centres where people can learn computer skills. Already in countries like Uganda and South Africa initiatives have been taken to establish community telecentres, which offer access to a variety of ICTs. The role of the private sector in enhancing computer accessibility in Africa is crucial. In many cities in Africa, private entrepreneurs have set up Internet cafés, which make it possible for many people who do not own computers to use Internet facilities.

## Computer usage in the African context

As noted elsewhere in this chapter, there exist several disparities with regard to the use of computers in the field of adult education in Africa. As observed in Chapter 9, while ICT is being used in the West to promote learning in the workplace, at home, on the road, in the business field and through collaborations with other learners, this is not the case in much of Africa. As the rest of the world is making use of ICT in the field of adult learning, very little is happening in Africa. This puts Africa at a great disadvantage. It has led to the digital divide between Africa and the rest of the world. Therefore, there exists a huge disparity in the use of technology between the North and the South. While globalisation is expected to benefit the world's entire community, this is not true when it comes to the use of technology in Africa. For instance, while almost every school in the North is equipped with computers, many adult learners in Africa have never even seen a computer.

The other problems associated with computer usage in Africa include the limited availability of computers; the transfer of old and outdated models of computers from the North to Africa; the high cost of computers and related accessories; frequent power failures in urban areas where electricity is available; lack of electricity in the rural areas where over 80 per cent of the population lives; lack of infrastructure; lack of finances to purchase computer equipment; and most importantly, the negative attitudes and fears associated with using computers (technophobia).

While ICT is important for Africa's development, the reader needs to be aware of the dangers of relying entirely on computers. Africa is disadvantaged in that few of the African languages can be read by computers. Most computer programs are not designed to work with languages such as Swahili or Kikuyu that are spoken by over 100 million people in the East and West African countries. This is a threat to African languages. Technology promotes the linguistic imperialism of English through computer software programs and the Internet. African scholars face a major challenge in developing software for African languages.

The Internet as a research tool is very important, but if not well used it is a threat to privacy, promotes international crime and has caused some corporations to incur major losses especially when junk mail interferes with the normal functioning of such corporations. In the West, where computers are heavily relied upon for work purposes, computer-related illnesses exist that affect users' health. In addition, a form of computer-generated physical and emotional burnout called technostress is caused due to the inability to adapt to new technology. Technostress threatens the performance and productivity of the workforce in the United States (Elder, 1987). The same could be true of Africa if the use of computers is adopted without establishing certain precautions. The point we would like to stress here is that computers are mere work tools and have some disadvantages that users should be aware of. As machines, computers cannot replace human thinking. Having given this brief discussion on the state of computer usage in Africa, we would like to demystify the computer by explaining what it is and how it functions.

## ⊞ ACTIVITY

1 Describe your own experience with computers. What fears did you have? How were these fears overcome?
2 After reading this section of the chapter, how has your attitude towards technology and computers been affected?
3 Explain how African governments should address the problem of the digital divide within countries, and between Africa and the rest of the world.

# WHAT IS A COMPUTER?

The computer is an important machine that has contributed to the current technological and knowledge revolution. While many people in Africa know what a computer is, some others, especially adults, have never had an opportunity to see or use this important tool. Figure 8.1 shows the 1990s model of a computer and its main parts. With advancements in technology, several kinds of computers now exist. Figure 8.2 shows a 2000 model of a computer.

A computer is a versatile machine that can be used to do many functions besides processing and storing information. As a data-processing tool, a computer is fast, efficient and reliable. It is a tool that accepts input data, processes it according to programmed logical and arithmetical rules, stores and outputs data and/or calculates results. Like all machines, however, computers are subject to errors and failures. Computers do not eliminate the need for backup paperwork or hard copies and are not smarter than people. Therefore

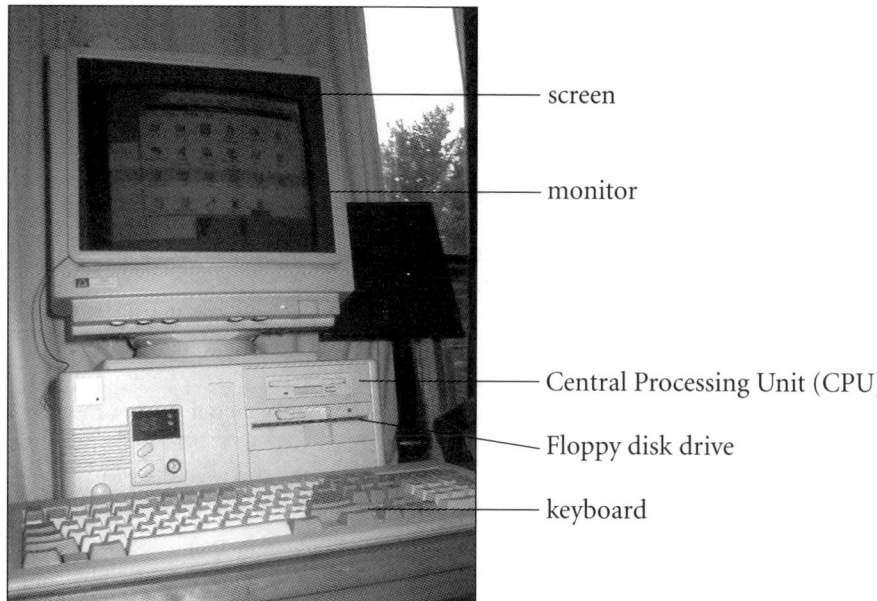

— screen

— monitor

— Central Processing Unit (CPU)

— Floppy disk drive

— keyboard

*Figure 8.1: A computer in the 1990s.*

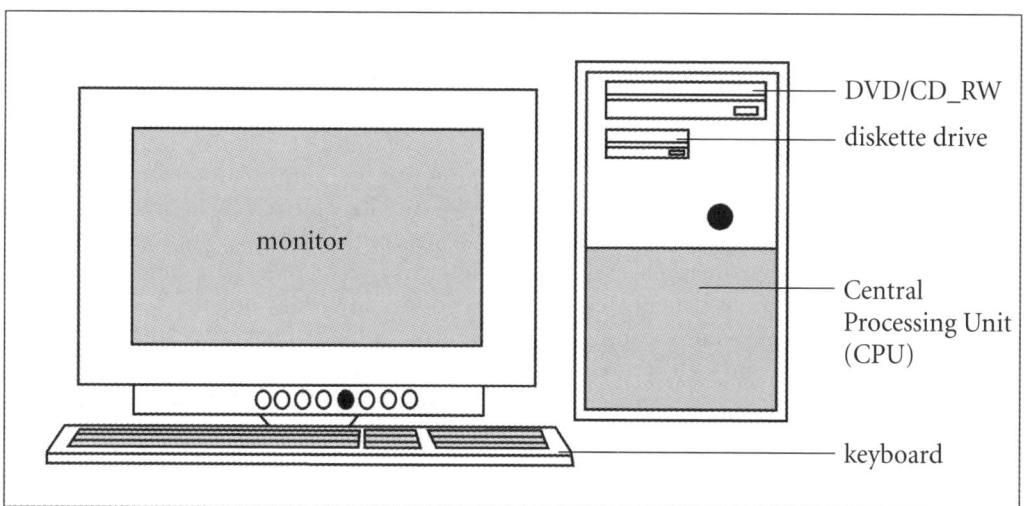

— DVD/CD_RW

— diskette drive

— Central Processing Unit (CPU)

— keyboard

monitor

*Figure 8.2: A computer in the year 2000.*

computers cannot replace human beings. A computer's operations are performed under the control of a stored program. A programme is a set of instructions that tells the computer what to do. It is usually held in the computer's internal memory while the instructions are being carried out. The general term used to describe programs is *software*. In a nutshell, a computer can be defined as a collection of machines (hardware) that will accept input data, process data and store and output the results, all under the control of a program (software). Having looked at this definition, one question springs to our mind: What is data?

The terms *data* and *information* are often used interchangeably, as meaning the same thing. However, there are major differences between these terms. Data is the 'raw' material for processing. It is unprocessed information. Data is collected and then processed into information. For example, the number of students enrolled in adult education programmes in Africa, the amount of fees paid by the students and the percentage of the workforce currently enrolled in adult and continuing education classes is raw data. This data can be processed into information to show whether the enrolment is increasing, constant or falling. When this is done, then it becomes information. Information is data processed in such a way as to create some meaning. It must have a purpose and so it is used for decision-making. Usually researchers process data to be able to answer their

research questions or hypotheses. Company executives, educational administrators and government cabinet ministers need information in order to make conscious and sound decisions. Without reliable data and quality information it is not possible to make sound decisions. Figure 8.3 shows how data is collected and processed into information.

Data processing refers to the methods and procedures whereby data is converted into information. For example, when students pay school fees by depositing money in a school bank account, they will complete a payment voucher and give the money to the bank cashier. They are given a deposit slip which is then taken to the college to use as evidence that the fees were paid. As far as the bank is concerned, the payment vouchers are data, that is, raw material that needs to be processed. The bank processes this data by using a computer and produces information for the student or school in the form of a bank statement. Caution must be used when employing the terms *data* and *information* since the two do not mean the same thing. It is data which goes into a computer and information that comes out.

Computers are widely used today because of their ability to process large volumes of data quickly, accurately and economically. Many organisations with an enormous load of paperwork do not have to employ many clerks to maintain and keep records. They rely on computers instead. When compared to people, computers

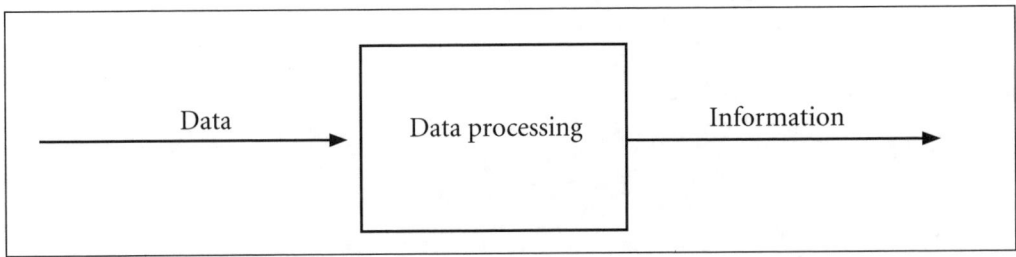

*Figure 8.3: The collection and processing of data into information.*

do not suffer from fatigue, boredom or hangovers. They are capable of processing large volumes of data accurately and for long periods of time without showing any negative effects except when there are occasional failures of an electronic component, a power failure or when viruses corrupt the software. Computers are particularly good at repetitive, time-consuming tasks with large amounts of data. For example, banking data tends to occur in large volumes requiring similar processing. Therefore, computers are very useful for processing banking data. In educational settings, computers are often used for management and instructional purposes. In this chapter, we show how computers can be used to promote adult education and training in Africa.

## Basic parts of a computer

A computer has four main parts, namely, an input device, a processing unit, a storage device and an output device (Figure 8.4). All computers must have these four parts in order to function as a computer system. The four main parts make up the computer hardware. *Hardware* refers to the physical equipment that processes information for use. The output devices consist of the mon-

itor, printers and plotter (an output device that produces drawings using a pen or pens and paper).

## ⌗ ACTIVITY

**List the various ways computers are used at home, in schools, in industry and in hospital settings. Explain why you think it would not be wise for a fully computerised university or hospital to revert back to manual ways of operation.**

## TYPES OF COMPUTERS

Computer types can be categorised based on their uses or sizes. There are two main types of computers based on their uses, namely, stand-alone computers and networked computers. A stand-alone computer is one that is not hooked up to other computers. It has only one terminal, that is, only one monitor, keyboard and processor. A stand-alone computer can also be referred to as a personal computer (PC), laptop, desktop or notebook depending on its size and portability.

A network or multi-user computer is a computer system that has one processor

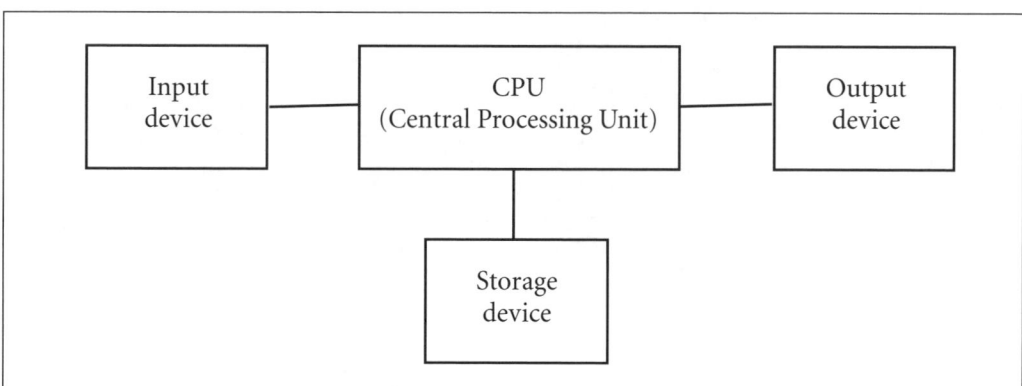

*Figure 8.4: Main parts of a computer.*

where shared information is stored. Several terminals or workstations are connected to a network. This processor is called a server. The terminals may or may not have processors, but they all have monitors and keyboards and they are all connected to the fileserver. A terminal that does not have a processor is called a *dumb* terminal. A terminal that has its own individual processor is called a *smart* terminal. Smart terminals can function either as a stand-alone computer or networked computer. When a networked system has more than one terminal, it is referred to as a *multi-user* system. If your institution has Internet facilities they are linked up using a server. When a computer system can run more than one programme at a time, it is called a *multi-task* system. The similarities and differences between computers are discussed in the section below.

## Computer sizes

The second way in which computers can be categorised is on the basis of their size. There are five main computer sizes. But, given the rapid technological development of the computer industry, a sixth one could come out before this book is published. Below, three basic computer sizes are discussed.

## Personal computer (PC)

A PC is the smallest computer available when measured by processing speed and internal storage capacity. This includes the smallest notebook computer, laptop and the larger desktop computers that are most common in many offices. Figures 8.5 and 8.6 show pictures of a laptop and desktop computer respectively.

## Miniframe computer

A miniframe computer is the next size larger than a PC. It is a network system that can have from two to twenty-five or more users or terminals connected to it (Figure 8.7). It can process information faster, store more information and run a wider variety of programmes or software than a PC. The

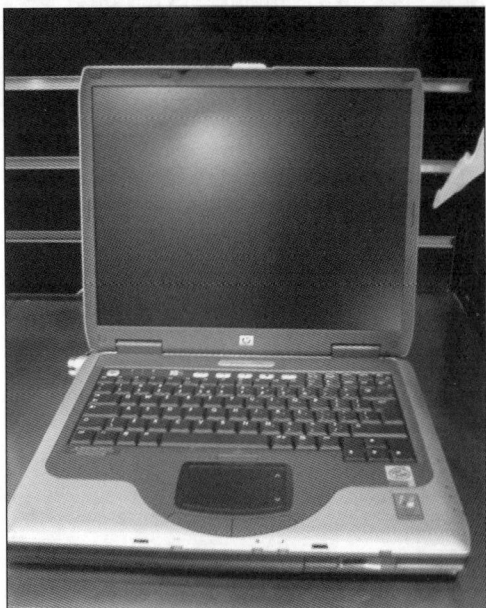

*Figure 8.5: A laptop*

*Figure 8.6: A desktop computer*

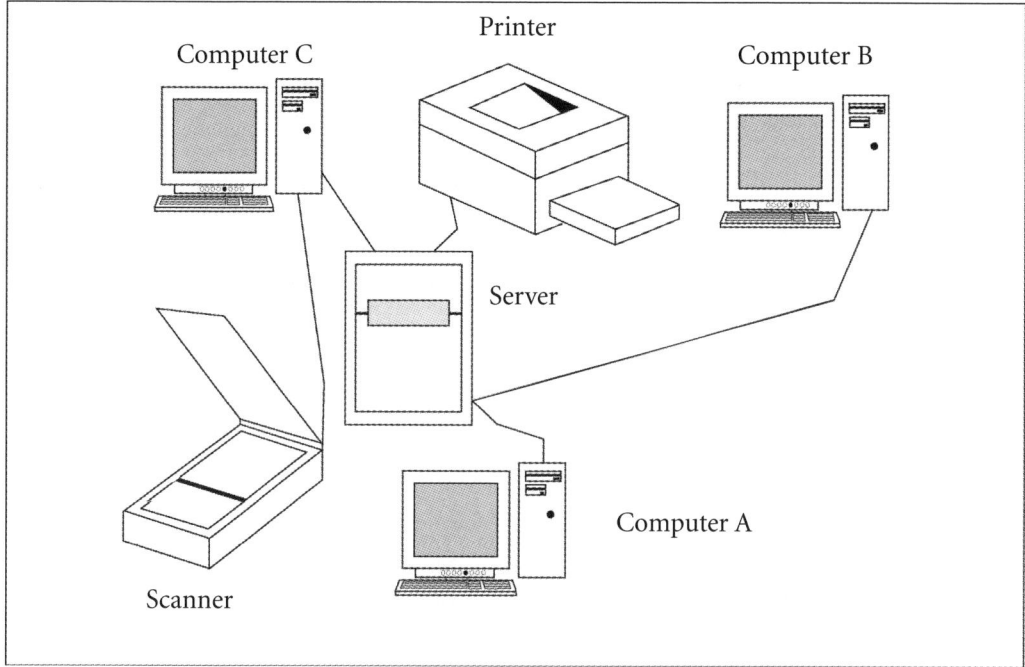

*Figure 8.7: Diagram of a computer network.*

fileserver for a miniframe is usually a small box about four to six inches wide and about two to three feet tall.

## Mainframe computer

A mainframe computer is the next size larger than a network system. It may have 100 or more users or terminals and can run faster, store more data and run many more programmes concurrently. The fileserver for a mainframe computer system can take up to one or more entire rooms. A mainframe computer could be found in your university library.

## ✳ ACTIVITY

Name the various parts of a computer from the diagrams presented in Figure 8.1.

## COMPUTER SOFTWARE

Software refers to a pre-packaged pro-gramme used to perform specific jobs on computers. Without the software, the computer machine would not be able to perform any functions.

## Operating system software

Operating system software is the software that is required to run the computer. Every computer must have this software. The computer uses it to coordinate opera-tions and for the storage of files onto the hard drive. The most popular operating system software for personal computers includes the Disk Operating System and the Windows System produced by Microsoft (MS-DOS).

# Application software

This is a program or combination of programs sold together as a package for use by computer operators. There are more than one million different application software packages on the market for IBM-compatible computers. This explains why the IBM PCs are very popular in Africa, just as they are in other countries of the world. For the purpose of this book, only eight common types of application software packages are discussed. These are:

1 *Word-processing software*
   Word-processing software is used for creating documents that were previously created using a typewriter, for example, letters, reports, memos, forms, newsletters and brochures. Examples of the most used word-processing software include Microsoft Word, Professional Write, WordPerfect and Note Pad.

2 *Electronic spreadsheet software*
   Electronic spreadsheet software consists of rows and columns used to input data. Electronic spreadsheet software is mainly used for accounting, bookkeeping and recordkeeping purposes. The screen created by this type of software is similar to the worksheets used by accountants. The software is designed to enable the user to input mathematical computations or formulas for the computer to perform using the numbers entered into the spreadsheet. Examples of electronic spreadsheet software available for use on a PC include: Excel, Quattro Pro, Quick-Books, LOTUS 1.2.3, and Quicken.

3 *Database management software*
   Database management software is used to manage or work with large amounts of information of similar types, such as files containing names of students enrolled in a programme of study, phone numbers, addresses and dates. Examples

of database management software packages are Paradox, Lotus Approach, Dbase, Rbase and FoxPro.

4 *Graphics software*
   Graphics software is used to create pictures, logos, or drawings. These types of software require large amounts of memory. Also, some printers are not capable of printing graphics. Examples of graphics software packages are: Microsoft Publisher, Harvard Graphics, Chart-Master, Draw Perfect, Paintbrush, Corel Draw and Draw Plus.

5 *Desktop publishing software*
   Desktop publishing software is used to create newsletters, brochures, letterhead, business cards or any type of printed material that combines graphics with texts. Examples of desktop publishing software packages are PageMaker, First Publisher, Newsroom Pro, and Ventura Publisher.

6 *Suites*
   This refers to a combination of software intended to give the computer user basic versions of word-processing, spreadsheet and database software all in one package. These are simplified versions that have a smaller number of features than the complete version of the same software purchased alone. Examples of combination software packages are Microsoft Works suite, WordPerfect Office suite, Lotus Approach and Microsoft Office suite.

7 *Games software*
   This is software that enables the computer user to play a variety of games. Some will require special hardware, or 'joysticks', to be added to the PC. The computer user can play golf, cards, chase, and Monopoly, among many others on the computer.

8 *Communication software*
   Communications software enables two or more computers to communicate

with each other. This is the software required when a computer is linked to a telephone line through a modem. A modem is a device that allows the computer user to send digital signals over a telephone line. The modem allows your computer to connect to and communicate with the rest of the world.

## ✳ ACTIVITY

Make an appointment with the librarian of the university or college where you live. During your meeting with the librarian identify the different forms of software packages available in the library and describe how they are used to serve library users.

## THE INTERNET

Many adult learners, teachers and educationists in sub-Saharan Africa have a lot of questions about the Internet. Such questions include: What is the Internet? Who owns the Internet? How does the Internet work? The Internet is the largest and most widely used computer network in the world (Poindexter, 1996). The Internet can be defined as a network of networks. Fibre optic cables, satellites, phone lines and other communication systems connect these networks. A network refers to two or more computers that are connected to enable users to share data and resources such as printers. A network server refers to a computer with special software and large file storage capabilities. Two or more connected networks form an Internet through which users can share information.

## The history of the Internet

Poindexter (1996) observed that the Internet began in the 1960s when the US Department of Defence was researching how to build a network of geographically dispersed computers that would continue to function even if one of the computers on the network failed to operate due to a catastrophe such as a military attack. In 1969 the Advanced Research Projects Agency (ARPA) created by the US Department of Defence, connected four computer networks to form a network called ARPANET. The decentralised structure of ARPANET made it easy for other networks to connect to it. Later, other government, academic and industrial networks were added to the ARPANET and it became known as the Internet, or the Net.

## Who owns and operates the Internet?

No single individual, institution, corporation, government or agency owns or operates the Internet. However, individuals, educational institutions, private corporations and government agencies own and operate each of the smaller networks that comprise the Internet. The Internet can be looked at as an electronic resource that contains a wealth of data and information. The freedom provided by the Internet has been considered dangerous to society if left uncontrolled, for example, criminals are using the Internet to transact their businesses. Therefore, the Internet has come under scrutiny and several groups have been formed to self-regulate the Internet instead of leaving governments to impose the regulations on people. The Electronic Frontier Foundation (EFF), which was established in the USA in 1990, addresses social and legal issues involving the electronic distribution of information on the Internet. The EFF focuses on civil liberties and protection of the First Amendment right to freedom of speech, as it applies to the electronic society of the Internet. The foundation is active in fighting government regulations and finding various ways to control the Internet. Another body that regulates the operation of the Internet is the Internet Society (ISOC), which was founded in 1992. ISOC is an international organisation that is trying to develop and implement standards for the Internet and its related technologies. With time the Internet should eventually have internationally accepted regulations binding its users (Laudon, Traver and Laudon, 1996). The Internet is considered an important communication resource. However, in the case of Africa, the United Nations Commission of Africa (ECA) found that, excluding South Africa, only 500 000 Africans have any access to the Internet. This is in contrast to North America and Europe where one in every five or six people currently uses the Internet. Only one in 1 500 people throughout most of Africa have access to the Internet (Africa One, 2000). While the Internet is considered to be a fast and cheap means of communication, this is not the case in Africa. Africa One (2000: 1) has noted that:

> Africans pay much more than Americans and Europeans for both telephone services and access to the Internet. International calls within Africa are generally routed via Europe, adding an estimated US $600 million to the continent's annual phone bill. An Internet account in Africa costs an average of $60 for five hours a month compared with about $29 a month for 20 hours Internet access in the United States.

There is an urgent need, therefore, to bridge the information gap currently existing between Africa and the rest of the world. One irony is that, coltan, the precious metal used in the manufacture of chips used in computers and in cellular phones, comes from the Democratic Republic of Congo in Africa. For Africa to compete effectively in the international arena, the finished mineral products need to be exported from Africa, instead of the current practice where precious minerals from Africa are exported in raw form and are later sold back to Africa as manufactured goods at a very high cost (Nafukho, 2003). The ICT era should empower African people to question current practices in international trade. Organisations like UNESCO who are devoted to international peace and understanding could play a big role in explaining Africa's predicament with ICT issues.

## How the Internet works

For the Internet to work, it requires a site or host. 'An Internet site, or host, is a network server that is connected to the Internet and allows people around the world to access its files' (Poindexter, 1996: 6). For the Internet to function, local hosts are attached to a major connection (or communication link) called a backbone. Without the local hosts and communication links, Internet communication would not be possible since every host site on the globe would need to connect directly to every other host in order to request information. The backbone quickly moves information from long distances and provides a cost-effective way to link local area networks (LANs) worldwide.

In order to access documents stored on web servers, you need software called a *web browser*, which is a programme that retrieves, interprets and displays web pages on the computer screen. Microsoft Internet Explorer and Netscape Navigator are powerful and easy-to-use web browsers capable of accessing Web documents, as well as any other type of Internet service.

As shown in Figure 8.8, computers A, B, C and D are linked by servers A and B using the Local Area Network (LAN). This could be in one university such as Makerere University in Uganda. People using the isolated network can communicate with those using networked computers by means of the Internet.

## The usefulness of the Internet

The Internet is an important tool for every learner and teacher in this ICT age. It provides many services that one can use to communicate with people around the world, to access and retrieve data and information, and to obtain software. Compared to other means of communication, the Internet is a fast and cheap means of communication. While the Internet has many advantages, five major examples of the usefulness of the Internet are now provided.

1  The Internet enables the user to send electronic messages to other users and receive messages. This is referred to as electronic mail (e-mail).
2  By using the Internet, one can run a programme on a remote host, play interactive games and access remote library material.
3  Users are able to search for documents, databases and information using the World Wide Web.
4  Users are able to transfer to computer files of text, graphics, music, animations or videos.
5  Users are able to participate in electronic discussion groups about a variety of topics.

The usefulness of the Internet especially to the field of adult education in Africa can

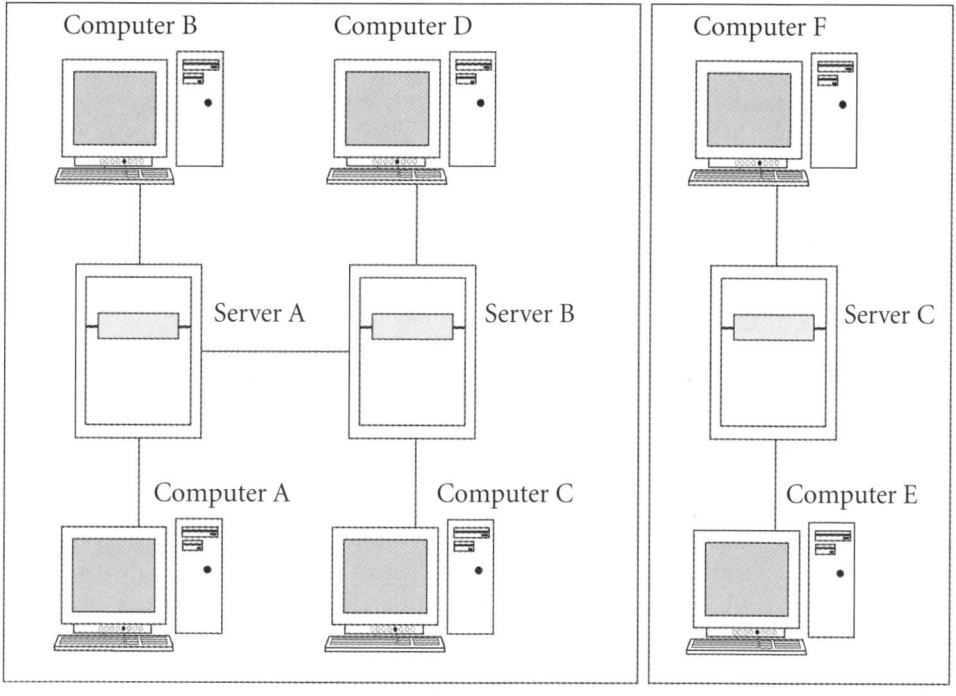

*Figure 8.8: A diagram that shows how a Local Area Network works.*

be demonstrated by its size. The Internet started in 1969 with four hosts only. By the year 2000, the US Internet Council's State of the Internet Report 2000, placed the number of African users at 2.5 million compared to 136 million in North America, 23 million in Europe and 69 million in Asia. More recently, the Internet has acquired the name 'information superhighway'. The worldwide network of computers linked by telephone lines, cables, microwaves and satellites makes up the information superhighway. The towns on the highway are the computers in the network. The roads that connect the computers are fibre optic cables, satellites and other communication systems. In fact, remote controlled Internet services are now available. The computers now use satellites to communicate and fibre optic cables are being replaced with remote controlled Internet access technology. One of the best known and most important telecom communications projects in Africa is the Africa One project. This is a private venture with an aim of putting a 32 000 kilometre optical fibre necklace around the entire continent of Africa. The project was expected to cost $1.9 billion (Africa One, 2000).

## ⌗ ACTIVITY

1 List the various ways you have personally benefited from the use of the Internet.
2 Visit a library or an Internet café and using the following descriptors/names search for information relevant to adult and continuing education in Africa: adult education, UNESCO, continuing education, lifelong learning, learning society, comparative education, Nyerere, Knowles, Youngman, Indabawa, Bhola, Houle, Lindeman, Opany, Karani, Nafukho, Amutabi and Otunga.

## PRACTICAL USES OF ICT

For a long time in Africa, the teaching and learning process relied mainly on pedagogical theories that focused on teacher-centred approaches. Knowles (1984) observed that this method of teaching was based on the assumption that learners needed to know only what the teacher taught them, resulting in a teaching and learning environment that promoted dependency on the teacher. Therefore, learning implied the transfer of knowledge from the teacher to learners with an empty mind (tabula rasa). The teacher was considered the content expert and provided answers to all the learning needs of the learners. With the availability of the Internet and many learning resources this is no longer the case. Information technology has led to a paradigm shift in instruction known as e-learning. Now the teacher is a facilitator of learning within a learner-centred environment. As noted in Chapter 1, using andragogy as a method of helping adults learn, the Internet and many learning resources available should help promote learning among adult learners. Learners should be encouraged to actively research the needed information. The teachers' role should be that of a coach and supporter who encourages students to use their personal knowledge and skills to create unique solutions to problems (Newby, Stepich, Lehman and Russel, 2000).

The advancement in ICT supports andragogy as a method of teaching. It also relies on the psychology of constructivism. Unlike some schools of thought that hold that knowledge exists independently of the individual, constructivism subscribes to the fact that learners can construct their own knowledge based on their own work and life experiences. Knowledge is constructed by the enrichment processes of the mind. This is a function of how well an individual reflects on his or her thinking, ponders questions, seeks answers to them and uses the opportunity to experiment with the knowledge acquired (Ropnarine and Johnson, 1987).

Teachers of adult learners should focus on teaching them how to learn by instilling a desire to learn. This can be done by acting as a guide in encouraging students to exercise higher-order thinking skills, such as problem-solving, reasoning and reflection (Nafukho and Kangethe, 2002: 167). The Internet is an invaluable tool of knowledge acquisition. For example, McKeown and Beck (1999) have observed that students develop the ability to learn in cooperative and collaborative learning environments. Adult learners should be given plenty of opportunities to think problems through, ask questions and find answers on the Internet. In addition, technology should help create learning environments that actively engage learners and encourage them to participate in the learning process. Therefore, both the Internet and computer-assisted instruction should be looked at as an enrichment factor which can have a great influence on how students learn, construct their own knowledge and eventually become citizens who participate in lifelong learning.

In the United States, the amount of technology in schools has increased significantly in the last ten years (Reiser, 2001). In Africa the same trend is being observed. A number of governments have put policies in place to promote computer usage. For example, in Kenya the new government that was elected in December 2002 introduced tax rebates on computer equipment imported as a method of making computers affordable. On the importance of incorporating technology in the field of education, empirical research shows that using technology in the classroom motivates students, encourages them to become problem solvers and creates new avenues for exploring information (Shelly, Cashman, Gunter and Gunter, 1999).

Technology has also been established to provide authentic and active learning environments. Shelly, Cashman, Gunter and Gunter (1999) observed that authentic learning experiences are instructional activities that demonstrate real-life connections by associating the concept being taught with a real-life activity or event. This is what adult learners need in their learning processes. Researchers note that learners provided with the opportunity to be involved derive ownership of the information with which they are presented because they are actively involved in the learning process.

The other major advantage of using ICT for instructing adult learners is that adult students are able to engage in multiple learning contexts incorporating visual, auditory, tactile and kinaesthetic learning processes. In such contexts, a variety of learning styles and individual needs are addressed making it easier to reach and benefit the diverse groups of adult students. The learner is engaged in an active process that fosters the use of what is learned in other contexts and situations. At the same time the learner develops problem-solving skills that can be used in real-world situations (Lowe, 2002: 165). ICT can be used to engage both students and their teachers in discussions aimed at promoting learning. For example, it enables students to have control of the flow of information and to review concepts, practise skills and conduct on-line research. Also, well-implemented instructional technology programmes engage learners and create excitement in the learning process. It can be a powerful tool for improving motivation and incentives for learning (Garmer and Firestone, 1996). Learners are able to obtain materials on-line using digital libraries. This improves the quality of their research work. We would, however, like to point out that information technology can only enhance learning and can never replace the teachers who play important roles as facilitators of learning.

While there is no doubt that the field of education in Africa stands to benefit from the use of technology as discussed above, we would like to mention practical examples of how this is happening in Africa. At the University of Dar-es-Salaam in Tanzania, the Carnegie Corporation provided $3.5 million that helped to install the required technology; purchased equipment; trained staff on how to use computers and the Internet; supplied more computers for student use; assisted in digitising the University Library's card catalogue; provided network security; and bought emergency power generators (Carnegie Corporation of New York, 2001).

Another good example of the promotion of technology usage in the area of education in Africa is the World Bank's global effort in 1997 to train teachers to use the Internet in 261 African schools. It was hoped that the trained teachers would in turn teach other African teachers and in this way spread their computer knowledge into the educational systems and African societies. The development of the *African Information Society Initiative* document by African ministers of social and economic planning and its endorsement by all countries in Africa is another positive and practical example of the promotion of the use of communication technology in the continent. Cisco Systems Inc., a well-established corporation in the field of computer networks, is currently helping Kenyan Internet Service Providers (ISPs) band together to establish and share Internet Exchange Points. The aim is to stop the current expensive practice where e-mail and web page requests among local ISP users in Kenya have to be done via Europe. Cisco hopes that its investment will reduce the cost of the Internet for African

users, make Internet accessibility faster and allow the creation of Internet information in African languages. In the case of South Africa, Cisco donated subsidised equipment and expertise.

In many African cities and major towns, there has been a rapid expansion of private institutions, that is, academies, colleges and institutes that offer courses in computing. Some of the institutions are franchised and offer Microsoft certificates. This is one of the fastest growing areas of adult learning in Africa today. The other practical example of Internet usage in the field of adult education in Africa is the Africa Virtual University discussed in the case study below.

## A case study of ICT usage for distance learning

In this section a practical example is provided of how adult education learners in Africa are already benefiting from the advancements in information technology. The African Virtual University (AVU) is a technology-based distance education network of universities in Africa, Europe and the United States of America. It was established by the World Bank in 1997. Its original objective was to provide an international virtual university expanding access to and improving the quality of tertiary education in Africa, especially in the fields of science, engineering and business (AVU, 1997). Light (1999:1) observes that the AVU was a timely project for Africa. The demand for quality education at tertiary level on the continent is high (AVU, 2003; Okech and Amutabi, 2002). The AVU project was built by using Information and Communication Technology (ICT), initially enabling students in six African countries to take courses and seminars taught by professors from universities around the world (AVU, 1997; Light, 1999). The professors deliver their lectures in front of television cameras in their own classrooms while the video is routed via fibre optics, ISDN lines or satellite to an uplink in Washington, DC, which then beams it via satellite to points in Africa (Okech and Amutabi, 2003; AVU, 1997). Students are able to talk with instructors in real time using standard phone lines. A student in one country with an AVU point, such as Kenya, Uganda or Zimbabwe, is able to ask a question to an instructor in the United States at leading universities such as Stanford or Harvard, while students listen at other AVU points in other countries such as Ghana, Tanzania or Uganda (AVU, 1997, 2003; Light, 1999). In its initial phase, which ended in 1999, the European and American faculty taught the lessons. The lessons were beamed to twenty-two universities in Africa (AVU, 2003). This was expected to expand in subsequent years as AVU moved into its second and third phases, beginning in mid-1999 and the start of 2002, respectively. Currently, the AVU project has expanded and is now offered in 31 learning centres in seventeen African countries. While the project may have logistical problems, its operation is a clear indication that information technology can be harnessed to promote learning in Africa, especially among working adults.

- See comments regarding AVUs in Chapter 9, under 'Economic restructuring', for a different viewpoint.

## A case study of ICT usage for community-based adult learning

The use of ICT in Africa has also led to the establishment of community telecentres. These are centres that provide access to the public for communication and information services using a variety of technologies including library services, phone, faxes and computers, as well as the Internet and e-mail (Whyte, 1999). They are located in

rural areas. Mayanja (1999) discusses the Nakaseke Community Telecentre in Uganda and shows how it has helped in providing ICT to the rural people. Another successful example of a community telecentre is the Mamelodi Telecentre in South Africa. The Mamelodi Telecentre benefited from strong community participation, as in the case of Nakaseke Telecentre (Mayanja, 1999). The Mamelodi Telecentre was spearheaded by the Council for Scientific and Industrial Research (CSIR) of South Africa, while Nakaseke was backed by a strong management team led by the Uganda National Commission for UNESCO. The management structure of Nakaseke Telecentre is composed of a local steering committee, a local core user group and a management committee at the national level (Mayanja, 1999). The common feature of the two community telecentres is that they are both integrated into the community and have developed a local capacity to appreciate and manage the telecentre. Mayanja observes that telecentres situated in remote areas of Africa have enabled people in these communities to leapfrog from traditional to modern information and communication technologies and an appreciation of the 'knowledge society'. He compares the impact of ICT in Africa to the industrial revolution that preoccupied Europe during the nineteenth century. For more information on telecentres please visit http://www.development.org/ict/telecentres.

## Key terms

**E-learning**   Learning that utilises ICT as the main medium of instruction. Examples may include on-line instruction or an adult learner browsing the Internet for educational purposes.

**Internet**   A network of computer networks.

**network**   Two or more computers that are connected to enable users to share data and resources such as printers.

**network or multi-user computer**   A computer system that has one processor where shared information is stored.

**network server**   A computer with special software and large file storage capabilities.

**web browser**   A program used to find and retrieve information on the Internet.

**World Wide Web (www)**   A hyper-media information system that provides easy access to a large number of documents.

## ⊞ ACTIVITY

**Using the Internet, list the countries and universities in Africa that are participating in the AVU project. Identify and discuss some of the advantages and limitations of the AVU project.**

## SUMMARY

In this chapter we have looked at the status of computer usage in Africa, including the constraints and possibilities. We also endeavoured to explain what a computer is, how it works and what the Internet is, how it was created and its main functions and advantages, especially in the field of education. We have also shown the value of ICT and E-learning to the field of adult education in Africa. A case study of how technology is being used to promote distance learning in Africa under the Africa Virtual University (AVU) project was presented. Also presented was a case study of how ICT is being used for adult learning at the community level.

## KEY POINTS

- A computer is a tool that can be used to process information faster, more efficiently and accurately.
- Computers are working tools and cannot replace teachers in the field of education and in society in general.
- A computer has four main parts, namely, an input device, a processing unit, a storage device and an output device.
- The Internet was created in the 1960s by the US Department of Defence.
- Developments in information and communication technology and in communication have led to a paradigm shift in the teaching and learning process where the teacher is a facilitator of learning and the student takes an active role in the learning process.
- Digital libraries enable learners to obtain materials on-line using the Internet. This can promote learning and improve the quality of research work.

## ⊞ ACTIVITY

**Suppose you were the Minister for Education, Science and Technology in your country. Outline the steps that you would take to increase the use of computers and the Internet by adult learners in the community and in the workplace.**

## FURTHER QUESTIONS

1 What are the main parts of a computer and how does the computer work?
2 Describe how the Internet works and, using relevant examples, discuss the importance of the Internet to the field of adult education in Africa.
3 Discuss how adult educators can benefit from the advancements in ICT and show how ICT can be used to improve teaching and learning in adult education programmes.
4 Explain how the link between ICT and adult education could be harnessed to bridge the digital divide between Africa and the rest of the world.

## SUGGESTED READINGS

Laudon, C. K., Traver, G. C. and Laudon, P. J. 1996. *Information technology and society*. New York: Course Technology Inc.

Knowles, M. 1984. *The adult learner: A neglected species*, (3rd edn.). Houston: Gulf Publishing.

# Chapter 9

# Globalisation and adult education in Africa

## OVERVIEW

This chapter attempts to define *globalisation* as a concept and phenomenon and discusses its impact on adult education in Africa. The chapter examines the influence of externally generated neo-liberal policies on adult education curricula, instruction, methods and programmes in Africa. It looks at the effects of global economic restructuring, such as the World Bank's Structural Adjustment Programmes (SAPs) on adult education. It explains how rapid technological and media changes have affected adult education in learning institutions and at the workplace, and shifted the dynamics of human resource development in African countries to global dictates of marketism (liberalisation and privatisation). This chapter shows how globalisation has created new roles and spaces for civil society in Africa, thereby affecting national politics, social interactions, cultural patterns and adult education. It explores some of the problems that African countries have encountered in dealing with globalisation in the realm of adult education.

## LEARNING OBJECTIVES

By the end of this chapter, you should be able to:

1  Define globalisation and explain how it has impacted on adult education in Africa.
2  Analyse the role of civil society in the development of adult education in Africa.
3  Discuss the role of adult education in the global exchanges between Africa and the rest of the world.
4  Explain the necessity of lifelong learning in a changing world.

## KEY TERMS

**globalisation**   The intensification and transformation of relations between nations and the emergence of strong global actors such as supra-national organisations. It refers to the fast sharing of benefits and problems on a massive scale never seen before through improved technology and the movement of ideas, ideologies and culture across the world.

**marketism**   The total embracing of market forces for determining supply and demand. It is the implementation of free market principles, trade liberalisation and privatisation, as advocated by organisations such as the International Monetary Fund and the World Bank.

**non-governmental organisations (NGOs)**   Non-profit-making or voluntary organisations established outside governmental control by private citizens involved in advocacy and philanthropic work and activities.

**community-based organisations (CBOs)**   Small, village-level associations established for meeting certain local objectives such as the provision of water, construction of roads, cattle-dips, sanitation facilities or income-generation.

**virtual learning**   Learning that takes place when a teacher and learner are separated by distance but are connected through information and communication technology for the facilitation of the learning process.

**civil society**   Voluntary associations of people, usually those at grassroots levels, which often undertake advocacy and lobbying, and express interest in the advancement of common concerns.

## ✴ BEFORE YOU START

1   **List five major economic activities in your country. Out of these activities, identify those that are connected to the global market.**
2   **List five ideologies present in your country, e.g. capitalism. Which ones are found only in your country and which ones originate from outside of your country?**

# THE IMPACT OF GLOBALISATION

*Globalisation* as a concept and phenomenon has quickly become the defining feature of societal dynamics in the world today. It has come to define activities in many realms of life, that is, in private and public spheres and in education. Much of the initial analysis of globalisation has focused on defining and explaining its causes, mechanisms, strategies, key actors and institutions involved, and the economic, political and environmental consequences. During the second half of the 1980s, globalisation as a subject attracted considerable debate from economists, educators, historians, political scientists, and other social scientists. Recently, scholars from all disciplines have examined globalisation more intensely. Globalisation relates to multiple levels of analysis, that is, economic, historical, social, cultural, educational, political, anthropological, environmental and technological, among others. As a concept, globalisation refers both to the compression of the time and space aspects of sociocultural, economic and political relations, as well as to an intensification of the awareness that the world is becoming smaller. Supra-national organisations exert a powerful influence, international law is more cogent and nation-states are increasingly weakened. Through globalisation, there are increased relations between citizens, ideas spread faster and technology, especially the media, is at the centre of interstate and individual relations. It has led to the increased spread of cultures, especially the dominant ones.

At its most basic level, globalisation is about the structural and institutional transformations that are occurring in the social, cultural, political and economic organisation of the world, that is in production and distribution and in decision-making in the global arena. It is a multidimen-sional process through which the world is increasingly tied together by networks of interdependence at regional, sub-regional and national levels. In many analyses, it is the economic and technological dimensions of globalisation that feature more prominently than the political, social and cultural dimensions. Although globalisation has many levels, its main manifestation includes the spatial reorganisation of economic production systems and the spread and dominance of the free-market concept. This means entrenchment of capitalist, neo-liberal ideology and the interpenetration of industries across borders, simultaneous technological revolutions in computers, telecommunications, transportation, international labour markets, massive transfers of populations and the emerging hegemony of Western culture.

Through the analysis of definitions, one can discern that there has emerged a clear distinction between pro-globalisation and anti-globalisation scholarship in the past ten years. It was Malcolm Waters who first clearly defined globalisation and invited global debate on this concept in academic circles in his book *Globalization* in 1990. He defined globalisation as a perpetration of Western dominant ideologies such as democracy and capitalism across the world. Some scholars (such as Guehenno, 1995; Frank, 2002; Ohmae, 1995; Wriston, 1992) see globalisation as defining a new epoch in human history in which 'traditional nation-states have become unnatural, even impossible business units in a global economy' (Ohmae, 1995: 5). Such views of globalisation generally privilege an economic logic and celebrate the emergence of a single global market.

Malawi-born Paul Tiyambe Zelza, South African scholar Shirley Walters, and Giddens and Rosenau are more sympathetic to the South. To them, contemporary patterns of globalisation have been historically unprecedented in that states and societies across the globe are experiencing profound change as they try to adapt to a more interconnected but highly uncertain world (Giddens, 1990, 1995 and Rosenau, 1997; Walters, 1997: 5; Zelza, 2003: 49). To Walters, it is the epitome of 'think global, act local' under new circumstances. Zelza sees globalisation as representing ensnaring and coercive structures represented by Western hegemony. Held and associates see globalisation as the 'widening, deepening and speeding up of worldwide interconnectedness in all aspects of contemporary social life, from the cultural to the criminal, the financial to the spiritual' (Held, McGrew, Goldblatt and Perraton, 1999: 2). Some scholars think that globalisation favours the North, arguing that the industrialised countries of the world have adapted to this techno-economic paradigm shift through various strategies and high levels of public and private sector cooperation. On the other hand, countries in the South, including African countries, are facing a tidal wave of changes and challenges in this new era of globalisation and economic, political, social and cultural restructuring which in many cases is overwhelming their capacity to cope.

Progressive, radical and neo-Marxist scholars view globalisation as a negative force that weakens authentic cultures, erodes the power of national governments and subordinates social and environmental goals to the economic imperatives of capitalism. For those who accept this stark portrait, there are few if any benefits to be gained from the closer economic integration of the world (Gray, 1999; Were and Amutabi, 2000; Zelza, 2003). It is, therefore, not surprising that the anti-globalisation movement has stirred strong emotions in Africa. Obviously globalisation does not have the same meaning among all scholars. While the term has become quite

widespread, there are confused and often conflicting definitions, usage and conceptions of the phenomenon, perhaps due to its multi-centred, multi-layered meanings, and historical roots and implications for the North and South, respectively.

For Africa, as Shirley Walters and associates and Paul Tiyambe Zelza have demonstrated, globalisation represents the dominant strands of the hegemonic paradigms of the North, such as the neo-liberal economic and political ideologies that have been imposed on Africa. Its main anchors are international, financial and corporate institutions and private Northern multinational corporations that are the most dominant players at the global level. In the present volume, globalisation represents the encapsulating patterns of the industrialised nations of Western Europe and North America for control of the world and the imposition of Western ideologies, dogmas, models and paradigms over the exploited, poverty-stricken states of the South. This reflects the fact that globalisation appears to be organised in institutions and structures of control that have continued to influence African governments and peoples. To this extent the debate on globalisation in Africa has focused on social, cultural, political and economic circles, where its effects have been most intense. Therefore, globalisation is seen to be spreading Northern hegemony and ideas to the South, in effect, a recolonisation of sorts and the creation of new spheres of influence in social, political and economic realms (Amutabi, 1997; Zelza, 2003).

In *Re-Thinking Africa's Globalization*, Zelza attacks the North for the exploitative nature of globalisation, which he perceives as negative in its entirety and from which Africa has nothing to gain. He argues that the structures of globalisation have been based in Africa for many centuries. He says that these became manifest more visibly during the transatlantic slave trade when Africans were forcefully shipped into the new world to participate in the development of capitalism. He argues that Africa has not negotiated itself into globalisation but has been coerced into it (Zelza, 2003: 43). Whereas neo-liberal ideologies such as democratisation have an increasing appeal for many countries in Africa, these ideologies come with a hidden agenda, such as free-market principles, trade liberalisation and privatisation, which are harming African countries while benefiting the North. Even where countries are not willing to democratise or liberalise or privatise, they are coerced into it. The role that the World Trade Organization (WTO) has started to play in world affairs, besides the International Monetary Fund (IMF) and the World Bank, is indicative of the coercive strand of globalisation. It should be noted, however, that while the term globalisation has become quite widespread, even in the popular media there are confused and often conflicting definitions and conceptions of the phenomenon. In order for this concept to maintain any analytical usefulness it must be unpacked, carefully defined and examined with regard to its impact on society, the economy and the world system.

Globalisation, for Africa at least, is forceful. It is apparent that African nations have no choice when the forces of globalisation arrive. That globalisation is moving hand in hand with the decline of the nation-state is becoming increasingly clear through the democratisation project in Africa and the way capitalist structures and institutions are following up quickly and becoming entrenched. In Africa democracy and capitalism are the moving spirits behind the globalisation phenomenon, which is rather paradoxical to the adult education movement. It is paradoxical because through democracy adult education has been re-

energised and found a new lease on life through civic education campaigns and outreach programmes in African countries. However, the new economic policies of liberation and free-market enterprise have reduced public spending on education. This is where adult education has been the most adversely affected. Civil society organisations, known as community-based groups (CBOs) and NGOs in Africa are the vehicles of democratic articulation and dissemination through adult education. Capitalism is withdrawing the development initiative from the state by reducing spending on social welfare, but instead privileging multinational organisations and NGOs.

These are challenges that are relevant to adult education, which calls for the rethinking of the asymmetrical relationship that has developed between technology, society and African economies through exposure to the transforming processes of globalisation. Economic modernisation and globalisation have led to important developments that the adult education sector must confront. Korsgaard has discussed the impact of globalisation on adult education, arguing that the level of competitiveness demanded by global dynamics will require skilled people, hence the need for adult education to meet these challenges. He says that 'adult education institutions have to play two roles: one to safeguard the cultural heritage and identity of their people, and the other to train the people to be able to compete in the global market' (Korsgaard, 1997: 16). Gouthro has pointed out that 'in this era of globalisation, adult educators are challenged to provide learners with the skills and knowledge they will need to function in a radically altered world' (Gouthro, 2000: 57). This is the imperative which adult education in Africa earnestly needs to confront.

## ACTIVITY

List the sectors of the economy which are the major foreign exchange earners for your country. What are the implications of these economic activities for adult education?

## ECONOMIC RESTRUCTURING

The effects of globalisation on adult education are most pronounced in the discourse surrounding the connections between adult education and the marketplace. Here, it is economic globalisation which has negatively affected African economies, especially from the 1990s, and this has in turn impacted on adult education in very profound ways. But to understand the full impact, a little background is necessary.

The postcolonial African economies experienced fairly respectable rates of growth for nearly a decade and then began to decline after the oil crisis of the mid-1970s. 'Between 1965 and 1974, the annual growth in the gross domestic product (GDP) per capita averaged 2.6%, from 1974 onwards it stagnated and by the end of the 1980s many African states had a lower GDP per capita than at independence, but still continued to grow' (Mkandawire and Soludo, 1999: 6). There were many problems related to the African economies. Firstly, there were trade-related factors (terms of trade and volatility of markets for African exports); secondly, there were climatic conditions (mainly drought); and thirdly, there was the prevalence of civil strife and wars on the continent.

Between 1961 and 1994, Africa was the only one of the major developing regions that suffered a decline in per capita levels of food production. Much of this decline was blamed on policies that favoured industry and urban development while penalising agriculture; land redistribution policies and inheritance laws that encouraged subdivision leading to smallholders; the peasantification of farmers; and unfavourable terms of trade and poor distribution networks in the countryside. Despite these, Africa made gains in development up to the late 1980s. It is the political and economic upheavals of the 1990s that have left their mark on the field of education, particularly adult education. A major source of change is the globalisation of the capitalist economy and its restructuring, which made extraordinary demands on education in general and adult education in particular.

The most obvious of these impacts were those necessitated by Structural Adjustment Programmes (SAPs) as promulgated by the World Bank and International Monetary Fund (IMF). SAPs led to the devaluation of currency and reduced government spending in social service ministries such as the education sector (Mkandawire and Soludo, 1990). African governments were forced to divest from education, and adult education was one of the casualties with regard to funding in many instances. SAPs led to the liberalisation and privatisation of government enterprises, including many educational activities. This led to the reduced role of the state in many sectors. It led to increased taxation and interest rates, the introduction of cost-sharing schemes, user fees, cost-recovery measures and wage restraints. All this affected adult education and training directly and indirectly.

Walters and Watters have made a persuasive argument for countries in Southern Africa with regard to the impact of SAPs. They have stated that SAPs have led to the orientation of education towards the needs of business, and stress the development of human resources necessary for economic growth. For adult education, the structural adjustment policies (SAPs) have ensured a cutback in services through 'a reduced role for the government, more emphasis on adult education for the development of the economy and encouraging the private sector to take a more important role in education provision' (Walters and Watters, 2000: 52). In some countries there have been staff retrenchments and cutbacks in funds available for on-the-job training, hence directly affecting adult education. Therefore, with SAPs, there appeared a new phase in education in Africa, that of commodification and a corporate mentality in education, which was seen purely in economic terms, and this has weakened the effectiveness of African governments in education (Nafukho, 1996). Coupled with privatisation, the burden of training workers in new technologies has shifted from workplace training and state initiatives to adult education courses paid for by the worker.

Structural Adjustment Programmes have impoverished people and made many in Africa destitute. The external debt burden for many African states has continued to rise. Many of these states have undergone many phases of currency devaluation in order to attract foreign investment. As a result, the power and investment of Western multinational corporations have increased. The multinational corporations of the North and the internationalisation of the market economy are exploiting the human and natural resources in Africa more than before. Structural adjustment has disrupted the social, economic and political fabric of African societies. SAPs have produced wide disparities and serious internal conflicts within families. Based on the rationing of family expenditure, many families place primary formal education first and adult education last. As a result, this has reduced the number of adult learners.

Due to SAPs, many learning institutions in Africa are under-resourced and lack basic communication facilities, especially in information and communication technology. The ratio of learners to computers, books, laboratory equipment and lecturers in African institutions is poor and therefore learning has been greatly impaired. Furthermore, the knowledge gap between Africa and the rest of the world is becoming wider. It is certain that the economic and social disparity between Africa and the rest of the world will widen at an even more rapid pace. African governments have failed to equip learning institutions so as to make them effective instruments of technological innovations, scientific and industrial research and development.

The African Virtual University (AVU) introduced by the World Bank has not solved problems of access and learning. The AVU has failed to bring high-quality education to a large number of students in Africa because modern information technology has not been utilised, thereby producing insufficient numbers of well-trained African scientists, technicians, engineers and business managers required for economic development. The high cost of fees and other demands on learners, and the AVU's location in exclusive campuses, has made these centres inaccessible to many students. The AVU learning package is comprised of live and pre-recorded lectures transmitted by satellite and viewed on TV screens, the on-line supply of handouts, the provision of textbooks, lecture guidelines, programme schedules on transmission and other materials that are transmitted electronically from outside Africa. This form of learning is very different to the way adult education has been organised in Africa. The cost of AVUs and Africa's increasing dependence on external resources and materials has limited the zeal for invention and innovation in Africa.

- See the reference to AVUs in Chapter 8 under 'A case study of ICT usage in Africa' for a different viewpoint.

The rise of market models in education has made education a luxury, a non-essential service. Retrenchments in the civil service and cost-sharing in the purchase of services has been the most pronounced of these impacts. For some families, cost sharing has meant that money that was allocated to finance adult education has gone into financing urgent needs, such as medicine. Faced with reduced financial allocations, most government ministries have removed the course training components from their programmes, impacting directly on adult education. As a result, government-owned adult education institutions have been forced to trim down their staff or close down altogether. In Kenya, some of these institutions, such as the Institute of Adult Education at Kikuyu near Nairobi, the Government Training Institute (GTI) at Maseno, and the Farmers Training Centre at Eldoret, have been converted into university campuses. With retrenchment and the removal of on-the-job training, many adult education programmes have suffered. This has reduced the pool of traditional learners but opened up opportunites for another realm of adult learning.

Reduction in the number of traditional adult education learners has taken place alongside the expansion of continuing education programmes in African countries, such as Uganda, Kenya, South Africa and Tanzania. This has occurred simultaneously with the restructuring of courses and programmes at universities so as to make them more marketable, thereby increasing privately sponsored students. This has included new courses such as MBAs (popular with multinational corporations), modularity (to achieve economies of scale) and the increased use of part-time and distance-learning programmes (to target those already in the workplace). The introduction of student loans and course fees has significantly raised the direct cost placed upon students and their parents, and has helped to change people's orientation towards the financing of education.

Despite the massive surge in enrolment in adult classes by privately sponsored students, there are dangers. Public universities in Uganda, Kenya, Zambia and Tanzania, for example, have to compete for students in order to sustain and extend their funding following reduced government allocations (Okech, 2000). Adult learning is used to place both individuals and countries in a more advantageous position so as to be able to compete for limited access to better employment opportunities. Whereas there is nothing wrong in marketing the strengths and particular qualities of these institutions, as Nafukho (2002) has argued, there is, however, a fundamental problem with the way such business models are being applied in these countries. The real danger is the widening gap between the rich and the poor, as only the rich make use of these 'second chance' opportunities. Gouthro has stated that 'education becomes a consumer good for the elite, a means for jockeying for higher status and privilege' (Gouthro, 2000: 59).

The other danger is that it is not the most qualified students who are entering these institutions of learning, but rather those who can afford to pay. The unthinking adoption of private sector models means less emphasis on community and equity, and more on individual advancement and the need to satisfy investors and influential consumers. Adult education has come to resemble a private, rather than public good. As might be expected, the marketisation and commodification of education may lead to compromised standards at African institutions of learning. Seeking to turn education into a commodity is simply an expression of neo-liberal economics and politics in Africa. Adult education that focuses on concerns outside of the marketplace is perceived as a luxury and is considered to be irrelevant in the competitive environment of globalised capitalism.

Widespread acceptance of the marketplace models can be seen in the way in which curricula are being formulated and shaped in African institutions of learning – many are becoming consumer-driven and client-responsive. Courses that are not popular on the market are being shelved; recruitment of staff at these departments is frozen in favour of the more 'popular' disciplines.

Distance education, especially 'e-learning', 'tele-learning', 'on-line-learning' and 'internet-learning' or 'virtual learning', is expanding in Africa's adult education arena, thanks to globalisation. These processes bring about independence of time, location and distance, and have immense benefits to the learner and instructor. Learning without being absent from the job is definitely an advantage. The fact that one can get lessons on videotapes, and receive and submit assignments on-line, assists with travel expenses. The fact that one can do assignments from any place and without being confined is also a new freedom that enables learners to be in charge of their learning 'in the classroom without walls'. But there are undoubtedly problems, as discussed in Chapter 8.

The first problem which bears repeating is one of access. According to many experts in distance education, access is usually the most important criterion for deciding on the appropriateness of a technology for distance learning. At present the telecommunication infrastructure in Africa is inadequate. National networks are limited in that they will inevitably preclude access for a large number of learners. AVU has the necessary equipment situated at its adult education centres in Africa, but the problem of access for the majority is still a problem it has to grapple with.

The second problem is related to the question of cost. The 'state-of-the-art-technologies' needed for on-line instruction, such as those with the AVU-type of connectivity which requires current and up-to-date computers and Internet servers, TVs, VCRs, and other sophisticated multimedia appliances, can be very expensive. They cost more money than many African struggling economies can buy and sustain, yet they are likely to benefit only a handful of students that can afford the cost.

## ⌗ ACTIVITY

**What is your favourite TV programme and how has it influenced you? What changes have occurred in your area that you would associate with the influence of television and the Internet? How are these affecting adult learning?**

## THE MEDIA AND CULTURAL GLOBALISATION

There has been a considerable amount of concern by governments in many African countries concerning the role of the Western media especially in terms of cultural and political influence. The South Commission has shown that through the media, the world is increasingly interconnected. Through this, the cultural influences coming from the North to the South are 'much stronger, more pervasive and in some respects pernicious' (South Commission, 1990: 6). Civil society has been a major beneficiary of the liberalisation of the media (Hall, 1996). The arrival of satellite television in Africa in the 1980s in people's homes meant that censorship, which was often employed by authoritarian regimes in Africa, would no longer be effective. Cable networks and international broadcast companies have become the major sources of information for many African people. The impact of the media on children and adults in Africa in the recent past has been significant. This has led to the rise of mass culture, a kind of pop culture that is promulgated by global media houses. Western soap operas are today dictating family tempo and romance in many African upper and middle class homes. Advertising has promoted mass consumption unprecedented in Africa's consumer history.

Today, television is increasingly playing a critical role in the life of the African people. In many middle class homes, the true tutor of children in urban areas in Africa today is not the schoolteacher or university professor but the television, which has spread into many homes, entertainment areas and social halls in urban centres. It would be inconceivable to claim middle class and 'advanced' status without claiming ownership of a television. Many products, ideas and lifestyles in Africa are consumed and disseminated through this medium. The other influences are film makers, advertising executives and pop culture purveyors. Video libraries and clubs are sprouting everywhere on the continent, full of pirated Hollywood movies. Thanks to television and films, American celebrities such as Arnold Schwarzeneggar, Chuck Norris, Michael Jackson and Michael Jordan, among others, are widely known in Africa, more so than some African presidents. The American CNN and British BBC are relied on and believed more than African networks. How do all these affect adult education? They affect adult education because learning equipment and technology in Africa is not updated and learners are unable to keep up with trends even if the educators are. Many African learners lack confidence in their own methods and learning aids.

Whereas the media, especially the Western media, has been on the forefront of the democratisation process in Africa and has been useful for learning, especially in adult education, reservations remain. There is concern that the media is estranged from the values of the African people and that it offers nothing but entertainment and distraction from reality, promoting utopianism. The radio, the television and the newspapers were for a long time used for propaganda purposes by many regimes in Africa. The liberalisation of the airwaves, the emergence of independent local networks and newspapers and the role of the movie industry have, however, countered this. Adult education has been very instrumental in all this, especially through the promotion of literacy skills and civil society mobilisation and campaigns, especially voter education. However, African values are disappearing under these internationalised cultural movements. African politicians have been isolated from their people as NGOs increasingly take up their places among grassroots people. New forms of cultural imperialism are appearing on the scene. Vernaculars and other local languages are disappearing and being replaced by foreign *lingua franca* such as English. What worries African cultural nationalists is the fact that everything today is market-driven without regard for African values and national interests (Habasonda, 2002).

## ✦ ACTIVITY

**List examples of cultural changes that you have observed that can be related to the impact of the international media.**

# THE ROLE OF CIVIL SOCIETY

In Chapter 4, it was stated that there are two major social actors in adult education in Africa – the state and civil society. Through globalisation, a struggle has emerged in Africa between the state and civil society in Africa over the control of citizens. The triumph of civil society has led to more democratisation and free space in many countries, although this has not been easy. To civil society in Africa, therefore, globalisation has been characterised by a unique paradox. On the one hand, it benefited from democratisation in Africa, on the other hand, marketism (which includes economic liberalisation and privatisation) and its attendant effects have negatively affected civil society.

However, it is the spread of democratic ideals by civil society that will be focused on here. It has challenged the dominant notion of the African state as omnipotent. In 1997, Stevenson stated that a transnational civil society of the globe's citizens was gradually emerging (Stevenson, 1997). Within this context, as Budd Hall has observed, there is a sense of duty and responsibility to others that is evident in globalised movements to assist others. He conceives of global civil society as a 'political space which has grown in response to and in resistance to the globalising forces of the day. It is of course the conceptual cousin of "civil society" [which is] the autonomous space for citizen action, organisation or theorisation' (Hall, 2000: 11).

How has civil society through adult education affected the democratic practice and process in Africa? The civil society movement stresses cooperation over competition, equity over personal gain, and is therefore a counter to marketism and its oppressive tendencies. Global civil society activists advocate for the peaceful spread of democratic ideals across the world and equality between races and genders (Youngman, 2000). They recognise within the context of the values of diversity, tolerance and pluralism the need for universal peace and justice, and of solidarity and responsibility by nations. Adult education is the engine of these expectations, because civil society is increasingly being perceived as an alternative focus by which educators and citizens can reassert democratic principles for justice and equity.

To be sure, adult educators have linked adult education to the development of democratic ideals in many societies where it has been successfully used. Beder says 'that a major purpose of adult education is to promote that democratic order is an idea with strong roots in the early adult education movement. The logic was as simple as it is powerful: Democracy can work only if the citizenry exercises rational, informed choice, for in the absence of informed, rational choice, propaganda prevails, and democracy lapses into totalitarianism' (Beder, 1989: 40). This is what has happened in Africa since the early 1990s. Indeed, true democracy requires active participation on the part of the citizenry. Since the electorate is adult, it is the purpose of adult education to assist in informing and developing critical skills. Skills are not sufficient without participation. This explains why civil society and adult education have been at the forefront of the democratic movement in Africa.

Civil society in Africa is composed of social and popular movements, popular organisations, non-governmental organisations (NGOs) and community-based organisations (CBOs). In many African countries, adult education has been the preferred mode of dissemination by civil society in defining and constructing alternatives for participation in decision-making processes and in local development. While civil society has sometimes stood in opposition to unjust government and economic policies, it is not intended to completely replace either of these two spheres. Rather, it is intended to bring about a power balance, to develop a new partnership and constructive engagement among three key actors – the government, the private sector (the corporate or business world) and the citizen. In Africa, this new dynamism has involved the development of grassroots movements within the community which are active in developmental issues and that lead to a sense of active citizenship. There has been a revival and re-emergence of citizen responsibility and sovereignty, whereby people are now engaged in determining the direction of change in their various countries. Past election results have shown increased voter turnout and more participation in electioneering compared to previous years. Civil society campaigns through adult education obviously share the credit.

## ✦ ACTIVITY

How has adult education through the influence of civil society assisted in disseminating democracy in Africa?

## SUMMARY

This chapter has explored the ongoing process of globalisation, including its alternative and contending perspectives. It has also commented on the various ways globalisation has impacted on adult education. This chapter has also shown that adult education has played a very significant role in recent democratisation activities in Africa, particularly through civil society organisations. It has also demonstrated that distance-learning and lifelong learning are becoming widespread in Africa due to demands generated by globalisation, especially marketism. It has also shown that

Africa's adult education programmes need to catch up technologically with the rest of the world if they are to realistically meet the demands placed on them by globalisation.

## KEY POINTS

- Globalisation has led to the increased spread of cultures, especially the dominant ones. Because there are increased relations between citizens, ideas spread faster and technology, especially the media, is at the centre of interstate and individual relations.
- In Africa, democracy and capitalism are the moving forces behind globalisation, and this has impacted on adult education both positively and negatively.
- Attempts to restructure the economy through the implementation of Structural Adjustment Programmes promulgated by the World Bank and the International Monetary Fund have negatively affected African economies and in turn adult education as well.
- In order to accommodate globalisation, adult education in Africa has shifted its emphasis from serving the community to viewing adult education as a means to satisfy investors and influential consumers. Marketism has therefore led to compromised standards at African institutions of learning.
- Distance-learning and the notion of 'classrooms without walls' are a positive effect of globalisation. This is because the dissemination of technological innovations, such as e-learning, tele-learning, on-line learning and internet-learning has brought about independence of time, location and distance to the student. However, there are also negative aspects to this development.
- The triumph of civil society through the influence of globalisation has led

to further democratisation in many countries. Through the medium of adult education, civil society has positively contributed to the improvement of citizens' freedom of determination and decision-making in their various countries.

## ▦ ACTIVITY

Discuss why you think there are many differences in the definition of globalisation.

## FURTHER QUESTIONS

1  What role has civil society played in adult education in Africa?
2  Explain why lifelong learning is becoming popular under globalisation in Africa.

## SUGGESTED READING

Burbules, N. C. and Torres, C. A. 2000. *Globalization and education: Critical perspectives*. London: Routledge.
Walters, S. ed. 1997. *Globalization, adult education and training: Impacts and issues*. London: Zed Books.

# Chapter 10

# Lifelong learning

## OVERVIEW

While adult education and its meaning have been well explained in the introductory chapters of this book, lifelong learning has been mentioned only in passing, albeit repeatedly. This was done deliberately since the concept of *lifelong learning* is considered very important and hence deserves special discussion. In this final chapter of the book, a strong case will be made for lifelong learning in Africa and the need for learning societies. The future of adult education in Africa lies in the promotion of lifelong learning. This chapter provides definitions of 'lifelong learning' and a 'learning society' from several scholars. In African contexts, what is lifelong learning? Is lifelong learning a new concept in Africa or has it existed since time immemorial? What legislation and policies should be addressed to promote lifelong learning in Africa? What innovative funding strategies should be implemented to develop and sustain lifelong learning programmes in Africa? While effort is made in this chapter to provide answers to these pertinent questions, the authors would like to engage the reader in providing some of the answers to these questions. It would be a mistake on the part of the authors to try and provide all the answers to the questions raised in this chapter. Issues pertaining to lifelong learning are ever-evolving and may not be completely addressed at any one time. This book concludes by actively engaging the reader in the concept of lifelong learning and learning societies.

## LEARNING OBJECTIVES

By the end of this chapter, you should be able to:

1 Discuss the place of lifelong learning in contemporary African societies.
2 Explain the meaning of lifelong learning and a learning society.
3 Describe lifelong learning activities initiated by governments in other parts of the world.
4 Explain policies related to lifelong learning.
5 Identify sources of funding for lifelong learning programmes in Africa.

*sesa woruban*

## KEY TERMS

**knowledge society**  A society in which people's lives are controlled by information and communication technologies, and in which decisions are made based on the information generated.

**lifelong learning**  Learning that takes place throughout the life-span, from the cradle to the grave.

**learning society**  A society in which all members participate in education and training throughout their life.

## ⌗ BEFORE YOU START

Think of sayings and proverbs in your community that reflect lifelong learning. Write down these sayings in your mother tongue and translate them into English and share them with other members of your class.

## ORIGIN OF LIFELONG LEARNING

The concept of lifelong learning is grounded in the four pillars of education expounded by Delors (1998): learning to know; learning to do; learning to live together; and learning to be. Lifelong learning refers to holistic learning for life and work. The concept of lifelong learning is as old as Africa itself. It goes back to the origin of human life on the continent of Africa. As shown in Chapter 2, African traditions encouraged continued learning. Children learnt from adults how to live and function in society and likewise adults learnt from children and fellow adults. Learning was an important part of life in Africa long before the arrival of the missionaries and colonialists. Youngman (2001: 7) has stated that 'it is evident that the practice of people learning throughout their lives was characteristic of pre-colonial African societies'. Omolewa (1981) in his study of Nigerian society concluded that the traditional Nigerian society made ample provision for facilitating adult development and provided a variety of informal and non-formal adult learning situations within a lifelong learning context. In Chapter 1, it was shown how people in Africa continuously learn, whether in non-formal or informal environments. Youngman (2001) further observed that the elders in African societies, especially grandparents, parents, uncles and aunts played a major role in passing on to younger adults and children essential knowledge, skills and values. Shiundu and Omulando (1992) noted that lifelong learning in traditional African societies was accomplished through peer alliances, as well as through interaction with older people deeply familiar with the various aspects of community laws, values and mores. Chapter 3 discussed the issue of African philosophy and wisdom and how it was passed on to others during marriage,

initiation, harvesting, planting, hunting and burial ceremonies. Therefore, like many other societies in the world, traditional African societies valued and promoted lifelong learning from one generation to the other.

While not all the learning that took place in traditional African societies may be relevant in contemporary societies, there is an urgent need to create a learning society in Africa in which lifelong learning is promoted for both investment and consumption motives (Nafukho, 1999). An investment motive of learning involves learning that equips learners with key competencies required at the workplace. The consumption motive, on the other hand, refers to learning for its own sake or learning for personal development. There is evidence to show that African societies were learning societies even before the introduction of Western types of education. Youngman (2000: 7) has stated that

> *In fact, it can be argued that pre-colonial African societies represent a particular form of the* learning society *and that it was the colonial intrusion which disrupted this pattern through separating education from daily activities and locating it in the Western institution of the school.*

From the above statement, we would like to point out that some aspects of traditional African culture should be incorporated in the current concept of lifelong learning. For instance, in several African societies, morality was a treasured topic that was taught by adults to the youth as they matured into adulthood. We feel that the traditional approach of teaching issues pertaining to morality in society could be used for teaching people in Africa, for example, with regard to issues pertaining to HIV/AIDS.

While the notion of lifelong learning has existed for centuries, its contemporary form and its adoption in various education policies all over the world can be traced to the 1960s. The landmark document in terms of articulation and promotion of the concept of lifelong learning was the report of the International Commission on the Development of Education, published in 1972 under the title *Learning to Be*. To emphasise the importance of lifelong learning to the entire world, Faure (1972: 183) stated that 'we propose lifelong education as the master concept for educational policies in the years to come for both developed and developing countries'. While lifelong learning was identified as being important for contemporary society, the concept remained marginal in practical terms despite the efforts of some scholars and international organisations such as UNESCO.

Mok and Chan (2002: 3) highlighted the fact that in the 1970s and 1980s 'intergovernmental organisations such as UNESCO played a very significant role in forming policy on lifelong learning'. Alanen (1981) and Mok and Chan (2002) reported that during the same time, there was lively debate on the views of UNESCO, the Organization for Economic Cooperation (OECD) and the European Community which focused on lifelong education, recurrent education and continuing education as being important aspects of educational systems. This debate extended to the 1990s. In the 1990s, the concept of lifelong learning gained renewed recognition in a number of Western and Asian countries. This renewed prominence of the concept has been attributed to 'changes in the nature of work and global competition; rapid technological development; demographic shifts; the increase in human knowledge and expanded social demand; cultural and lifestyle changes; and political concerns of opportunity and social inclu-

sion' (Youngman, 2001: 1). The G-7 *Charter on Lifelong Learning* entitled 'Basic Principles' states that 'meeting our societal and economic goals will require a renewed commitment to investment in lifelong learning' (US Government, 1999: 1).

UNESCO has played a central role in influencing policy towards lifelong learning. In November 1994 UNESCO held its First Global Conference on Lifelong Learning in Rome, Italy. Federico Mayor, then director-general of UNESCO, advocated the idea of lifelong learning. In Europe, the European Union chose the theme of lifelong learning for the year 1996. Referring to the importance of lifelong learning in the twenty-first century Mok and Chan (2002: 4) affirm that

*A dominant theme in current education policy, especially in Europe and North America has been the creation of access to lifelong learning through the educational system; while international organisations (IGOs), trans-national corporations (TNCs) and non-governmental organisations (NGOs) have been pushing lifelong learning to the educational agendas of national governments.*

In the case of Africa, Youngman (2001) has observed an international trend of increased policy emphasis on lifelong learning. For example, in 1996 the Africa Regional Consultation for UNESCO's Fifth International Conference on Adult Education (CONFINTEA V) produced the *Dakar Declaration on Adult Education and Lifelong Learning*. In this important declaration, the demand for lifelong learning was reported as being on the increase in Africa. In addition, lifelong learning was considered as being a fundamental right and a prerequisite for individual development and social change. In 1998, the Seventh Conference of Ministers of Education of African Member States had as its theme *Lifelong Education in Africa – Prospects for the Twenty First Century*. While policy rhetoric supports the need for lifelong learning in Africa, in practice, African leaders and scholars face a major challenge in transforming this policy into practice. For instance, Youngman (2001) discusses the important question of providing lifelong learning for all in Africa. How can this important concept be integrated and provided through formal education, informal education, non-formal education and through transition from school to work? There is an important need to recognise that education does not end with formal schooling and that, instead, it is a lifelong process. Adult and continuing education is therefore in support of lifelong learning. Africa's growth and survival in the global economy will be shaped by lifelong learning policies implemented by African governments. While the lifelong learning models, policies and approaches that are currently being implemented in the West should not be copied wholesale, scholars in Africa have a major challenge in shaping the direction of lifelong learning based on the current needs of African societies.

## ✳ ACTIVITY

**List the various activities that educational institutions, training centers, churches, civic education groups, human rights groups, employers, employees and trade unions can engage in to promote lifelong learning in the community where you live.**

## MEANING OF LIFELONG LEARNING

'The emphasis on lifelong learning is well placed given the rapidly changing pace of technological, social, economic and political realities of the modern world' (Avoseh,

2001: 479). Lifelong learning is now accepted universally as an important concept for every human being and it therefore needs to be defined. It is a truism that human beings learn throughout their life, that is, from the cradle to the grave (Gustavsson, 1997). We develop our abilities and adapt to the environment into which we are born and raised. Most of what human beings learn occurs in their everyday life. This may be at home, in the street, in the church, on the farm or in the workplace. Gustavsson (1997: 239) argues that 'the notion of *lifelong learning* implies a broad approach to knowledge and has a holistic view of education in which formal and informal types of learning can be integrated with one another and considered in one context'. Thus, the concept of lifelong learning needs to be examined in two dimensions, namely, horizontally, between the home, the local community, the economic environment and the mass media; and vertically, between different levels of learning such as elementary, secondary and college education.

Larsson (1997: 251), in an attempt to explain the meaning of *lifelong learning*, notes that the question of everyday learning is not a new one. It is a concept with many meanings used by a variety of actors. He argues that lifelong learning is a 'concept that links the most fundamental aspects of learning to specific life contexts'. Dave (1972) noted that lifelong learning needs to be conceptualised as integrative. This view claims that people learn no matter where and when, although in different ways. Gustavsson and Osman (1997) pointed out the fact that the expression 'everyday life' means everything around us that seems familiar, close and perceived as self-evident and unquestionable. In other words, it refers to the immediate interpretations made about the world around us. Such interpretations are based on our knowledge, but what is knowledge? Rousseau cited in Gustavsson and Osman (1997: 281) states that '… knowledge begins with the senses and self-made experiences. Knowledge is viewed as a product of a person's self-activity and creative power rather than a passive reflection of the outer world through sensory perceptions'. Lifelong learning therefore can be looked at as that 'form of learning that occurs throughout life and that is crucially important for enriching personal lives, fostering economic growth and maintaining social cohesion. The aim of this kind of learning is to equip the individual with the necessary foundations and to improve the motivation for continued learning' (Paye, 1996: 1).

## ✳ ACTIVITY

Write a definition of lifelong learning in your own words.

## A LEARNING SOCIETY

In order for lifelong learning to become a reality in society, there is a need to create a learning society. African governments should use lifelong learning as a conceptual framework for conceiving, planning, designing, coordinating and implementing activities aimed at promoting learning for all people in society. Mok and Chan (2002: 4) have observed that 'different scholars may have diversified interpretations of a learning society, some of them stress the economic functions of a learning society, while others attach significant weight to social and political dimensions'.

One of the first scholars to develop the idea of a learning society was Hutchins. In his book *The Learning Society*, Hutchins defines a learning society as 'a society in which everybody has begun a liberal education in educational institutions and is

continuing liberal educational learning either in such institutions or outside them, for a society in which there are true universities, centres of independent thought and criticism, is one in which values may be transformed' (Hutchins, 1968: 134). A learning society has also been defined as 'one in which everyone participates in education and training throughout their life' (Ball, 1991: 6). This definition focuses on access or providing lifelong education for all, an issue that Youngman (2001) questions. Is it realistic to provide lifelong education for all especially in African countries with limited financial resources? Edwards (1995: 187) has observed that a learning society is one that has the following key characteristics:

- an educated society committed to active citizenship, liberal democracy and equal opportunities;
- a market in which educational institutions provide educational services to individuals enabling them to compete in the economy; and
- networks which enable learners to develop their interests and identities by drawing on a wide range of resources.

These characteristics address issues such as why a learning society is an ideal in the first place. The United Kingdom's Economic and Social Research Council (ESRC) defines a learning society as a society 'in which all citizens acquire a high-quality general education, appropriate vocational training and a job (or series of jobs) worthy of a human being, while continuing to participate in education and training throughout their lives' (cited in Tight 1996: 46). On the importance of a learning society, Apps (1988: 19) notes that a learning society is:

- a practical idea for human beings living in a rapidly changing world where a lifetime of learning is a requirement for survival;

- an attitude that learning need not only occur for practical reasons but can happen for its own sake;
- a unifying attitude, and an approach for bringing together an ever more diverse society; and
- a metaphor for a new age with regard to defining the relation of education to learning, and the recognition that educational opportunities, and therefore learning potential, go well beyond what is provided by those institutions that are ordinarily associated with education.

Stein and Imel (2002) maintain that learning societies have four common themes, namely, the place where learning takes place; the content learned; the production of knowledge; and the structure of learning societies. Space, which relates to the time and place in which problems are situated, is important. Content relates to the community's daily life and allows learners to express personal concerns. Knowledge learnt should be locally produced and all learners in a society should be encouraged to produce useful knowledge. Learning communities, if well supported, should positively influence decision-making processes in society. This means that the structure of lifelong learning should have informal, non-formal and formal orientations.

On the importance of a learning society, Ranson (1994: ix) has stated that 'in the periods of social transition, education becomes central to our future well-being. Only if learning is placed at the centre of our experience can individuals continue to develop their capacities, institutions are enabled to respond openly and imaginatively to periods of change, and the difference between communities become a source of reflective understanding'. This statement sounds like the best prescription for African countries faced with social, political and economic changes. It can

be persuasively argued that encouraging and supporting learning societies which combine traditional African cultures with Western type education could resolve many conflicts facing Africa. For example, in the year 2002, Kenya surprised the world by holding one of the most democratic, peaceful and transparent elections in Africa. While the Kenyan people were praised for this great achievement, no one has explained one of the main reasons for this remarkable achievement. It is the heavy investment that Kenyans and the Kenyan government have made in education that contributed significantly to this important and peaceful transition. As a result, the general consciousness of the Kenyan populace has risen tremendously. Civic group leaders and church leaders are highly educated people and have always provided challenges to the general Kenyan population on the need to manage change peacefully.

A learning society creates socially competent people who can question what is happening around them, and creates the social capital that every society needs. Learning that takes place throughout an individual's life may not only equip learners with knowledge, but should also address social and ethical issues in society.

The need for a learning society is also necessitated by the change that is taking place as a result of the knowledge revolution. Miller (1985) and Nasbitt and Aburdene (1990) observe that in a knowledge society (a society in which people's lives are controlled by information and communication technologies, and in which decisions made are based on information generated), change is a key factor, and hence the need for lifelong learning. Change may outdate present skills, as well as creating new demands and presenting new opportunities for individuals. As seen in Chapter 8, technological advancements are now a major force that is driving change in Africa and all the countries of the world. Changes in technology create a 'domino effect' in the workplace, in the home and for the individual. Our world requires each adult to update knowledge and skills frequently. This necessitates lifelong learning. In the United States of America, for instance, the amount of new knowledge being generated is enormous so that remaining in one job for a long time is not practical (Laudon, Traver and Laudon, 1996). This also encourages lifelong learning, which may be formal or informal (Merriam and Brockett, 1997). Countries in the European Union have implemented lifelong learning policies so that these countries can be competitive in the world economy.

The current increase in knowledge being generated creates a demand for additional education. The dynamics and rate of technological change support the concept of lifelong learning. It is also true that as technology increases the skill and knowledge requirements of jobs, education can no longer be confined to traditional formal schooling (Oduaran, 2002). People naturally develop new desires and seek new expressions of self-change based on the everyday experience of living (Gallagher, 1992). Every nation of the world needs to organise its educational system in such a way that any individual may obtain additional skills as demanded by the environment in which they operate. This means people will continue learning long after leaving formal schools. Therefore, governments and learning institutions have to be prepared to meet the increased demand for lifelong learning.

Lifelong learning has become essential in Africa for a number of reasons, such as:

- the social changes taking place in African families and communities;
- diseases such as HIV/AIDS;
- demographic changes leading to younger children being orphaned with no adult to take care of them;
- ethnic conflicts;
- economic pressure from outside Africa by those with vested interests in valuable minerals such as diamonds, gold and oil that are found in abundance in Africa;
- technological changes driven by advances in information and communication technologies and political instability; and
- increased demand for education at all levels.

These issues arise from within and without Africa. The only way to address them is through continued learning, hence the need for lifelong learning. Avoseh (2001: 479) has observed that 'the more I understand lifelong learning as a way of life, as a process of breaking barriers and of combating social exclusion, the more I am convinced that it is more about the rediscovery of Africa and the revival of traditional African pedagogy and values'.

The lifelong learning approach responds directly to the demands of the new era and is in line with the needs of modern economies and societies in which individuals, as well as organisations, have to adapt and renew themselves continuously through learning. Continued learning through lifelong learning programmes has the potential to foster and unleash the innovative energies of individuals in African societies. In the increasingly interdependent world that Africa finds itself in, individual choices and collective policy decisions must draw on information, research, evaluation and analyses that go beyond national frontiers (Bryant and White, 1982). This calls for an appropriate knowledge base critical for informed decision making. The lifelong learning approach should therefore be at the centre of African societies.

## ACTIVITY

1 List several activities which take place in your family, learning institution and community that you think promote life-long learning.
2 Suggest several strategies that should be undertaken by the government to promote lifelong learning in your community and country.
3 Plan to attend a village or town hall meeting that is aimed at addressing a social and community issue facing the people involved. At the end of the meeting, list the various lifelong learning needs raised in the meeting.

## GLOBAL LIFELONG LEARNING

The legislation and policies to support lifelong learning in Africa require urgent attention. The first issue that needs to be addressed is where to house adult education programmes. In several African countries, adult education programmes are housed in ministries of labour, youth, sports and home affairs. Lifelong learning programmes should be housed in the ministries of education, science and technology. However, since lifelong learning transcends all ministries, a multidisciplinary approach should be used. Before identifying specific legislation and policies that need to be put in place, examples from other continents of the world will be drawn upon. For instance, how have Western or Asian countries addressed legislation and policies aimed at supporting lifelong learning?

Mok and Chan (2002) have observed that while it was difficult to reach a consensus on the notion of a *learning society* and the ideas of *lifelong learning, learning society* and *continuing education*, these concepts have become increasingly important

in shaping the direction of educational development in the West and in Asia. The same trend is being witnessed in Africa. European countries came up in 1995 with the European Commission White Paper entitled: *Teaching and Learning – Towards the Learning Society*. The White Paper pointed out that three factors of change were being witnessed in European countries, namely, 'the impact of the information society, the impact of internationalisation and the impact of the scientific and technical world' (European Commission, 1995: 5–6). As a way forward, the White Paper proposed five policy actions necessary for establishing a learning society in European countries. According to the European Commission (1995: 9–11, 53–72) these are:

1 Encourage the acquisition of new knowledge in specific ways which include establishing an accreditation system covering technical and vocational skills; increasing student mobility; and the development of multimedia educational software.
2 Bring school and business sectors closer together by developing apprenticeship/trainee schemes in order to provide vocational training.
3 Combat exclusion by offering second-chance schools and extending the scope of the European voluntary service.
4 Treat capital investment and investment in training on an equal basis.

In the case of Asia, several countries have continued to review their educational systems with a focus on creating learning societies (Mok and Chan, 2002). In Hong Kong, for example, the *Education Blueprint for the 21st Century* was published in 1999. The Hong Kong Education Commission (1999: 15) stated that the overall aims of education for the country in the twenty-first century were

*To enable everyone to develop their full potential in all areas covering ethics, intellect, physique, social skills and aesthetics, so that each individual is ready for continuous self-learning, thinking, exploring, innovating and adapting to changes throughout life; filled with self-confidence and team spirit; and is willing to strive incessantly for the prosperity, progress, freedom and democracy of society, and to contribute to the future well-being of the nation and the world at large.*

While reforming educational systems in Africa, it is important that policy makers draw from what is happening in other parts of the world. Every country and continent is faced with unique problems. For instance, in several East Asian countries, usually referred to as Asian Tigers, such as Hong Kong and Taiwan, the economic crisis of the 1990s made these countries re-examine the role of education in managing economic and social crises. In the case of Hong Kong it was noted that 'our young people must be outward-looking, imbued with a spirit of exploration, able to make use of IT, able to master different kinds of knowledge, and willing to strive to improve through continuous learning. To enhance our competitiveness, Hong Kong has to shift to high value-added and technology-based production and services. It is people who are creative, versatile, knowledgeable and multi-talented that are needed (Education Commission, 1999: 9). While these sentiments may be relevant in Asia, African policy-makers and educational leaders may find the words even more relevant to the situations facing several African societies. In Taiwan, another successful Asian economy now faced with an economic crisis, the Ministry of Education published an education report aimed at promoting lifelong learning and establishing a learning society. The report clearly articulates various

implementation strategies for achieving lifelong learning (Mok and Chan, 2002). The Ministry of Education in Taiwan produced a White Paper that outlined fourteen programmes aimed at promoting and implementing strategies for achieving lifelong learning. Mok and Chan (2002: 19) report that the action programmes focus on the following issues:

- full integration of information for learning;
- trial launch of the lifelong learning card (passport);
- deregulation of admission channels;
- promotion of learning organisations in enterprises;
- organising reading clubs through the assistance of libraries;
- establishing recurrent education systems;
- widespread establishment of lifelong learning centres;
- promotion of foreign-language learning among the populace;
- establishing of learning organisations within the civil service;
- promotion of lifelong learning within correctional institutions;
- promotion of learning families;
- promotion of learning communities;
- integration of relevant regulations and the drafting of a 'Lifelong Education Law'; and
- establishment of accreditation systems for learning achievement.

While some of these programmes may be too ambitious for several African countries, policy-makers, educational planners and educational implementers in Africa should reflect on the relevance of these kinds of innovative programmes for Africa. Implementation of some of the programmes above would ensure accessibility to learning centres and institutions would promote lifelong learning as a way of life.

## ⊞ ACTIVITY

From the strategies for promoting lifelong learning in Taiwan, identify those that you think are relevant to Africa, and explain why you think Africa should try them out.

## POLICY ISSUES IN AFRICA

While examples of practical policy issues undertaken by countries outside Africa for the promotion of lifelong learning have been given, focus needs to be placed on policy issues in Africa. Firstly, as shown in Chapter 5, many countries in sub-Saharan Africa have different educational systems, as well as social, political and economic environments which differ from those in other parts of the world. These policies should, however, be implemented with great care and consideration of every country's specific situation. They should serve as resources for educational policy-makers. Given the critical contribution of education to a nation's development, every government in Africa should prioritise education. Supporting, promoting and providing lifelong learning opportunities should not be left only to international organisations and non-governmental organisations. African governments should provide conceptual and legal frameworks for policies that create an enabling environment for other agencies and stakeholders to operate in. Governments should also encourage strong partnerships between business and industry, NGOs and civil society.

Governments in Africa should initiate guided policies for decentralisation in the education sector. This will give individual educational institutions autonomy to develop educational plans aimed at serving the communities where the institutions are situated. Government should, how-ever, play a proactive role in reviewing and restructuring the educational systems, as has been done in Hong Kong and Taiwan. Africa requires purposeful governments that recognise the important role of lifelong learning. While traditional African societies promoted learning societies, the introduction of Western-type education and its requirement for monetary investments has undermined traditional educational systems, often replacing them and thereby denying access and opportunities to many people in Africa. Given this situation, the need for educational reform in Africa to make lifelong learning available to everyone in society is imperative. While this may sound impossible it can be achieved if there is government will and support.

Regarding the policy environment in connection with lifelong learning in Africa, Youngman (2001: 8) argues that a number of factors must be taken into account. He observes that

*Firstly, the nature of the state must be analysed. Is the state 'developmental' in terms of using public policy and planning to intervene in developmental processes, or is it 'minimalist' in terms of prioritising the role of market forces in economic and social development? Countries that implement Structural Adjustment Policies imposed by the World Bank and IMF reduce state intervention and the provision of social services, and hence are unlikely to regard lifelong education as an important area of state activity.*

While the above observation is true of most African countries, lifelong learning is a basic human right and every effort should be made to engage everyone in society in some form of learning. Direct implementation of Structural Adjustment Policies has led to negative impacts on lifelong learning in countries such as Tanzania and Zimbabwe.

What is now required is for every individual African country to conduct policy analysis studies to determine the status of adult education. So far, countries like Nigeria, Ghana, Botswana, Kenya, Namibia and South Africa are conducting such studies. On the importance of a lifelong education policy, Youngman (2001: 8) states that 'educational policy must be analysed with respect to the extent to which it embodies the principle of lifelong education for all'. Using the Botswana example, the current education policy in Botswana as expressed in the *Revised National Policy on Education* endorses both the philosophy of education as a lifelong process and the goal of creating a learning society (Youngman, 2000: 9). This should be the right channel for all governments in Africa. As seen in the earlier sections of this chapter, the issue of lifelong learning is receiving the attention of many African governments. Following the Asian example cited earlier, the need for a White Paper on educational reforms and restructuring in individual states in sub-Saharan Africa should be recommended. Such a White Paper should focus on the following pertinent issues:

- the need for stable partnerships between stakeholders;
- the need for stronger advocacy;
- reforming the entire school education system to include aspects of lifelong learning;
- strengthening the administrative support of educational institutions;
- encouraging business enterprises to participate in lifelong learning;
- launching of research and policy studies on lifelong learning;
- establishing a legal framework for lifelong learning;
- increasing lifelong learning opportunities; and

- integrating lifelong learning into the family, community and workplace.

## Case study

The Government of the Republic of Namibia in 2003 adopted a National Policy on Adult Learning. The government and non-governmental organisations which participated in CONFINTEA V declared that adult learning is a vital element in strategies aimed at achieving sustainable and equitable development within the perspective of lifelong learning. In the Second National Development Plan (NBP2), 2001/2–2005/6 the government stated its priorities clearly in the National Development Objectives and National Development Strategies for NDP2. The plan shows that education and the training of adults and out-of-school youth is an essential component of the approaches required for achieving these objectives and strategies. Adult learning in Namibia has been recognised as being important for meeting national development priorities. These priorities include: economic priorities, social priorities, environmental priorities, political priorities and human resource development priorities. This is an excellent example of the government playing a leading role in recognising the important role of lifelong learning.

## ⬚ ACTIVITY

**What are the responsibilities of governments in Africa with regard to providing policies that will assist in fostering lifelong learning?**

# FUNDING LIFELONG LEARNING

The success of lifelong learning programmes in Africa requires political will and financial support. However, no matter how sound an educational plan may be, without financial support its implementation will be hampered. This brings us to the important issue of raising money in creative ways for investment in lifelong learning. Firstly, education is too important an activity to leave its funding to third parties. Instead, the state should play a leading role in this regard. A country that cannot educate its own people cannot compete in the current global economy. This is the reality that African leaders and African people must be prepared to face. While Africa is faced with many problems, the best way to address those problems is through learning and the promotion of learning societies. This means that education should receive special attention in funding. Both the individual and the government must be prepared to make sacrifices by investing more of the limited financial resources available into education. There is no other path to Africa's survival but through lifelong learning.

At institutional levels, a challenge goes out to every learning institution in Africa to devise innovative ways of raising additional funds to supplement government resources (Nafukho, 2004). Doing so will ensure that institutions will be able to operate the learning programmes they have designed for the promotion of learning in society. Individuals who are able to invest in their learning by directly paying for their own education must be encouraged to do so. While a number of African leaders and successful business people in Africa have enormous wealth, little effort has been made to encourage such individuals to make direct contributions to this important sector of education. Innovative and honest fundraising approaches should be promoted in Africa to reach such individuals. While the issue of innovative strategies for raising funds for education has been criticised as making education a commodity, the reality is that education as an important and durable investment requires financial resources. The United Nations' Article 26 cited by Oduaran (2002: 25) and titled *The Right to Education* states that

> *Everyone has the right to education. Education shall be free, at least in the elementary and fundamental stages. Elementary education shall be compulsory. Technical and professional education shall be generally available, and higher education shall be equally accessible to all on the basis of merit ...*

While this is the ideal regarding the supply of education by UN member countries, the reality in Africa is that most governments cannot meet the direct demand for education even at an elementary level. This is a challenge to both the governments and policy makers.

International organisations like UNESCO, UNICEF and the Institute for the International Co-operation of the German Adult Education Association (IIZ/DVV), to mention a few, are already playing a leading role in the funding of adult learning programmes in Africa. Such organisations must be encouraged to continue with their investments. If every human being made a deliberate effort to invest in their own learning and that of their neighbour the world would be a much better place to live in, including Africa. The following funding strategies for lifelong learning programmes in Africa are suggested:

- Governments in Africa should introduce education taxes that would raise revenue for funding lifelong learning for all in society. The revenue generated should go to a special education fund for lifelong learning and not into the general pool as has happened previously.

- There must be involvement by the private sector in supporting lifelong learning through direct contribution and through the financial support of employees with regard to receiving further training.
- Encouragement must be given for the establishment of entrepreneurial activities in all learning institutions. The revenue generated should help fund various lifelong education programmes. This is already proving successful in a number of learning institutions in Africa (Nafukho, 2004).
- Voluntary giving by private members of society who have been endowed with immense financial resources should be promoted.
- Reforms should be made in the tax system, with a focus on recognising individuals who make contributions to educational institutions. African governments should offer tax rebates to organisations that make charitable contributions to individuals and to learning institutions.
- Learning institutions in Africa should form strong alumni associations with a focus on lifelong learning. Such associations should help in raising funds for investment in community learning. The professional associations of adult educators discussed in Chapter 7 should play a role here.
- African governments should make a strong case to their debtors regarding the need for a percentage of all debt repayments to be channelled back into promoting and developing lifelong learning.

- The spirit of volunteerism in African countries should be encouraged. In most African countries, the retirement age is 55 years. This is a prime age. Individuals retiring should be encouraged to offer voluntary services by teaching in community learning centres, in adult literacy classes and in other educational institutions. This is a major way of helping governments meet the learning needs of people in society.
- Community-based computer learning centres should be established by African governments as a strategy for reducing the digital divide between people living in urban areas and those living in rural areas.

As mentioned at the beginning of this chapter, issues pertaining to lifelong learning and its funding require critical thinking and examination. We would like to engage our readers in this important debate on lifelong learning for all in Africa. It would be a great mistake on our part to assume that we have all the answers related to funding lifelong learning programmes in Africa. Instead, we want to challenge our readers to offer some innovative ideas based on their personal experiences. Regarding policies related to schooling and the promotion of lifelong learning, African governments have been found to have good policies on paper. The problem is one of policy implementation. African policymakers must be challenged to implement several good policies already in existence. For policy implementation to be successful, functional systems must be established. Without well-established systems, lifelong learning goals and strategies cannot be implemented. There is an urgent need in Africa to build a database from primary and secondary research results on the prevailing status of lifelong learning, workforce development and education efforts. By doing this, professionals in the field of adult education will have a strong foundation from which to operate.

## ⊞ ACTIVITY

1  In this chapter, we emphasised the importance of lifelong learning. Based on the knowledge of your society's economic background, suggest various ways of funding lifelong learning programmes in your community, town and country.
2  What successes and weaknesses do you foresee in the strategies that you have suggested above?

## SUMMARY

In this final chapter of this book, the origin of lifelong learning the world over and specifically in Africa was explained. The meaning of lifelong learning was provided and its importance to contemporary African societies was discussed. We also explored the meaning of a learning society and demonstrated that African societies were learning societies even before the introduction of Western education. We also discussed the importance of learning societies in Africa. In this chapter the issue of funding lifelong learning in Africa was also examined.

## KEY POINTS

■ African traditional cultures encouraged lifelong learning for all in society, but this important cultural behaviour was disrupted by the introduction of the Western type of schooling.

■ Lifelong learning in traditional Africa was the responsibility of the elders, especially grandparents, parents, uncles and aunts who played a major role in passing on to younger adults and children essential knowledge, skills and values.
■ Educational reforms in Asia and in Western societies have focused on the role of lifelong learning in managing rapid change taking place in those societies.
■ There is a need for urgent reforms in the educational systems in Africa with a focus on the creation of learning societies and the encouragement of lifelong learning.
■ African governments must give priority to funding lifelong learning programmes.
■ Innovative ways of funding lifelong learning programmes need to be developed.

## ⊞ ACTIVITY

1  Explain how the field of adult education in Africa can be developed in order to create learning societies in Africa.
2  Describe how distance and open learning modes of instruction could be used to promote lifelong learning in Africa.
3  List the issues and problems that require urgent attention in your country with regard to the field of adult education and the promotion of lifelong learning.

## FURTHER QUESTIONS

1  Discuss the role of lifelong learning programmes in your community and at the workplace.

2  What legislation and policies should be developed in your country to promote lifelong learning?

3  Explain, using practical examples, how lifelong learning programmes in your country should be funded.

4  Explain why you think it is possible to provide lifelong learning for all in your country.

## SUGGESTED READINGS

Laudon, C. K., Traver, G. C. and Laudon, P. J. 1996. *Information technology and society*. New York: Course Technology Inc.

Merriam, S. B. and Brockett, R. G. 1997. *The profession and practice of adult education: An introduction*. San Francisco: Jossey-Bass.

Shiundu, J. and Omulando, S. 1992. *Curriculum: Theory and practice in Kenya*. Nairobi: Oxford University Press.

# References

Abun-Nasr, J. 1975. *A history of the Maghrib.*
London: Cambridge University Press.

Adekanmbi, G. and Modise, O. 2000. 'The state of
adult and continuing education in Botswana.'
In *The state of adult and continuing education
in Africa.* eds., S.A. Indabawa, A. Oduaran, T.
Afrik and S. Walters, pp. 65–78. Windhoek:
Department of Adult and Non-formal
Education, University of Namibia.

Africa One, 'Wiring a continent for the 21st
century: The Africa one project overview',
viewed 22 July 2003, http://www.africaone.com/
english/about/about.cfm.

African Virtual University. 1997. *A Project of the
World Bank.* Feasibility Study Report, 23 April.
Washington, DC: The World Bank.

Afrik, T. 2000. 'Significant post-independence
developments in adult and continuing
education in sub-Saharan Africa'. In *The state
of adult and continuing education in Africa,*
eds. S.A. Indabawa, A. Oduaran, T. Afrik and S.
Walters, pp. 19–30. Windhoek: Department of
Adult and Non-formal Education, University of
Namibia.

Afshar, H. 1991. 'Women and development: Myths
and realities: some introductory notes'. In
*Women, development and survival in the Third
World,* ed. H. Afshar, pp. 1–10. New York:
Longman.

Aggarwal, J. C. 1985. *Theory and principles of
education.* New Delhi: Vikas Publishing House.

Ajayi, J. A. 1989. *Africa in the nineteenth century.*
Oxford: Heinemann.

Ajayi, J. A. and Crowder, M. 1985. *History of West
Africa.* London: Longman.

Alemayehu, R. 1988. 'Adult education and the Third
World: An African perspective'. In *Radical
approaches to adult education: A reader,* ed. T.
Lovett, pp. 281–201. London: Routledge.

Allison, C. B. 1995. *Past, present: Essays for teachers
in the history of education.* New York: Peter
Lang.

Amin, S. and Moore, R. 1988. *Eurocentrism.* New
York: Monthly Review.

Amutabi, M. 1997a. 'Plight of adult education in
Kenya'. In *Globalization, adult education and
training: Impacts and issues,* ed. S. Walters, pp.
196-201. London: Zed Books.

Amutabi, M. N. 1995. *Challenging the orthodoxies:
The role of ethnicity and regional nationalism in
leadership and democracy in Africa.* Conference
Paper, UNESCO Conference on Nationalism
and Ethnicity in Africa, Kericho, 28–31 May 1995.

Amutabi, M. N., et al. 1997. 'Introduction'. In
*Globalization, adult education and training:
Impacts and issues,* ed. S. Walters, pp. 1–14.
London: Zed Books.

Amutabi, M. N. 2000. 'Globalization and the
politics of GNP and GDP in twenty-first
century Africa: A critical reflection'. In *Africa in
the beginning of the twenty-first century,* ed. G. P.
Okoth, pp. 269–286. Nairobi: Nairobi University
Press.

sesa woruban

Apps, J. W. 1973. *Towards a working philosophy of adult education.* Syracuse: Syracuse University.

Apps, J. W. 1988. *Higher Education in a learning society: Meeting new demands for education and training.* San Francisco: Jossey-Bass.

Avoseh, M. B. M. 2001. 'Learning to be active citizens: Lessons of traditional Africa for lifelong learning.' *International Journal of Lifelong Education*, Vol. 20, No. 6, pp. 479–486.

'The African Virtual University (AVU): Pilot phase programme', 1997, viewed 22 May 2003, http://physinfo.ulb.ac.be/!UVA!/AVU_pilot-phase.html.

'The African Virtual University: education for the knowledge age', 2003, viewed 22 May 2003, http://www.avu.org.

Ball, S. J. 1994. *Education reform.* Buckingham: Open University Press.

Baranshamaje, E. 1995. *The African Virtual University (AVU).* Concept paper. Draft of 7 June 1995. Washington, DC: The World Bank.

Baranshamaje, E., et al. 1995. *Increasing Internet connectivity in sub-Saharan Africa: Issues, options and World Bank group role.* Draft of 29 March 1995. Washington, DC: The World Bank.

Barbules, N. C. and Torres, C. A. 2000. *Globalization and education: Critical perspectives.* London: Routledge.

Barnes, T. 1999. *'We women worked so hard': Gender, urbanization, and social reproduction in colonial Harare, Zimbabwe, 1930–1956.* Portsmouth: Heinemann.

Becker, H. S. 1962. 'The nature of a profession.' In *Education for the professions*, ed. N. B. Henry, pp. 27–46. Chicago: University of Chicago Press.

Beder, H. 1989. 'Purposes and philosophies of adult education'. In *Handbook of adult and continuing education*, eds. S.B. Merriam and P.M. Cunningham, pp. 30–50. San Francisco: Jossey-Bass.

Bernal, M. 1987. *Black Athena: The Afroasiatic roots of classical civilization*, Vol. 1. New Brunswick, WNJ: Rutgers University Press.

Bhola, H. S. 1997. Trans-national forces and national realities of adult basic education and training (ABE). In *Convergence*, Vol. 30, pp. 41–51.

Bhola, H. S. 2000. 'Inventing a future for adult education in Africa'. In *The state of adult and continuing education in Africa*, eds. S. A. Indabawa, A. Oduran, T. Afrik and S. Walters, pp. 207–215. Windhoek: Department of Adult and Non-formal Education, University of Namibia.

Blaut, J. M. 1992. *The debate on colonialism, eurocentrism and history.* Africa World Press.

Blaut, J. M. 1993. *The colonizer's model of the world.* New York: Guildford.

Bogonko, N. S., Otiende, J. E. and Sifuna, D. M. 1986. *History of education: Education foundations, Part One.* Nairobi: Nairobi University Press.

Bogonko, S. N. 1992. *A history of modern education in Kenya (1895–1991).* Nairobi: Evans Brothers Kenya Ltd.

Bown, L. and Olu-Tomori, S. H. 1979. *A handbook of adult education for West Africa*. London: Hutchinson Library.

Bryant, C. and White, G. L. 1982. *Managing development in the Third World*. Boulder, Co: Westview Press.

Brookfield, S. D. 1986. *Understanding and facilitating adult learning: A comprehensive analysis of principles and effective practices*. San Francisco: Jossey Bass.

Burke, T. 1996. *Lifebuoy men, lux women: Commodification, consumption and cleanliness in modern Zimbabwe*. London: Duke University Press.

Bwatwa, Y. D. 1990. *Adult education methods: A guide for educators*. Dar-es-Salaam: Dar-es-Salaam University Press.

Carnegie Corporation of New York. 2001. 'Africa goes online', *Carnegie Reporter*, 1 (2), Spring, http://www.carnegie.org/reporter/02/africa/index4.html.

Cervero, R. M. 1988. *Effective continuing education for professionals*. San Francisco: Jossey-Bass.

Cervero, R. M., Wilson, A. L. and Associates. 2001. *Power in practice: Adult education and the struggle for knowledge and power in society*. San Francisco: Jossey-Bass.

Chege, W. 1999. World mourns death of Tanzania's founder: Julius Nyerere was an inspiration to a generation of Africans. *The Toronto Star*, 15 October, p. A24.

Chukwu, C. N. 2002. *Introduction to philosophy in an African perspective*. Eldoret: Zapf Chancery Research Consultants and Publishers.

Collins, R. O. 1997. *Eastern African history: African history in documents*. Princeton: Markus Wiener.

Courtney, S. 1989. 'Defining adult and continuing education'. In *Handbook of adult education and continuing education*, eds. S. B. Merriam and P. M. Cunningham. San Francisco: Jossey-Bass.

Craig, S. 1992. 'Considering men and the media'. In *Men, masculinity and the media*, ed. S. Craig, pp. 1–7. Newbury Park: Sage Publishers.

Cropley, A. J. 1980. *Towards a system of lifelong education: Some practical considerations*. Hamburg: UNESCO Institute of Education.

Currid, C. 1989. A 3-step plan of attack on corporate computerphobics. *PC Weekly*, No. 8, p. 81.

Dailey, N. 1984. 'Adult learning and organizations'. *Training and development*, No. 38, pp. 66–68.

Darkenwald, G. G. and Merriam, S. B. 1982. *Adult education: Foundations of practice*. New York: Harper and Row.

Datta, K. and Murray, A. 1989. 'The rights of minorities and subject peoples in Botswana: A historical evaluation'. In *Democracy in Botswana*, eds. J. Holm and P. Molutsi, pp. 58–73. Gaborone: Botswana Society.

Dave, R. H. 1972. *Foundations of lifelong education*. New York: Pergamon Press.

Davenport, J. 1993. 'Is there any way out of the andragogy mess?' In *Culture and process of adult learning*, eds. M. Thorpe and R. E. Hanson. London: Routledge.

Delors, J., et al. 1998. *Learning: The treasure within*. Paris: UNESCO.

Dennis, C. 1991. 'Constructing a "career" under conditions of economic crisis and structural adjustment: The survival strategies of Nigerian women'. In *Women, development and survival in the Third World*, ed. H. Afsher, pp. 88–103. New York: Longman.

Diawara, T. A. 2002. ECHO: World Summit on sustainable development. *Bilingual Quarterly Newsletter of the Association of Africa Women for Research and Development*, No's. 10–11, December. Dakar: AAWORD.

Diop, C. A. 1967. *The African origin of civilization: Myth or reality*. New York: Lawrence Hill and Company.

Djait, H. 1981. 'Written sources before the fifteenth century'. In *Methodology and African prehistory*, ed. J. Ki-Zerbo, Vol. 1, pp. 87–113. London: Heinemann, UNESCO and University of California Press.

Draper, J. A. (ed.) 1998. *Africa adult education: Chronologies in Commonwealth countries*. Cape Town: CACE, University of the Western Cape, South Africa.

Education Commission. 1999. *Education blueprint for the twenty-first century: Review of the academic system: Aims of education*. Hong Kong: Government Printer.

Edwards, R. 1995. 'Behind the banner: Whither the learning society'. In *Adult learning*, Vol. 6, No. 6, pp. 187–189.

Eglash, R. 1997. 'When math worlds collide: Intention and invention in ethno-mathematics'. *Science, Technology and Human Values*, Vol. 22, No. 1, pp. 79–97.

Elder, V. B. 1987. Gender and age in technostress: Effects on white-collar productivity. *Government Finance Review*, Vol. 3, pp. 17-21.

Elias, J. L. and Merriam S. B. 1995. *Philosophical foundations of adult education*. 2nd ed. Malabar: Krieger Publishing Company.

Emeagwali, G. T. 1989. 'Science and public policy'. *Journal of International Science Policy Foundation*, Vol. 16, No. 3.

European Commission. 1995. *European commission White Paper: Teaching and learning – towards the learning society*. Luxembourg: Office for Official Publications of the European Community.

Fafunwa, A. B. 1967. *New perspectives in African education*. Lagos: Macmillan and Co. (Nigeria) Ltd.

Fafunwa, A. B. 1974. *History of education in Nigeria*. Ibadan: NPS Educational Publishers.

Fafunwa, A. B. 1982. 'African education in perspective'. In *Education in Africa: A comparative survey*, eds. A. B. Fafunwa and J. U. Aisiku. London: Allen and Unwin.

Fafunwa, A. B., Macauley J. I. and Sokoya, J. A. (eds.). 1989. *Education in mother tongue: The Ife Primary Education Research Project*. Ibadan: University Press Limited.

Faure, E. 1972. *Learning to be*. Paris: UNESCO.

Flexner, A. 1915. *Is social work a profession?* Proceedings of the National Conference of Charities and Corrections at the Forty-second annual session held in Baltimore, Maryland, 12–19 May, Chicago: Hildmann.

Forde, D. 1976. *African worlds: Studies in the cosmological ideas and social values of African peoples*. Oxford: Oxford University Press.

Frank, T. 2002. *One market under God: Extreme capitalism, market populism, and the end of economic democracy*. London: Vintage.

Freire, P. 1970. *Pedagogy of the oppressed*. New York: Herder and Herder.

Freire, P. 1973. *Education for critical consciousness*. New York: Seabury.

Freire, P. 1995. *Pedagogy of hope*. New York: Continuum.

Gallagher, S. 1992. *Hermeneutics and education*. Albany, NY: State University of New York Press.

Garmer, A. K. and Firestone, C. M. 1996. Creating a learning society: Initiatives for education and technology. Washington, DC: Aspen Institute Forum.

Geiger, S. 1997. *Tanu women: Gender and culture in the making of Tanganyikan nationalism, 1955–1965*. Portsmouth: Heinemann.

Giddens, A. 1990. *The consequences of modernity*. Cambridge: Polity Press.

Giddens, A. 1995. *Beyond left and right*. Cambridge: Polity Press.

Gordon, A. A. 1996. *Transforming capitalism and patriarchy: Gender and development in Africa*. Boulder, CO: Lynne Rienner.

Gouthro, P. 2000. 'Globalization, civil society and the homeplace'. *Convergence*, Vol 33, No's. 1–2, pp. 57–77.

Gray, J. 1999. *False dawn: The delusions of global capitalism*. London: Granta.

Green, A. 1999. *Education, globalization and the nation state*. London: Macmillan.

Green, K., Graham, R., Schneider, M. and Bunn, S. E., 2003. 'World's fastest network launched to connect TeraGrid sites', viewed 22 July 2003, http://www.teragrid.org/news/030403.html.

Greenstreet, M. and Siabi-Mensah. 1998. 'Ghana'. In *African adult education: Chronologies in Commonwealth countries*, ed. J. A. Draper, pp. 33–34. Cape Town: CACE, University of Western Cape.

Guehenno, J. M. 1995. *The end of the nation-state*. Minneapolis: University of Minnesota Press.

Gumede, E. 1997. 'On the periphery: The needs of rural women'. In *Globalization, adult education and training: Impacts and issues*, ed. S. Walters. pp. 233–236. London: Zed Books.

Gush, C. and Walters, S. 1998. 'South Africa'. In *African adult education: Chronologies in Commonwealth countries*, ed. J. A. Draper, pp. 77–86. Cape Town: CACE, University of Western Cape.

Gustavsson, B. 1997. 'Lifelong learning reconsidered'. In *Globalization, adult education and training: Impacts and issues*, ed. S. Walters, pp. 237–248. London: Zed Books.

Gustavsson, B. and Osman, A. 1997. 'Multicultural education and lifelong learning'. In *Globalization, adult education and training: Impacts and issues*, ed. S.Walters, pp. 179–187. London: Zed Books.

Gyekye, K. 1997. *Tradition and modernity*. Oxford: Oxford University Press.

Habasonda, L. M. 2002. 'The pitfalls of gender activism in Africa'. *Agenda: Empowering women for gender equity*, No. 54, pp. 99–105.

Hall, B. L. 1973. 'University adult education: A time for broadening participation'. In *Adult education and national development*, eds. B. L. Hall and K. Remtulla, pp. 69–70 Nairobi: Kenya Literature Bureau.

Hall, B. 1996. 'Adult education and the political economy of global economic change'. In *Towards a transformative political economy of adult education*, eds. P. Wangoola and F. Youngman, pp. 105–106. De Kalb: LEPS Press.

Hall, B. 1998. 'Please don't bother the canaries'. Paulo Freire and the International Council for Adult Education, *Convergence* Vol. 31, No. 1–2, pp. 95–103.

Hall, B. L. 2000. 'Global civil society: Theorizing a changing world'. *Convergence*, Vol. 33, Nos. 1–2, pp. 10–32.

Hamilton, N. W. 2002. *Academic ethics: Problems and materials on professional conduct and shared governance*. Westport, CT: Greenwood Press.

Hart, M. U. 1992. *Working and educating for life: Feminist and international perspectives on adult education*. London: Routledge.

Hartmann, H. 1981. 'The unhappy marriage of Marxism and feminism: Towards a more progressive union'. In *The unhappy marriage of Marxism and feminism: A debate of class and patriarchy*, ed. L. Sargent, pp. 1–35. London: Pluto Press.

Hatcher, T. 2002. *Ethics and HRD: A new approach to leading responsible organizations*. Cambridge: Perseus Publishing.

Held, D., McGrew, A., Goldblatt, D. and Perraton, J. 1999. *Global transformations: Politics, economics and culture*. Stanford: Stanford University Press.

Hinzen, H. 2000. 'Innovation and continuity in international cooperation by German adult education centres in the 1990s'. *Adult education and development*, Vol. 55, pp. 107–122.

Hirst, P. H. 1974. *Knowledge and the curriculum*. New York: Routledge.

Houle, C. O. 1980. *Continuing learning in the professions*. San Francisco: Jossey-Bass.

Hountondji, P. J. 1983. *African philosophy: Myth and reality*. Bloomington: Indiana University Press.

Huntingford, G. W. B. 1963. 'The peopling of the interior of East Africa by its modern inhabitants'. In *History of East Africa*, eds. R. Oliver and M. Gervase, pp. 58–93. Oxford: Clarendon Press.

Hutchins, R. M. 1968. *The learning society*. Harmondsworth: Penguin.

Imbo, S. O. 1998. *An introduction to African philosophy*. Lanham: Rowman & Littlefield Publishers Inc.

Indabawa, S. A., Oduaran, A., Afrik, T. and Walters, S. (eds.) 2000. *The state of adult and continuing education in Africa*. Windhoek: Department of Adult and Non-formal Education, University of Namibia.

Indire, F. 1982. 'Education in Kenya'. In *Education in Africa: A comparative survey*, eds. A. B. Fafunwa and J. U. Aisiku, pp. 115–139. London: Allen and Unwin.

Jarvis, P. 1990. *An international dictionary of adult and continuing education*. New York: Routledge.

Kane, L. 2000. 'The state of adult and continuing education in Senegal'. In *The state of adult and continuing education in Africa*, eds. S. A. Indabawa, A. Oduran, T. Afrik and S. Walters, pp. 155–160. Windhoek: Department of Adult and Non-formal Education, University of Namibia.

Kani, A. 1992. 'Arithmetic in pre-colonial Central Sudan'. In *Science and technology in African history*, ed. G. Emeagwali. New York: Edwin Mellen.

Karani, F. A. 2000. 'Research priorities in adult and continuing education in Kenya'. In *The state of adult and continuing education in Africa*, eds. S. A. Indabawa, A. Oduaran, T. Afrik and S. Walters, pp. 107–114. Windhoek: Department of Adult and Non-formal Education, University of Namibia.

Karanja, W. 1992. 'Market women and children in Nigeria: Some notes from Lagos'. *Women and reproduction in Africa, Occasional Paper Series*, No. 5, pp. 15–40. Dakar: AAWORD.

Kassam, Y. 1983. 'Nyerere's philosophy and the educational experiment in Tanzania'. *Interchange on Education Policy*, Vol. 14, No. 1, pp. 56–68.

Kelly, T. 1992. *A history of adult education in Great Britain*. Liverpool: Liverpool University Press.

Kirui, D. K. 1998. 'Kenya'. In *Africa adult education: Chronologies in Commonwealth countries*, ed. J. A. Draper, pp. 42–45. Cape Town: CACE, University of Western Cape.

Ki-Zerbo, J. 1981. 'African pre-historic art'. In *General history of Africa: Methodology and African prehistory*, ed. J. Ki-Zerbo, Vol. 1, pp. 656–687. London: Heinemann,UNESCO and University of California Press.

Ki-Zerbo, J. 1990. *Educate or perish: Africa's impasse and prospects*. Dakar: UNESCO-UNICEF.

Knowles, M. 1984. *The adult learner: A neglected species*, 3rd edn. Houston: Gulf Publishing.

Knowles, M. S. 1970. *The modern practice of adult education: Andragogy versus pedagogy*. New York: Association Press.

Knowles, M. S. 1980. *The modern practice of adult education: From pedagogy to andragogy*. Revised and updated, Eaglewood Cliffs, NJ: Cambridge.

Knowles, M. S. 1984. *Andragogy in action*. San Francisco: Jossey-Bass.

Knowles, M. S., Holton, E. L. and Swanson, R. A. 1998. *The adult learner*. Woburn, MA: Butterworth-Heinemann.

Koroma, P. A. 1998. 'North-South cooperation in adult education: A case study of the partners and the Institute for International Cooperation of the German Adult Education Association'. *Adult education and development*,Vol. 50, pp. 63–69.

Korsgaard, O. 1997. 'The impact of globalization on adult education'. In *Globalization, adult education and training: Impacts and issues*, ed. S. Walters, pp. 15–26. London: Zed Books.

Kuper, L. 1971. 'African nationalism in South Africa'. In *The Oxford History of South Africa, 1870–1966*, eds. M. Wilson and L. Thompson, pp. 424–475. Oxford: Oxford University Press.

Larsson, S. 1997. 'The meaning of lifelong learning'. In *Globalization, adult education and training: Impacts and issues*, ed. S. Walters, pp. 250–261. London: Zed Books.

Lassiter, J. E. 1999. *African culture and personality: Bad social science, effective social activism, or a call to reinvent ethnology?* African Studies Quarterly, Vol. 3, No. 2.

Laudon, C. K., Traver, G. C. and Laudon, P. J. 1996. *Information technology and society*. New York: Course Technology Inc.

Lawson, K. H. 1991. In *Adult education: Evolution and achievements: A developing field of study*, eds. J. M. Peters, P. Jarvis and Associates, pp. 282–300. San Francisco: Jossey-Bass.

Letseka, M. 2000. 'African philosophy and educational discourse'. In *African voices in Education*, eds. P. Higgs, N. C. G. Vakalisa, T. V. Mda and N. T. Assie-Lumumba, pp. 179–193. Cape Town: Juta.

Levtzion, N. 1971. 'The early states of Western Sudan to 1500'. In *History of West Africa*, eds. J.F.A. Ajayi and M. Crowder, pp. 120–157. New York: Columbia University Press.

Lewis, L. H. 1980. 'Adults and computer anxiety: Fact or fiction'? *Lifelong learning*,Vol. 11, No. 8, pp. 5–12.

Lieb, S. Principles of adult learning. 1999. Viewed 1st October 2002, http://www.hcc.hawaii.edu/intranet.

Light, D. 1999. 'Pioneering distance education in Africa'. *Harvard Business Review*, Vol. 77, No. 5, p. 26.

Lindeman, E. C. 1926. *The meaning of adult education*. New York: New Republic.

Lindeman, E. C. 1989. *The meaning of adult education*. Norman: Oklahoma Research Centre for Continuing Professional and Higher Education, University of Oklahoma.

Lovett, T. (ed.). 1988. *Radical approaches to adult education: A reader*. Beckenham: Croom Helm.

Lowe, J. 2002. 'Computer-based education: is it a panacea'? *Journal of research on technology in education*, Vol. 34, No. 2, pp. 163–171.

Lutta-Mukhebi, M. C. and Amutabi, M. N. 2000. 'Globalisation of communication and media technology on democracy in Kenya'. Conference paper presented at the 6th Congress of the Organisation of Social research in Eastern and Southern Africa (OSSREA), 23–28 April, Dar-es-Salaam, Tanzania.

Mabogunje, A. L. 1971. 'The land and peoples of West Africa'. In *History of West Africa*, eds. J. F. Ade Ajayi and M. Crowder, Vol. 1. pp. 1–33. New York: Columbia University Press.

Makgoba, M.W. 1997. *Mokoko, the Makgoba affair: A reflection on transformation*. Florida Hills: Vivlia Publishers and Booksellers.

Makgoba, M. (ed.). 1999. *African renaissance: The new struggle*. Sandton and Cape Town: Mafube and Tafelberg.

Mamdani, M. 1990. 'A Glimpse of African studies made in USA', *Bulletin* No. 2, pp. 66. Dakar: CODESRIA.

Manthoto, L. H., Braimoh, D. and Adeola, A. A. 2000. 'The state of adult and continuing education in Lesotho'. In *The state of adult and continuing education in Africa*, eds. S. A. Indabawa, A. Oduaran, T. Afrik and S. Walters, pp. 155–160. Windhoek: Department of Adult and Non-formal Education, University of Namibia.

March, C. 1996. *A tool kit: Concepts and frameworks for gender analysis and planning*. Oxford: Oxfam.

Marcus, H. G. 1994. *A History of Ethiopia*. Oxford: University of California Press.

Masolo, D. A. 1995. *African philosophy in search of identity*. Nairobi: East African Publishers.

Matiru, B. 1987. 'Distance education in Kenya: A Third World view.' In *Distance education and the mainstream: Convergence in education*, eds. P. Smith and M. Kelly, pp. 57–73. London: Croom Helm.

Mayanja M., 1999. 'Nakasckc tclcccntrc: Tracing how far we have come', viewed 1 October 2003, http://www.nakaseke.or.ug.

Mayo, P., 1999. 'Julius Nyerere and education: A tribute.' *The Sunday Times (Malta)*, 31 October.

Mbigi, L., 1997. 'New life for a new year.' In *Sawubona*, December 1997, pp. 37.

Mbiti, J. S. 1969. *African religions and philosophy*. New York: Praeger Publishers.

Mbiti, J. 1970. *African religions and philosophy*. New York: Anchor Books.

Mbiti, J. S. 1991. *Introduction to African religion*. Portsmouth: Heinemann Educational Books.

McIntyre, C. 1996. *Guide to Zambia*. Saybrook, CT: Globe Pequot.

McKeown, M. G., and Beck, I. L. 1999. 'Getting the discussion started.' *Educational Leadership*, Vol. 57, No. 3, pp. 25–28.

Merriam, S. B. and Brockett, R. G. 1997. *The profession and practice of adult education*. San Francisco: Jossey-Bass.

Miller, M. D. 1985. *Principles and a philosophy for vocational education*. Columbus: The National Centre for Research in Vocational Education.

Mkandawire, T. 1988. 'The road to crisis, adjustment and de-industrialisation: The African case'. *Africa Development*, Vol. 13, No. 1, pp. 5–32.

Mkandawire, T. and Soludo, C. C. 1999. *Our continent, our future*. Trenton, NJ: Africa World Press.

Mohapeloa, J. 1982. 'Education in Lesotho'. In *Education in Africa: A comparative survey*, eds. A. B. Fafunwa and J. U. Aisiku, pp. 140–161. London: Allen and Unwin.

Moumouni, A. 1968. *Education in Africa*. London: Andre Deutsch.

Mok, K. H. and Chan, D. 2002. 'The quest for quality education and learning society in Hong Kong, Taiwan and Shanghai'. Paper presented at the Pacific Circle Consortium 26th Annual Conference, 1–3 May, Seoul, Korea.

Mudakiri, T. 1996. 'The political economy of adult education in Zimbabwe: A case study.' In *Towards a transformative political economy of adult education: Theoretical and practical challenges*, eds. P. Wangoola and F. Youngman, pp. 161–187. DeKalb: LEPS Press.

Muhammad, S. I. 1989. 'Women, the family and the wider society'. In *Women and the family in Nigeria*, eds. A. Imam, R. Pittin and H. Omole, pp. 29–36. Dakar: AAWORD.

Mukudi, E. 1993. 'Women and education'. In *Democratic change in Africa: Women's Perspectives*, eds. J. A. Oduol and M. Nzomo, pp. 83–92. Nairobi: Africa Centre for Technology Studies .

Mulenga, D. 2001. 'Mwalimu Julius Nyerere's contribution to education'. *International Journal of Lifelong Education*, Vol. 26, pp. 446–470.

Mulira, E. E. K. 1978. *Adult literacy and development: A handbook for teachers of adults*. Nairobi: Kenya Literature Bureau.

Mumba, E. 1998. 'Zambia'. In *The state of adult education in Africa*, eds. S. A. Indabawa, A. Oduaran, T. Afrik and S.A. Walters, pp. 94–97. Windhoek: Department of Adult and Continuing Education, University of Namibia.

Mushi, P. A. K and Bwatwa, Y. D. M. 1998. 'Tanzania'. In *Africa adult education: Chronologies in Commonwealth countries*, ed. J. A. Draper, pp. 88–93. Cape Town: CACE, University of Western Cape.

Mwenegoha, H. A. K. 1974. *Mwalimu Julius Kambarage Nyerere: A bibliography*. Dar-es-Salaam: Foundation Books Limited.

Nabudere, D. W. 1996. 'Class, race, and ethnicity in adult education in Africa'. In *Towards a transformative political economy of adult education: Theoretical and practical challenges*, eds. P. Wangoola and F. Youngman, pp. 161–187. DeKalb: LEPS Press.

Nafukho, F. M. (In press). *The United States' African Growth and Opportunity Act: A new path for Africa's economic recovery*. Dakar: CODESRIA.

Nafukho, F. M. 1995. 'The need for optimal mix of theoretical instruction and practical work experience in Kenyan public universities'. Proceedings of Kenya DAAD Scholars National Conference on Strengthening the Relationship between the Universities and Industry, 28 November – December, Nairobi.

Nafukho, F. M. 1996. 'Structural adjustment programmes and the emergence of entrepreneurial activities among Moi university students'. *Journal of Eastern African Research and Development*, Vol. 2: 26, pp. 79–90.

Nafukho, F. M. 1998. 'Entrepreneurial skills development programmes for unemployed youths in Africa: A second look'. *Journal of Small Business Management*, Vol. 36, No. 1, pp. 100–103.

Nafukho, F.M. 1999. 'The place of lifelong learning in Kenya: Need to build bridges between private agencies, public agencies and universities'. In *Conference Proceedings of the 16th Annual Meeting of the Association of Third Studies. On the theme Rhetoric versus Action: The Challenge of Policy Implementation*, eds. Skidmore-Hess and M.W. Jones, pp. 119–127. Durham, North Carolina: North Carolina Central University.

Nafukho, F. M. 2004. 'The market model of financing state universities in Kenya: Some innovative lessons'. In *African universities in the twenty-first century*, eds. P. T. Zeleza and A. Olukoshi, pp. 126–139. Pretoria: University of South Africa Press.

Nafukho, F. M., and Kang'ethe, S. 2002. *Training of trainers: Strategies for the twenty-first century*. Eldoret: Moi University Press.

Naisbitt, J. and Aburdene, P. 1990. *Mega trends 2000: Ten new directions for the 1990s*. New York: William Morrow Company Inc.

National University of Lesotho. *A history of adult education*. Maseru: Institute of Extra-mural Studies.

Ngo-Birm, B. S. and Minya, A. P. 2002. 'For an improved autonomy of women.' In *ECHO: World Summit on Sustainable Development*. Dakar: AAWORD.

Newby, T. J., Stepich, A. S., Lehman, J. D., and Russell, J. D. 2000. *Instructional technology for teaching and learning*, 2nd edn. Columbus: ASPEN.

Nickell, G. S. and Pinto, J. N. 1986. 'The computer attitude scale'. *Computers in human behaviour*, Vol. 2, pp. 301–306.

Njoroge, R. J. and Bennaars, G. A. 1994. *Philosophy and education in Africa*. Nairobi: Trans Africa Press.

Nondo, C. S. and Muti, E. J. 1998. 'Zimbabwe'. In *Africa adult education: Chronologies in Commonwealth countries*, ed. J. A. Draper, pp. 98–103. Cape Town: CACE, University of Western Cape.

Nottingham Andragogy Group. 1983. *Towards a developmental theory of andragogy*. Nottingham: Department of Adult Education, University of Nottingham.

Nyamnjoh, F. 2001. 'Delusions of development and the enrichment of witchcraft discourses in Cameroon'. In *Magical interpretations, material realities: Modernity, witchcraft and the occult in post-colonial Africa*, eds. H. Moore and T. Sanders, pp. 28–49. London: Routledge.

Nyamnjoh, F. and Jua, N. 2002. 'African universities in crisis and the promotion of democratic culture: The political economy of violence in African educational systems'. In *African Studies Review*, Vol. 45, No. 2, pp. 1–26, September 2002.

Nyasani, J. M. 1997. *The African psyche*. Nairobi: University of Nairobi and Theological Printing Press.

Nyerere, J. K. 1967. *Education for self-reliance*. Dar-es-Salaam: The Government Printer.

Nyerere, J. K. 1976. Declaration of Dar-es-Salaam: Liberated man, the purpose of development. *Convergence*, Vol. 9, No. 4, pp. 9– 48.

Obanya, P. 1990. *The dilemma of education in Africa*. Dakar: UNESCO-BREDA.

Ochieng-Odhiambo, F. 1997. *African philosophy: An introduction*. Nairobi: Consolata Institute of Philosophy.

Oduaran, A. 2000. 'Research and scholarship in adult and continuing education in Africa'. In *The state of adult and continuing education in Africa*, eds. S. A. Indabawa, A. Oduaran, T. Afrik and S. Walters, pp. 31–47. Windhoek: Department of Adult and Non-Formal Education, University of Namibia.

Oduaran, A. 2002. *Learning to live and living to learn in the 21st century*. Inaugural Lecture Series. Gaborone: University of Botswana.

Ohmae, K. 1990. *The borderless world*. London: Collins.

Ohmae, K. 1995. *The end of the nation state*. New York: Free Press.

Okech, M. 2000. 'Costing and financing high education for development in sub-Saharan Africa: Kenya's case'. *International Education Journal*, Vol. 4, No. 3, pp. 1–4, 3 September 2000.

Okech, M.O. and Amutabi, M. 2002. *Privatization of higher education in Kenya: Prospects and problems*. Paper presented at the International Symposium on African Universities in the 21st Century. University of Illinois at Urbana-Champaign.

Oliver, R. 1969. *The missionary factor in East Africa*. London: Lowe and Brydone.

Omolewa, M. 1981. *Adult education practice in Nigeria*. Lagos: Evans Brothers Publishers.

Omolewa, M. 1998. 'Nigeria'. In *Africa adult education: Chronologies in Commonwealth Countries*, ed. J. A. Draper, pp. 54–64. Cape Town: CACE, University of Western Cape.

Omolewa, M. 2000. 'Setting the tone of adult and continuing education in Africa'. In *The state of adult and continuing education in Africa*, eds. S. A. Indabawa, A. Oduaran, T. Afrik and S. Walters, pp. 11–16. Windhoek: Department of Adult and Non-formal Education, University of Namibia.

Ornstein, A. C. and Hunkins, F. P. 1988. *Curriculum: Foundations, principles and issues*. Boston: Allyn and Bacon.

Oruka, O. H. 1990. *Sage philosophy: Indigenous thinkers and modern debate on African philosophy*. Leiden: E. J. Brill.

Ostergaard, L. 1990. *Gender and development: A practical guide*. London: Routledge.

Oxenham, J. 2000. 'Signals from Uganda: What an evaluation suggests for adult educators'. *Adult education and development*, Vol. 55, pp. 229–260.

Paterson, R. W. K. 1979. *Values, education and the adult*. London: Routledge and Kegan Paul.

Paterson, R. W. K. 1989. 'Philosophy and adult education: Theory and practice in the study of adult education'. In *The epistemological debate*, ed. B. P. Bright, pp. 13–33. London: Routledge.

Paye, J. C. 1996. 'Strategies for a learning society.' In *The OECD Observer*. Vol. 199, pp. 4–6.

Peters, R. S. 1966. *Ethics and education*. London: Allen and Unwin.

Poggeler, F. (ed.) 1990. *The state and adult education*. Frankfurt: Peter Lang.

Poindexter, S.E. 1996. *The Internet: Using Netscape navigator software*. Cambridge: International Thomson Publishing Company.

Prosser, R. 1967. *Adult education for developing countries*. Nairobi: East African Publishing House.

Rabakoarivelo, V., Rakotozafy, H. and Randraimahaleo, S. 'The state of adult and continuing education in Madagascar'. In *The state of adult and continuing education in Africa*, eds. S. A. Indabawa, A. Oduaran, T. Afrik and S. Walters. Windhoek: Department of Adult and Non-formal education, University of Namibia.

Ranson, S. 1994. *Towards a learning society*. London: Cassell.

Ranson, S. 1998. 'Lineages for the learning society'. In *Inside the learning Society*, ed. S. Ranson. New York: Cassell.

Redman, D. W. 1976. *A study of Ujamaa and nationhood*. New York: Orbis Books.

Reiser, R. A. 2001. 'A history of instructional design and technology: Part 1: A history of instructional media'. *Educational technology research and development*, Vol. 49, No. 1, pp. 53–64, viewed 8 May 2002, http://www.area-ham.org/index.html.

Republic of Kenya, 1993a. *Adult education: A gender analysis*. Women's Bureau/SIDA Project. Issue No 3. Nairobi: Ministry of Culture and Social Services.

Republic of Kenya. 1993b. *Literacy: A gender analysis.* Women's Bureau/SIDA Project. Issue No. 5. Nairobi: Ministry of Culture and Social Services.

Republic of Namibia. 2003. *National policy on adult learning.* Windhoek: Government of the Republic of Namibia.

Richburg, B. K. 1995. 'Why is Africa eating Asia's dust'? In *Developing World*, ed. J. R. Griffiths. Guildford: Dushkin Publishing Group.

Ropnarine, J. L. and Johnson, J. F. 1987. *Approaches to early childhood education.* Columbus: Merrill.

Rosenau, J. 1997. *Along the domestic-foreign frontier.* Cambridge: Cambridge University Press.

Said, E. 1994. *Culture and imperialism.* London: Vintage.

Sanger, C. 1999. Africa's great teacher dies at 77. *The Globe and Mail*, 15 October, p. A12.

Schmidt, E. 1992. *Peasants, traders, and wives: Shona women in the history of Zimbabwe, 1870–1939.* Portsmouth: Heinemann.

Savenye, W. C. and Robinson, R. S. 1996. 'Qualitative research and methods: An introduction for educational technology'. In *Handbook of research for educational communications and technology*, ed. D. H. Jonassen. New York: Macmillan.

Schuller, T. 1992. 'Age, gender, and learning in the lifespan'. In *Learning across the lifespan: Theories, research, policies*, eds. A. Tuijnman and M. Van der Kamp. pp. 17–32. Oxford: Pergamon Press.

Sebatena L. A. and Moore, B. 1998. 'Lesotho'. In *Africa adult education: Chronologies in Commonwealth countries*, ed. J. A. Draper, pp. 46–51. South Africa: CACE, University of Western Cape.

Seepe, S. 2000. 'Africanisation of knowledge: Exploring mathematical and scientific knowledge embedded in African cultural practices'. In *African voices in education*, eds. P. Higgs, N. C. G. Vakalisa, T. V. Mda and N. T. Assie-Lumumba, pp. 118–138. Western Cape: Juta.

Senge, P. 1990. *The fifth discipline: The art and practice of the learning organization.* New York: Currency Doubleday.

Senghor, L. 1963. 'Negritude and African socialism'. In *St. Anthonys Papers*, ed. K. Kirkwood, No. 15, pp. 16–22 , London: Oxford University Press.

Senghor, L. 1966. 'Negritude'. In *Optima,* Vol. 16, No. 1, p. 18.

Shelly, G. B., Cashman, T. J., Gunter, R. E. and Gunter, G. A. 1999. *Teachers discovering computers: A link to the future.* Cambridge: Course Technology.

Sherman, M.B. 1982. 'Education in Liberia'. In *Education in Africa: A comparative survey*, eds. A.B. Fafunwa and J.U. Aisiku, pp. 162–187. London: Allen and Unwin.

Shifferaw, M. 1992. 'African women and reproduction of knowledge through formal schooling: A case study of Zambian female education in secondary schools'. *Women and reproduction in Africa*, Occasional Paper Series, No 5, pp. 79–109. Dakar: AAWORD.

Shiundu, J. and Omulando, S. 1992. *Curriculum: Theory and practice in Kenya.* Nairobi: Oxford University Press.

Shu, S. 1982. 'Education in Cameroon'. In *Education in Africa: A comparative survey*, eds. A. B. Fafunwa and J. U. Aisiku, pp. 28–48. London: Allen and Unwin.

Suret-Canale, J. 1971. 'The Western Atlantic Coast'. In *History of West Africa*, Vol. 1, J. F. Ade Ajayi and M. Crowder, pp. 386–439. New York: Columbia University Press.

Shutte, A. 1993. *Philosophy for Africa.* Cape Town: University of Cape Town Press.

Smith, M. K., 'The meaning of adult education: A brief guide and bibliography', 2001, viewed November 2002, http://www.infed.org/lifelonglearning/b-adedgn.htm.

Smith, M. K., 'Julius Nyerere, lifelong learning and informal education', viewed May 2002, http://www.infed.org/thinkers/et-nye.htm.

South Commission. 1990. *The challenge of the South: The report of the South Commission.* Oxford: Oxford University Press.

Stein, D. S., and Imel, S. 2002. 'Adult learning in community: Themes and threads.' *New directions for adult and continuing education*, Vol. 95, pp. 93–97.

Stevenson, N. 1997. 'Globalization, national cultures and cultural citizenship'. *The Sociological Quarterly*, Vol. 1, pp. 41–66.

Svendsen, K. E. and Teisen, M. 1996. *Self-reliant Tanzania.* Dar-es-Salaam: Tanzania Publishing House.

Tahir, G. 1985. *Nigerian national policy on education: An examination of the adult and non-formal education components and possible policy options.* A paper presented at the C.O.N. Seminar, Nsukka.

Tahir, G. 2000. 'Continuing education policy provisions and options in Nigeria'. In *The State of adult and continuing education in Africa*, eds. S. A. Indabawa, A. Oduaran, T. Afrik, and S. Walters, pp. 147–154. Windhoek: Department of Adult and Non-formal Education, University of Namibia, Windhoek.

Thomas, N. S. 1969. *Proverbs, narratives, vocabularies and grammar: Anthropological Report on the Ibo-speaking peoples of Nigeria, Part III.* New York: Negro Universities Press.

Thompson, A. R. 1981. *Education and development in Africa.* London: Macmillan.

Thompson, L. J. 1988. 'Adult education and the women's movement'. In *Radical approaches to adult education: A reader*, ed. T. Lovett, pp. 59–84. London: Routledge.

Tight, M. 1996. *Key concepts in adult education and training.* London: Routledge.

Tomlin, M. E. 1997. 'Changing what and how we teach for a changing world.' *Adult Learning*, 8 (5 & 6), pp. 19–21.

Townsend-Coles, E. K. 1998. 'Introduction'. In *Africa adult education: Chronologies in Commonwealth countries*, ed. J. A. Draper, pp. 5–8. Cape Town: CACE, University of Western Cape.

Tuchsherer, K. 1999. 'Africa, cradle of writing'. *Africana Bulletin*, No. 42. December 1998/ January 1999. Boston: Boston University.

Turay, E. 1998. 'Sierra Leone'. In *Africa adult education: Chronologies in Commonwealth Countries*, ed. J. A. Draper, pp. 68–76. Cape Town: CACE, University of Western Cape.

UNESCO. 1976. *Recommendation on the development of adult education.* Adopted by the General Assembly at its nineteenth session, 26 November. Paris: UNESCO.

UNESCO. 1995. *Audience Africa: Social development Africa's priorities.* Final Report. Paris: UNESCO.

UNESCO. 1996. *The Dakar declaration on adult education and lifelong learning.* Dakar:UNESCO.

UNESCO. 1997. *Adult education. The Hamburg declaration. The Agenda for the future.* Confintea. Fifth International Conference on Adult Education, 14–18 July 1997. Hamburg: UNESCO Institute of Education.

UNESCO. 2003. Recommitting to adult education and learning. viewed 30 September 2003, http://www.UNESCO.org/education/uie/pdf/recommitting.pdf.

United Nations Development Programme (UNDP). 2002. *Human development report.* New York: Oxford University Press.

University of Botswana. 2002. viewed September 2002, http://www.ub.bw/departments/education/ae.html.

Usher, R., Bryant, I. and Johnston, R. 1997. *The postmodern challenge: Learning beyond the limits.* London: Routledge.

US Government. 1999. 'G-8 Summit – G-7 Charter on lifelong learning', viewed 10 July 2003, http://www.sate.gov/www/issues/economic/summit.

Van Sertima, I. 1999. 'The lost science of Africa: An overview'. In *African renaissance: The new struggle*, ed. M.W. Makgoba, pp. 305–330. Sandton and Cape Town: Mafube and Tafelberg.

Visanathan, N., et al. 1997. *The women, gender and development reader.* London: Zed Press.

Wagner, D. A. 2000. Literacy and adult education: executive summary. *Adult education and development*, Vol. 55, pp. 129–139.

Waters, M. 1990. *Globalization.* London: Routledge.

Walters, S. and Watters, K. 2000. 'From adult education to lifelong learning in Southern Africa over the last twenty years'. In *The state of adult education in Africa*, eds. S. A. Indabawa, A. Oduaran, T. Afrik and S. Walters, pp. 49–61. Windhoek: Department of Adult and Non-formal Education, University of Namibia.

Wangoola, P. and Youngman, F. (eds.) 1996. *Towards a transformative political economy of adult education: Theoretical and practical challenges.* DeKalb: LEPS Press.

Welton, M. 1993. 'The contribution of critical theory to our understanding of adult learning'. In *An update on adult learning theory: New directions in adult and continuing education*, ed. S. B. Merriam, No. 57. San Francisco: Beacon Press.

Were, E. M. and Amutabi, M. N. 2000. *Nationalism and democracy for people-centred development in Africa*. Eldoret: Moi University Press.

Westwood, S. 1988. 'Domesticity and its discontents: feminism and adult education in past time (1870–1920)'. In *Radical approaches to adult education: A reader*, ed. T. Lovett, pp. 59–84. London: Routledge.

Whippel, J. B. 1964. 'The uses of history for adult education'. In *Adult education: Outlines of an emerging field of university study*, eds. G. Jensen, A. Liveright and W. Hallenbeck, pp. 201–213. Washington, DC: Adult Education Association of the USA.

White, T. J. 1970. 'Philosophical considerations'. In *Handbook of Adult Education*, eds. R. M. Smith, G. F. Aker and J. R. Kidd, pp. 121–135. New York: Macmillan.

Whyte A. 1999. *Acacia research guidelines for assessing community telecentres*. Toronto: International Development Research Centre.

Wiredu, K. 1996. *Cultural universals and particulars: An African perspective*. Bloomington: Indiana University Press.

Women's Bureau 1989. *Statistics and indicators on women in Kenya*. KEN/WB/STAT/SERIES D No. 2. Nairobi: Ministry of Culture and Social Services.

World Bank. 1997a. The African Virtual University (AVU). In *Pilot phase operation*. Washington, DC: The World Bank.

World Bank. 1997b. The African Virtual University. In *Knowledge is power*. Washington, DC: The World Bank.

World Bank. 1998. *World development report. Knowledge for Development*. Washington, DC: The World Bank.

World Bank. 2000. *Higher education in developing countries: Peril and promise*. Washington, DC: The World Bank.

World Bank. 2002. *World development report*. Washington, DC: The World Bank.

Wriston, W. 1992. *The twilight of sovereignty*. New York: Charles Scribner's Sons.

Young, K. 1992. 'Household resource management'. In *Gender and development: A practical guide*, ed. L. Ostergaard, pp. 135–164. London: Routledge.

Youngman, F. 1996. 'Towards a political economy of adult education and development in Botswana'. In *Towards a transformative political economy of adult education*. eds. P. Wangoola and F. Youngman, pp. 191–222. Dekalb IL: LEPS Press.

Youngman, F. 1998. 'Botswana'. *African adult education: Chronologies in Commonwealth countries*, ed. J. A. Draper, pp. 26–32. Cape Town: CACE, University of Western Cape.

Youngman, F. 2000. *The political economy of adult education and development*. London: Zed Books.

Youngman, F. 2001. 'The prospects for lifelong education for all in Africa: the case of Botswana'. *Inchiesta*, Vol. 30, No. 129, pp. 42–50.

Zelza, P. T. 1993. *A modern economic history of Africa*, Vol. 1. Dakar: CODESRIA.

Zelza, P. T. 2003. *Re-thinking Africa's globalization*. Trenton: Africa World Press.

Zewde, B. 1991. *A history of modern Ethiopia, 1855–1974*. London: James Currey.

Zinn, L. M. 1990. 'Identifying your philosophical orientation'. In *Adult learning methods*, ed. M. W. Galbraith, pp. 39–58. Malabar: Krieger Publishing Company.

# Index

Page references in italics indicate diagrams and illustrations.

nkonsonkonson

Southern Africa Development Community
(SADC)   38
Structural Adjustment Programmes (SAPs)   61, 69,
70, 139–140, 158
Sudan   14, 35, 62, 67, 79, 100
suites   124
Swaziland   82, 89

T
Taiwan   29, 157
Tambo, Oliver   37
Tanzania
  see also  Nyerere, Julius Kabarage
  adult education programmes   25–26, 141
  democracy   69
  ICT usage   130
  impact of SAPs   158
  indigenous knowledge   30, 31
  literacy   34, 89, 91
  political use of language   66
  pre-colonial technology   100
  universities   71, 82, 141
Teaching and Learning – Towards the Learning
  Society   156
telecentres   131
Timbuktu   23
Togo   14, 62
traditional society   10–11, 68, 100, 150
  see also  Indigenous Education Systems;
  Indigenous Knowledge Systems

U
ubuntu   12–13, 49, 55, 62
Uganda
  adult education programmes   67, 71, 141
  conflict   34, 62, 67
  democracy   69
  ICT usage   131
  indigenous knowledge   30, 31
  literacy   89, 91
  professional associations   110
  universities   71, 82, 141
UNESCO
  lifelong learning   151
  literacy programmes   38
  role in adult education   14, 83, 160
  World Conferences on Adult Education   7, 35,
  36, 37

UNICEF   15, 83, 160
universities   13–14, 26–27, 71, 82–83
  see also  Africa Virtual University (AVU)
  MBA programmes   103, 141
University of South Africa (UNISA)   68, 70

W
Wamba dia Wamba, Ernest   37
web browser   126
Wiredu, Kwasi   51
women   60–61, 66–67, 68, 79
  see also  gender
  women's movements   67, 94
Women in Development (WID)   94
word-processing software   124
World Bank   12, 14, 32, 70, 83, 130
  see also  Structural Adjustment Programmes
  (SAPs)
World Health Organization (WHO)   83, 103
World Trade Organization (WTO)   32, 138

Z
Zaire   38
Zambia
  democracy   69
  distance education   82
  ethnicity   62
  indigenous knowledge   30
  matriarchy   91
  universities   14, 27, 141
  use of education in liberation   36
Zimbabwe
  adult education   26, 27, 62
  conflict   79
  distance education   82
  impact of SAPs   158
  indigenous knowledge   30
  MINEDAF V conference   (1982) 38
  use of education in liberation   36, 37